Affinity as a Value

Affinity as a Value

Marriage Alliance in South India, with Comparative Essays on Australia

Louis Dumont

The University of Chicago Press
Chicago and London

Louis Dumont is Directeur d'Etudes at the Ecole Pratique des
Hautes Etudes en Sciences Sociales, Paris. Among his many
books, two have been published in English by the University of
Chicago Press—*From Mandeville to Marx: The Genesis and Tri-
umph of Economic Ideology* (1977), and *Homo Hierarchicus:
The Caste System and Its Implications* (revised edition, 1980).

The University of Chicago Press, Chicago 60637
The University of Chicago Press, Ltd., London
© 1983 by Louis Dumont
All rights reserved. Published 1983
Printed in the United States of America

90 89 88 87 86 85 84 83   5 4 3 2 1

Library of Congress Cataloging in Publication Data

Dumont, Louis, 1911–
   Affinity as a value.

    Bibliography: p.
    Includes index.
    1. Kinship—India—South India—Addresses, essays,
lectures.   2. Australian aborigines—Kinship—
Addresses, essays, lectures.   3. Marriage—India—South
India—Addresses, essays, lectures.   I. Title
GN635.I4D85   1983   306.8'3'0954   82-13468
ISBN 0-226-16964-2

Contents

Preface

The idea of gathering between two covers the studies here presented has been with me for some ten years. As the major essay, "Hierarchy and Marriage Alliance in South Indian Kinship" (1957) had gone out of print and the Royal Anthropological Institute graciously agreed to let me reprint it, it was natural to think of assembling around it both the earlier analysis of vocabulary ("Dravidian Kinship Terminology," 1953) and the article "Nayar Marriages as Indian Facts," which had appeared only in French (1961). It was natural also to add as a supplement the two pieces on Australia—one of which, the Kariera analysis, existed only in French—for while these papers, like the South Indian ones, focus on intermarriage, they bring forth at the same time an important difference between the two kinds of systems, on which I shall be insisting hereafter.

The intention was, and is, not only to bring together studies that belong together and may thus reinforce each other,[1] but also to

1. This was done in less complete form in French (Dumont 1975a).

offer a kind of stocktaking, an account of the reception of these texts in the little community of researchers dealing with South India and of the subsequent development of studies and ideas in the field.[2] Having in the meantime turned away from Indian studies, I have been remiss in carrying out the project, but this very delay has an advantage in the latter regard. The lively discussion these views have aroused has not died down, and it is now possible to survey from a greater distance a wider span of research and perhaps to isolate more significant trends in the history of the subject.

A word should be said about the title chosen for this collection. Originally the institution with which the texts essentially deal was called "marriage alliance," and there is no reason to change this designation. But after all there is a way of bringing it nearer to common sense. With us modern Westerners, affinity is subordinated to consanguinity, for my brother-in-law, an affine, becomes an uncle, a consanguineal relative, for my children. In other words, affinity is ephemeral, it merges into consanguinity for the next generation. As values are by definition conceived as permanent, durable, I may say that affinity is inferior to consanguinity, or *undervalued in relation to it*. Now my thesis is that the specificity of the South Indian kinship system lies in the fact that affinity there is transmitted from generation to generation, is thus permanent or durable, and so has *equal status* with consanguinity, or a value equal to it. It should not be thought at this point that the thesis is generally admitted, although it will be seen that the importance of affinity in this field is increasingly recognized (see chapter 4).

From the present point of view, at any rate, it is clear that affinity is a value in South India, and is not one with us. The irony of the situation is that, in this matter, we Westerners, equalitarians as we are, practice subordination—the relation between consanguinity and affinity is exactly what I have defined elsewhere as a *hierarchical relation*—while South Indian people, who live in a hierarchical society, look at the two entities in question with equanimity, and make a simple, straightforward, symmetrical distinction between them where we maintain a hierarchical distinction. Moreover, as will be seen in chapter 4, my fundamental

---

2. Some early literature was reviewed in the pages of *Contributions to Indian Sociology*; cf. Dumont 1961 and 1964.

objection against a contemporary interpretation is that it covers up and even contradicts this point.

I next wish to stress the separation maintained in this book between South India and Australia. In the first place, the texts dealing with India are based, directly or indirectly, on field experience, while the two articles on Australia are only analyses based on the literature. Moreover, there are internal reasons for maintaining a distance between the two areas. What justifies bringing them together is a pronounced similarity that has led researchers in the past to neglect their difference, as did both Radcliffe-Brown and Lévi-Strauss. Radcliffe-Brown, from the vantage point of his Australian experience, wrote of the "Australian-Dravidian" type of terminology. He overlooked, even after it had been brought to his attention, an apparently minute difference in terminological structure between Kariera and Dravidian (see below, correspondence at the end of chapter 1). This has led me to set out clearly the difference in structure (chapter 5). As to Lévi-Strauss, he took hold of the Australian holistic model—without analyzing it in his own terms as is done below, in chapter 6—and he proceeded to generalize it. Thinking that wherever cross-cousin marriage is found it must be accompanied by a holistic model of a sort, he presumed, when such a model was not evidenced in the people's representations, to ascertain its presence empirically from the outside. (He somehow retracted, later on, in a rather cryptic passage in *La pensée sauvage*. See Lévi-Strauss 1962, 333, quoted in Dumont 1971, 132.) The fact is that this cannot be done (cf. below, end of chapter 5). While Australia has *global* models of the society, we are left, in India and elsewhere, with representations attached to an individual ego, representations that are in that sense irremediably *local*, and there is no way to infer the global from the local.

While, from the present point of view, Australia is characterized by a global model of the society as made up of intermarrying *groups* (or marriage sections as they were sometimes called), India has only *categories*, which regulate the repetition of intermarriage—or, as I call it, the marriage alliance—but which operate in each case by reference to a particular locus and thus exclusively take the form of what is called in anthropological jargon "cross-cousin marriage." Strictly speaking, in the Australian case we cannot speak of marriage alliance as here defined. The two articles on Australia included here, especially the first, the Kariera analysis, should mark both the similarity and the difference.

This had to be specified because the ghosts of "dual organization" and of "circulating connubium" have long haunted Indian studies and have perhaps not ceased to do so. If, for the sake of visualizing some kind of relation between the two types, we indulge for a moment in evolutionary speculation, we cannot even assert that dual organization has necessarily preceded the kind of categorial dualism found in South India. We can only say that the reverse is impossible, that is, that the Australian type is not subsequent to a Dravidian type: the global can generate the local; the local cannot generate the global but only modify it.

The three texts dealing with India are reproduced in the chronological order of publication (chapters 1, 2, and 3). Chapter 4 is new and incorporates a general account of their reception and a discussion of related issues. All the texts are reproduced essentially in their original form, except for printing errors and the like. The footnotes, however, especially for the first two texts, differ from the original ones although they incorporate most of their substance. After twenty years or more, some of the notes appear to have been merely circumstantial, and have been omitted. More important: certain imperfections in the texts demanded the addition of new footnotes, for several reasons: (1) in the rare cases where the text has needed an alteration, a note signals the fact; (2) where, as is most frequently the case, the imperfection in the text has been reproduced, it is adverted to in a note; the same holds for reservations; (3) inclusion, in the notes, of the reactions of critics has generally been avoided; but where a critic's remark is specifically directed to one passage or one word, it has been accommodated in a footnote.

Apart from the general discussion in chapter 4, special comments are appended to chapters 1 and 3. Chapter 1 has met with wide incomprehension, due no doubt to its technical character and to the shortcomings of the original text, the earliest in this collection. It therefore receives an extended comment aiming mainly at explanation or elucidation and incorporating the discussion of the technical objections of critics. The essay on the Nayar (chapter 3) also bears on a special domain and accordingly has an appended comment discussing the reception of the text and the criticisms addressed to it.

The two papers on Australia have been reproduced as they were, including the notes; only a short postscript has been added.

The first two texts here reproduced were written in 1952–53, while I was a member of the Institute of Social Anthropology in Oxford. They benefited from the distant but effective encouragement of Evans-Pritchard and the help of David Pocock. The last stage in the preparation of this edition took place in the ideal conditions provided by a fellowship at the Center for Advanced Study in the Behavioral Sciences at Stanford in the fall of 1981. I am grateful to the Center and its director, Gardner Lindzey, and to the National Science Foundation for its financial support (grant no. BNS76-22945). Thanks are due to the editors and/or publishers of the original versions of chapters 1, 2, 3, 5, and 6 for permission to reproduce (see footnotes on the opening pages of those chapters). Finally, I thank Marta Nicholas, who kindly checked the new English versions.

South India

1

The Dravidian Kinship Terminology as an Expression of Marriage

This paper springs from two sources. Field acquaintance with Dravidian kinship vocabulary made me feel very strongly its systematic, logical character; I could not help thinking that it centered in marriage, and that it should be possible to express those two features in a simple formula. But, in trying to do so, a considerable resistance from current anthropological ideas was experienced. Therefore a few general and critical remarks suggest themselves.

Preliminary

Its main features are well known: classification according to generations, distinction of sex, distinction of two kinds of relatives inside certain generations, distinction of age.

This paper was read before the Fourth International Congress of Anthropological and Ethnological Sciences, Vienna, 1952; it is reprinted from *Man* 1953, Art. 54, by permission of the Royal Anthropological Institute. I should now prefer to speak of "vocabulary" rather than "terminology," and shall do so, as far as possible, in the Comment that follows the paper. But it was found unpractical to change the expression throughout the original paper(s). The phrase "as an expression of marriage" is unduly unilateral, as vocabulary also constitutes a chart for (inter-) marriage, but in the context of the time it meant in the first place "not an expression of groups" (of the unity of the "sibling group," or of the descent group), but of a relation, i.e. (inter-)marriage.

Since Morgan, who based his second or *"punaluan"* family on the Dravidian and the Seneca-Iroquois systems, this type of vocabulary, known as Seneca or Dakota-Iroquois type, and one of the most widely spread, has challenged anthropologists. Rivers, studying the Dravidian system, saw that its main feature was the distinction of parallel and cross cousins, and rightly connected some of its features with cross-cousin marriage, but, to account for it as a whole, he turned toward a hypothetical previous stage of dual organization. Less satisfactory descriptions, when found in modern literature, witness to the difficulty scholars encounter in becoming familiar with this important and relatively simple vocabulary. As late as 1947 we find maintained the denomination of "bifurcate merging" type introduced previously with the explanation: "bifurcate, because paternal and maternal kin are distinguished, merging as far as there is a partial merging with the parents," a definition obviously inaccurate and misleading, as the distinction is not between paternal and maternal sides, which are, on the contrary, treated exactly according to the same principle, as already made clear by Rivers. Even when the "principle of the solidarity of the sibling group" is emphasized, we return to the same confusion, since in that view the paternal aunt is assimilated with the father, the maternal uncle with the mother.[1]

All this would require an explanation, and some of what I believe to be the factors producing these misconceptions will be found below. But perhaps it may be said in general that the terminology was not considered for a moment in itself but in terms of other aspects of kinship, in fact related to but different from it; at the same time it was still felt as irrational and one hastened to explain without accurately describing. This is so true that when Kirchhoff, on the contrary, only wants to describe it, he comes close to the explanation. He states, in his type *D*, that there is "a common word for father and father's brother, but another word for mother's brother" (etc., in two columns.)[2] Let us proceed from this point to some further observations. Here, in the father's generation, there are two kinds, and two kinds only, of male relatives. They are two *classes*, and we should not, because the father and the mother's

---

1. Morgan 1877, 424–52; Rivers 1914, 47–49, 73; see also Rivers 1907, 611–40. "Bifurcate-merging": Lowie 1928, 265f; cf. Murdock 1947, 56–68. "Solidarity of the Sibling Group": Radcliffe-Brown 1950, p. 25.

brother respectively fall into these two classes, by stressing them in fact substitute the idea of a dyadic relationship for that of a class, as we do if we suppose, for example, "mother's brother" to be the basic meaning, and the others to be extensions.[3] Moreover, the "mother's brother" is also the "father-in-law," and the common assumption that the affinal meaning is here secondary, the cognatic meaning being primary, is based upon nothing but the common notion that one's kinship position necessarily precedes one's marriage, an idea quite out of place here, as only the analysis of the system can reveal the real meaning of the category. All these arbitrary assumptions arise from our own way of thinking, *unconsciously* superimposed upon the native way of thinking. We must, therefore, refuse to indulge them and keep before us the question: what is the principle of the opposition between those two classes of relatives exemplified by what we call father and mother's brother? Provided that we consider this opposition as standing in its own right and do not assume that the principle of the opposition lies in the relation with the Ego, and provided that we view it against the background of the whole system (see note 9 below), we can find some approach to the answer. Briefly, in this case the relationship between father and mother's brother is:

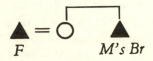

$$F \qquad M's\ Br$$

and it is very likely that the principle of the opposition lies in that relationship. Possibly our preconceived ideas resist such a view, but should they not give way if the facts impose it? This relationship we shall call an alliance relationship,[4] as the relationship

2. Kirchhoff 1932, 41–72; cf. Lowie 1950, 63.
3. For a strong protest against this kind of "extension," see Hocart 1937, 545–51.
4. More rigorously, in this passage one should have spoken of affinity only, and should have introduced "marriage alliance" only later on, when the diachronic dimension of affinity in the system is directly visible. Instead the text supposes

arising between two male (or two female) persons and their siblings of the same sex, when a "sister" (a "brother") of one is married to the other:

$$\Delta(= \overset{\ulcorner\urcorner}{\bigcirc}) \Delta$$

or, more generally: $\Delta [=] \Delta$

and

$$\bigcirc [=] \bigcirc .$$

It expresses the fact that if marriage creates a relation between two persons of different sexes, it connects also their groups. As an equivalent formula I shall speak also of two men (or women) having an alliance relationship as male (or female) affines.

There is another way of expressing the same fact, which, although not altogether wrong, is I think less accurate, and the criticism of which will throw some more light on the anthropologist's unconscious resistance to the classificatory idea. It is possible to extend the distinction between parallel and cross cousins and to speak of parallel and cross relatives, the principle of the distinction being that "there is, or there is not, a change of sex when passing from the direct line to the collateral line." I followed this doctrine in a monographic study of kinship in a Tamil-speaking community.[5] But the whole passage, although tending to a synthetic view, is, I am afraid, obscure. Moreover, the formula is not satisfactory for two reasons: (i) in spite of the fact that the natives do, when tracing relationships, pass from one line to another, these

---

that alliance is given synthetically as it were with the first considered occurrence of the relationship. It should be clear that (marriage) alliance means "affinity including the diachronic dimension" it receives in this case (cf. below, chap. 2). The fact of not having mentioned in this connection the similar early interpretation of Fison brought me a somewhat disobliging but not quite undeserved reproach from Scheffler (Scheffler 1971, 237). It was inexcusable, as I must have seen, at some stage at least, Fison's article (cf. now Barnes 1975, 39 and note 134).

5. Formula from Lévi-Strauss 1949, 165. I hoped in 1953 that my emphasis on marriage would be found in keeping with the general inspiration of that work. Cf. Dumont 1950, 1–26 (with many misprints); see pp. 5–12 as a first attempt in the present direction.

are not among their basic categories and are not in the least expressed in their theory: (*ii*) the system has much to do with marriage, and this should appear more clearly, if possible, in its formula. In fact, it is the anthropologist alone who is responsible for the introduction of this unsatisfactory concept of a "change of sex"; he does so because he wants to trace through a relative of the opposite sex a relationship which the native conceives—when he thinks classificatorily—in a different manner. For instance we introduce the mother as a link between Ego and his mother's brother, where in fact the latter is just opposed to the father. Two errors converge here: (*i*) the "extension" tendency confuses a class with the actual mother's brother, (*ii*) the introduction of the latter's compounded, western, descriptive name brings in the mother, who is only relevant at this level as the link by which the relation between father and mother's brother comes into existence. If, however, we agree to consider the terms for the two sexes separately (as is normal in a system where the terms for females are distinct, and not mere feminine forms of the terms for males), and in a classificatory perspective, the difficulty vanishes.

After this lengthy but necessary discussion, we can now define the problem.

Limits and Nature of the Analysis

Since Morgan, it has been recognized that the terminological systems used by most of the communities speaking one of the four written Dravidian languages (about 70 million people) are very much alike. What does this amount to, when each language uses different terms, when again in each language the actual list of terms differs slightly from one group to another, and when, moreover, only a few such lists are recorded from among the vast number of those which exist? Is it possible to abstract anything like a common terminological system? It is, thanks to the systematic character of a remarkably constant structure. And it will not be denied that the attempt will be logical rather than statistical. Not all groups conform to the perfect schema outlined below—for instance, some Tamil Brahmins alter the system considerably by the introduction of a number of individualizing terms, or Nayar at the present day do not distinguish between cousins (according to Mlle Biardeau)—but on the whole most lists can be said to center in a common scheme, from which they differ slightly and individually. Both the Tamil lists and the published Kanarese examples illustrate it almost perfectly.[6]

The limits of the analysis will be drawn close to the vital nucleus of the system: I shall consider only the common classificatory features within a range of five generations.

One important point is that the nature of the task compels us to consider the distinctiveness of the terms denoting the classes, quite irrespective of their concrete linguistic form. This is fortunate, because it allows the analysis to develop at the basic level of the structure of the system, whereas such analyses usually become mixed up with linguistic considerations as well as with considerations of attitudes or institutions which belong to a different level of analysis and which are excluded here by the very diversity of the background. The need to stress the cross-cousin marriage will appear the more striking as our analysis develops.

A brief explanation is needed of the expression used above: "the distinctiveness of the terms denoting the classes." The distinctiveness of the terms is the main matter, as they are used to distinguish (i.e. to oppose) classes. But conversely, linguistic differences which are not used to oppose classes are irrelevant here, and it is for this reason that I add the words "denoting the classes." For instance, different words applied to exactly the same relatives are irrelevant, or again secondary differences within a class (obtained by affixation, etc.) are irrelevant insofar as they do not alter its unity (because for instance the class word or root is kept in all). Again, linguistic resemblances may exist between terms of different classes, insofar as the classes are not in direct opposition. All such facts are of interest, and may even be found to be common to all our terminologies; but they do not form part of the basic structure. (Considerations of space preclude these points being developed and exemplified here as they should be.) Our situation is similar to that of the phoneticist: just as he retains among phonetic particularities only those which differentiate meanings, we here

6. Most complete are Morgan's lists (Morgan 1871, 518f.) for Tamil, Telugu, and Kanarese. References to recent monographs in Dumont 1950 (not restricted to written languages, but for Kanarese see Srinivas 1942; for Malayalam see Aiyappan 1937 and 1944). Lists of "common" terms, unspecified and unlocalized, are found in grammars, etc. I have taken here into account lists collected by me from several Tamil groups, unpublished.

retain from linguistic particularities only those which differentiate relatives, and even (for the time being) the fundamental classes of relatives only.

The system as just defined classifies all relatives of five generations from grandfather to grandson into sixteen classes by using sixteen distinctive (sets of) terms. The generations are as a rule absolutely distinguished; there is no assimilation of relatives belonging to different generations. Additionally, Ego's generation is split into two by distinguishing relatives older and younger than Ego: this distinction of age will be treated as analogous to the distinction of generations. (The distinction of age in other generations, e.g. the father's, is marked, not by distinct terms, but by prefixed adjectives; hence it is not relevant here, as stated in our previous point.) Some of the terms have a masculine and a feminine form, some have only one form, either masculine or feminine, and this is the rule wherever the central, critical distinction which follows is fully maintained. In each generation (or age) group, the relatives of the same sex are distinguished into two classes. In the chart (fig. 1), every class is designated by a letter, from *A* to *P,* and they are distributed symmetrically to stress the opposition.

Although, for the reader's convenience, I give the ordinary equivalents, we shall not rely upon them in the least, but on the contrary try to deduce the meaning of each class from its situation in the whole.

Some qualifications are necessary, as regards the value of the chart. Class *D* has a tendency to split among the Tamil groups that I studied, but the cleavage is never the same, and the two terms on which it is based are largely interchangeable, so that already in Tamil it is not possible to take it as a general feature. In the region *HILM* I had to choose between two variants, the other variant not applying distinction of age to this group. Both will be found equally consistent. For *N* and *O* this is the Tamil situation, while elsewhere the central distinction and the distinction of sex are more in evidence.

We now proceed to discover, or rather confirm, the nature of the principle of the central opposition, and thus define the fundamental meaning of each class (as distinct from its linguistic meaning; see above), and to try to understand the way in which the different distinctions are combined, and the range of their application.

Generation	△	○		○	△
grandfather		A (+fem.A')			
father	B	C		D	E
Ego { >Ego / <Ego } Ego	F / J	G / △ Ego ○ / K	█	H / L	I / M
son		N(+fem.N')		O[=k+N]*(+fem.O')	
grandson		P(+fem. P')			

*This line gives the disposition in Tamil, where k probably means "marriage." Strictly, in this case considered alone, N and O form a single category.

Fig. 1. A are the "grandfathers," B the "fathers," C the "mothers," D the "father's sisters" and "mothers-in-law," E the "mother's brothers" and "fathers-in-law," F the "brothers" older than Ego, J the younger, I and M, "male cross-cousins," older and younger; G, K, "sisters," and H, L, "female cross-cousins" respectively older and younger; N "parallel sons" (fem. for the "daughters"); O "cross-sons" (fem. for "cross-daughters"). (Note: this figure and its caption have been amended. Ego, male and female, were not located in the figure.)

Father's Generation

We have seen already that the alliance relationship defines the mother's brother by reference to the father. But the father himself is defined by reference to the Ego. Let us consider now the nature of the latter relation and both together. In doing so we should not forget that, although we have taken the particular, genealogical father as example, we are dealing in fact with the "fathers" as a class. In the relation, or as I prefer to say, in the opposition, between Ego and Ego's father, there are two elements, one of which is common to them both, while the other differentiates them; the element which is common to both terms of the opposition I call the "basis" of the opposition, the differentiating element I call the "principle" of the opposition. The principle is clear: it is the distinction between two successive generations. But what is the basis, what is it that is common to Ego and Ego's father? Obviously, the answer lies in the context: what they have in common is opposed to what makes their relation (more precisely the father's relation) with the mother's brother, i.e. to the alliance (fig. 2).

Father and Ego are related by a link which excludes alliance, and which I propose to call "kin link." One qualification regarding sex must be added: whereas the "fathers" and the "mother's brothers" are respectively male sibling groups, the sex of Ego is irrelevant (the terms for father, etc., being the same irrespective of the sex of Ego). The two generations opposed to one another in the kin group are one generation of male siblings, and the generation of their children, both male and female. In other words, the distinction of sex, if it is the preliminary condition of the distinction of kin, is unrelated to the distinction of generation; this should be remembered.

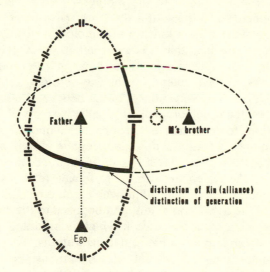

Fig. 2.

If we now consider together the two oppositions between Ego, his father and his mother's brother, we see that Ego and the father are similar in kin and different in generation, while father and mother's brother are similar in generation and different in kin (i.e. are allied). Each of the two elements (generation and kin) serves under its negative (differentiating) form as principle of one opposition, and under its positive (uniting) form as the basis of the other.

The two concrete oppositions not only have one term in common (the father), but their concatenation is built upon two abstract oppositions operating crosswise: (*i*) community and difference in generation; (*ii*) community and difference in kin, i.e. kin and alliance. The latter, in which the category of alliance is brought to light by opposition to the kin category, is of paramount importance. Compared with Morgan's Malayan system, where the two categories are not distinguished, it emphasizes the importance of alliance, i.e. of marriage as a relation between groups.[7] Moreover both ideas are given together, and spring from one another: no kin without alliance, no alliance without kin.

A few more remarks may be added. (*i*) We understand why there are no special terms (at the present level) for affines: the basic meaning of the terms for the "cross" category is affinal—my mother's brother is essentially my father's affine. (*ii*) We have in fact taken the two oppositions as a way leading *from Ego* to the father and from the father to the mother's brother; are we then perhaps not entitled to speak of a structure *sensu stricto*? But here lies the characteristic of a kinship terminology as compared with other kinship groupings, that it is a constellation revolving around the Ego. The only difference from customary views on the subject lies in the way we have taken, not the way through the mother, as suggested by our own vocabulary, but, I believe, the native way, as imposed by the terminology. (*iii*) What is here called kin has, of course, nothing to do with actual groups, being only an abstraction arising from the oppositions; this again centers in Ego, and is only a part of what the terminology suggests as such, because we had to abstract it on the male side; turning to female relatives, we shall finds its feminine counterpart. The whole could be called "terminological kin" to avoid confusion, and opposed to "terminological affines". This is only a framework which is used and shaped by each group according to its particular institutions.

In the same generation, we can deal exactly as above with the opposition between the "mother" and the "father's sister," and connect it with the opposition between Ego and Ego's mother. We

7. This is admittedly a very bad expression, which only the early date of the paper can perhaps in some manner excuse. What is meant is that marriage introduces between the relatives of both spouses a more or less collective affinity—or alliance—relationship. The less we speak of "groups" here, the better; cf. the discussion in chapter 4 below.

shall leave out the intermediary link, this time the father, as a mere agent bringing about (and hence contained in) the alliance relationship between the two women. The kin group arising here will be formed of a generation of female siblings, the mothers (opposed to their female affines), and of the generation of their children of both sexes. This kin category is not different from the preceding one; it is the same, opposed to alliance as above, though we take another view of it in accordance with the distinction of sexes in the system. In order to insist upon the classificatory character, we give here (fig. 3), a generalized scheme; a similar one could, of course, be drawn for males.

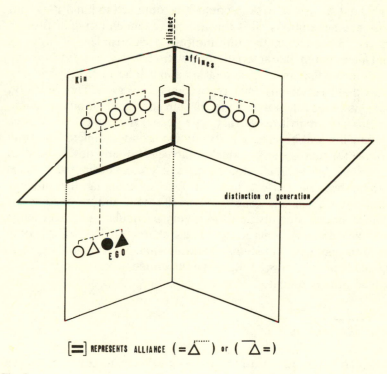

Fig. 3.

Having ended the part of the demonstration which is most likely to arouse controversy, and before extending it to the other generations, we may pause here and get a first glimpse of the whole. There will be no difficulty, as one can imagine, in showing that Ego's "cross cousins" are essentially Ego's affines, just as the "mother's brother" proved to be essentially the father's affine. This means that the alliance which we considered horizontally in one generation acquires a new, a vertical dimension, and runs through generations.

Alliance as an Enduring Institution: Cross-Cousin Marriage

It is not another alliance, but one and the same relationship transmitted from one generation to the next, inherited; what we have considered up to now as an alliance relationship was only a horizontal section of it. And could it be opposed to kin if it did not transcend generations? It is this alliance as an enduring institution that is embedded in the terminology, that provides it with its fundamental and characteristic opposition.

But to say that an alliance relationship is inherited is the same as to say that a certain marriage regulation is observed. Theoretically, to maintain the relation, one marriage in each generation is enough, but the more marriages of that type occur, the firmer the alliance relationship will be. The most immediate and complete, the total formula for that is "cross-cousin marriage" of any description. In fact, what we are accustomed to call cross-cousin marriage is nothing but the perfect formula for perpetuating the alliance relationship from one generation to the next and so making the alliance an enduring institution—a very particular and queer name for a fact of a very general and logical character. Indeed, it is only the anthropologist's customary and peculiar vocabulary, expressing alliance in terms of kin, which conceals this simple truth instead of revealing it.

Other Generations

How can we in our turn reproduce in other generations what we said in the father's generation? If the alliance relationship may be supposed to be similar, the generation relationship will be different.

In the grandfather's generation, cross-cousin marriage (or an equivalent) leads one to suppose an affinal link between Ego's two grandfathers, and this is the very reason why they cannot be distinguished, and why there is normally only one term for both of them, for both are kin in one way, and affines in another: mother as well as father is kin to Ego, and so are their fathers,[8] who have at the same time an alliance relationship, so that we may consider one of them A as kin, and the other B as affine, or, equally, B as kin and A as affine: the two categories merge in that generation and the distinction of kin does not apply to it. The same may be said about grandsons: alliance works as a principle of opposition for (two or) three generations only, whereas all relatives merge in the fifth and the first.[9]

In the son's generation, we should expect to find a mirror image of the father's generation, with two terms for males and two for females. In Tamil the distinctions within the generation are seriously weakened. Both the alliance and the sex distinctions cease to be radical and are marked only by affixes, there is only one (fundamental) category. Only on a secondary level can we follow up the distinctions and distinguish, apart from sex, between "parallel sons," i.e. sons of a (a = Ego and same-sex consanguine relatives of same generation), and "cross sons," i.e. sons of b and sons-in-law of a (b = same-sex affinal relatives of same generation)—the sons-in-law of b being equivalent to sons of a.[10]

In Ego's generation (males), something interesting happens if we try to apply the same procedure as in the father's generation: on one side the alliance opposition is present, the male affines being sister's husband and wife's brother as well as sons of the father's (male) affines and of the mother's (female) affines. On the other side, the generation opposition vanishes, as Ego and his brothers might be considered indifferently, but a new principle is invoked in order to replace as it were the waning principle, i.e. relative age is

8. On the face of it, "and so are their fathers" does not follow from the previous statement, which is valid, that "mother as well as father is kin (i.e. a consanguine) to Ego," for we have no right to reduplicate as it were the filiation relationship upward. To demonstrate that the assertion is valid, we have to draw the logical implications for the grandparent-grandchild relationship of the immediate filiation relationship acknowledged between parent and child. Through Ego, Ego's parents and Ego's children are consanguines to each other, that is to say, if we move the point of reference one generation down, that each of the four grandparents can be taken as kin to Ego. Q.E.D.

9. This feature is fundamental, and our analysis rests largely upon it. The whole structure is different when grandson and grandfather are identified, as in Kariera (with two terms for each).

10. The foregoing paragraph replaces the insufficient original.

distinguished, and the generation is split into two halves under
Ego's older brother and Ego's younger brother. The two distinctions (generation and age), one of which relieves the other, have a
common background of age connotation and are closely connected.

Now we can proceed with the elder brother as with the father: he
is opposed to Ego, as older, and he is opposed to the "cross
cousin, older than Ego" as a sibling to an affine. The same for the
younger brother, opposed to a "younger cross cousin" (fig. 4a),
but we here cross the generation axis of the structure, and the age
order between Ego and his kin is inverted.

As previously stated, our chart gives for the affines here only
one of the two variants actually found. The other variant presents
no distinction of age among the affines and has only one term for
males equivalent to *HL*. For this we can account very simply: in
that variant, Ego's generation is taken as a whole, the male affine is
opposed directly to Ego, and the age distinction, although introduced among brothers, does not replace structurally the generation
distinction, and is not extended to the affines (fig. 4b).

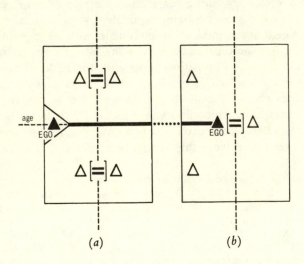

(a)   (b)

Fig. 4.

Moreover, it is in this part that the actual terminologies differ
most from our chart. Several factors are at work, one of which is of
a classificatory nature. It is a tendency to stress the relative sex of
the person compared to the Ego, as is quite natural where

prospective mates are found. This tendency combines in various ways with the elder-younger distinction, and the matter is still more complicated by other factors, so that it requires a special treatment.[11]

In the preceding paragraph we have already anticipated the classification of female relatives, which should be extended from the mother's to the other generations. This is not necessary, as the structure is symmetrical (with the exception just mentioned).

Conclusion

I have shown, I hope, that the Dravidian kinship terminology, and with it other terminologies of the same type, can be considered in its broad features as springing from the combination in precise configurations of four principles of opposition: distinction of generation (qualified as an ordered scale), distinction of sex, distinction of kin identical with alliance relationship, and distinction of age.

The third distinction (which alone is in no way biological) is the most important; the system embodies a sociological theory of marriage taken in the form of an institution following the generations, and supposes—as well as favors—the rule of marrying a cross cousin as a means of maintaining it. Hence also the fact, well preserved in Indian groups, that the two categories of kin and affines comprehend all relatives without any third category. This may be understood without resorting to dual organization; the opposition between kin and affines constitutes a whole—the affine of my affine is my brother; marriage is in a sense the whole of society, which it unites, and at the same time separates in two from the point of view of one Ego.[12]

No wonder, then, if India makes it the paramount ceremony, and perhaps it is also an explanation for the stability and vitality of the Dravidian terminology which has puzzled many anthropologists since Morgan.

11. I regret this omission the more, since the relative sex designation is one point where the system comes closer to that of the Kariera (see below chapter 5).
12. This happens only when certain conditions are present; cf. below, chap. 2, "How the Terminology is Applied."

Correspondence

Following its publication of the above, Man *published a letter from A. R. Radcliffe-Brown (*Man *1953, no 169) and the author's rejoinder (*Man *1953, no 224). Both are reproduced here by permission of the Royal Anthropological Institute.*

SIR,—I cannot claim that I understand the article on Dravidian kinship terminology by Mr. Dumont though I have read it carefully several times. I should like to be enlightened as to its meaning, and I suspect that there are others in the same position as myself.

As I understand it the fundamental point is the distinction between relations of kinship and what are called "alliance relationships" which are described as "the relationship arising between two male (or two female) persons and their siblings of the same sex when a 'sister' (a 'brother') of one is married to the other." "As an equivalent formula," Mr. Dumont writes, "I shall speak also of two men (or women) having an alliance relationship as male (or female) affines." It appears that the relation between a father and son (or mother and son) is one of kinship and so is the relation between siblings. But the relation of a man to his maternal uncle is described as an alliance or affinal relation, since he is the brother-in-law of the father. The "mother's brother," we are told, "proves to be essentially the father's affine." It appears similarly that the real relation of a father's sister to Ego is that she is in an "alliance relationship" with Ego's mother, being her husband's sister. The mother's brother and the father's sister and their children the cross cousins are therefore not kin, but relatives by alliance or affines. "There will be no difficulty in showing that Ego's 'cross cousins' are essentially Ego's affines, just as the 'mother's brother' proved to be essentially the father's affine."

We are not told whether the father's brother and the mother's sister are to be regarded as kinsfolk. Presumably not, since the mother's sister is the wife's sister of the father and therefore an alliance relative. It is customary in English to speak of uncles and aunts as kinsfolk. But when the maternal uncle is referred to as "mother's brother" this is described by Mr. Dumont as "the anthropologist's customary and peculiar vocabulary expressing alliance in terms of kinship," and so concealing the "simple truth" that the real relationship is that the maternal uncle is the brother-in-law of the father.

When Mr. Dumont asks us to abandon our "customary and peculiar vocabulary" and speak of the maternal uncle not as a brother of the mother but as a brother-in-law of the father he ought to give us some adequate reason for making the change and explain what will be the advantages. This he has not done. He is asking us to repudiate the idea of cognatic kinship by which persons are cognates if they are descended, through males or through females, from a common ancestor or ancestress. A mother's brother's son is just as much a cognate as a father's brother's son but is classified by Mr. Dumont as an "affine." Why?

Mr. Dumont speaks of the Dravidian kinship terminology as belonging to the "Dacota-Iroquois" type. In my teaching on kinship for more than a quarter of a century I have indicated to students that we ought to recognize what I called the "Australian-Dravidian" type of terminology existing in Australian tribes, in the Dravidian peoples and in some Melanesian societies. The characteristic feature of the type is that there are no terms for relatives by marriage, or in the few instances in which such terms are found they are not classificatory but specific for the individual relationship. In the Kariera tribe of Western Australia a man is only permitted to marry a woman who is his *nuba,* the daughter of a man who is his *kaga* and a woman who is his *toa.* After the marriage his wife is still his *nuba* and her father and mother are still his *kaga* and *toa.* Just as he practised rigid avoidance of his *toa* (of any *toa*) before he married, he continues to avoid her after his marriage. The terms "*nuba,*" "*kaga*" and "*toa,*" which are applied to large numbers of persons, are not terms for relatives by marriage.

Mr. Dumont says that in speaking of uncles and aunts as brothers or sisters of the father and mother we *unconsciously* superimpose our own way of thinking upon the native way of thinking. The evident implication is that the Dravidian peoples think of the maternal uncle not as a brother of the mother but as the brother-in-law of the father. It is impossible to believe that this is true of the Nayars where one of the maternal uncles is the head of the *taravad,* exercising authority, and the father is, or formerly was, no more than the *sambandham* lover, or one of the lovers, of the mother. I can assure Mr. Dumont that amongst the Australian natives the maternal uncle is thought of as the brother of Ego's mother and not as the brother-in-law of the father. It is certainly true that my own maternal uncle is the brother-in-law of my father, and that some other man whom I call "mother's brother" may be the husband of my father's sister. But in neither instance is he thought of as being "essentially" a relative by marriage. In fact the Australian aborigines have no terms to indicate relatives by marriage, "alliance" relatives or affines. Yet there is clearly great similarity between Australian and Dravidian systems of kinship terminology.

A. R. RADCLIFFE-BROWN

SIR,—Professor Radcliffe-Brown has honored me by criticizing at some length my article on "Dravidian Kinship Terminology." What can I say in its defense? In the first place I dealt solely with a type of *terminology* common among *South Indian* castes. On this I feel that none of my distinguished critic's arguments has a direct bearing, as I considered neither kinship *behavior,* nor *Australian* aborigines. When the assumption is renewed that Dravidian and Australian terminologies belong to the same type, I would ask that some attention be given to the difference I mentioned [note 9]. The only Indian group which Professor Radcliffe-Brown refers to is the Nayar. They were not included by me [sources, note 6], and their terminology differs widely from the type studied (see K. Gough in *J. R. Anthrop. Inst.* 82, part 1 [1952]:82f.).

I attempted to show that the simplest way of accounting for the basic distinction between two kinds of relatives in the systems which I considered is to say that it is based on affinity, e.g. the father and the mother's brother are distinguished as being affines to one another. The extra-terminological (and therefore strictly speaking irrelevant) Nayar data adduced by Professor Radcliffe-Brown would not seem to go against this, but rather to accord with it: there, the mother's brother is a close relative, while the father on the contrary is "no more than the *sambandham* lover . . . of the mother." (Incidentally, *sam-bandham,* "con-junction," means in Sanskrit and in common South Indian usage "marriage," "affinity.") True, the ordinary positions—which alone I mentioned—of father and mother's brother are here reversed, but the principle of the distinction stands, and this is the main matter.

Professor Radcliffe-Brown extends to kinship in general categories which I defined only on the terminological level: the system of kinship terms distinguishes two categories: the principle of the distinction lies in alliance (or affinal) relationship defined as "the relationship arising between two male (or two female) persons . . . when a sister (a brother) of one is married to the other." As against this relationship is defined a relationship excluding alliance, which is called arbitrarily "kin" relationship. Then the *kinship* terms fall into two categories: "terminological kin" and "terminological affines." It is relatively easy to confuse the issue by disregarding the definition of "kin" and identifying "kin" with kinship in general. Professor Radcliffe-Brown ironically asks in which category the mother's sister fits. The answer should be obvious, but, to clear up any doubts, she is present in fig. 3 of my text. He suggests that she might be considered as the father's affine. But this is clearly impossible, as they do not belong to the same sex, whereas affinity is considered only between persons of the same sex in the above definition, which was quoted by Professor Radcliffe-Brown himself a few lines earlier. Also, while I wrote of the "anthropologist's customary and peculiar vocabulary" only in relation to cross-cousin marriage, this is given by Professor Radcliffe-Brown as applying to the maternal uncle.

Is that all? Let us try to see where the disagreement actually lies. Two points seem important. First, Professor Radcliffe-Brown insists on knowing "how the maternal uncle is thought of" by the people. This, I submit, is not a matter of terminology, but of behavior. Two different approaches are contrasted here: in the first one, Professor Radcliffe-Brown takes the maternal uncle as the prototype of a whole class of relatives, and inquires into the concrete linguistic form of the term (e.g. "male mother," etc.), the way the people think of that particular relative, etc. In the other approach, we take the terminological system as a whole and try to determine from its structure what the content of each of its categories is. The latter method obviously implies that the system as a whole is logically consistent, and one might object to that assumption, if one were inclined to consider the kinship vocabulary as being merely a rough reflection of patterns of behavior. But is this possible in a case where the assumption of consistency is verified? Here, there is some advantage in treating the two sexes separately. In English, it might perhaps be said that the aunt is a female uncle, etc. But it does not lead us very far unless we recognize that the difference between the father and the uncle, the mother and the aunt, the brother (or sister) and the cousin, the son (or daughter) and the nephew (or niece) is one and the same, and is the difference between the direct line and the collateral lines. Here is the main distinction, the axis of the system. Once we have acknowledged this, is not the question how an Englishman "thinks of" his paternal aunt a different matter altogether? But, if the English system is logical, then is not the Dravidian type (my fig. 1) as logical as the English? If so, then what is the structural principle on which it is based? I may have been mistaken in its identification, but the task of seeking it is inescapable.

A second reason of disagreement lies in contrary assumptions about the importance of affinity. From the fact that in a given system "there are no terms for relatives by marriage," Professor Radcliffe-Brown seems to conclude that any affinal content is absent from the terms of that system. Limited as my experience is compared with his, I should conjecture on the contrary that in such a case many terms have an affinal content, which may be important even though unsuspected or understressed by the anthropologist. This is true already of the Kariera examples adduced: "a man is only permitted to marry a woman who is his *nuba* . . . , after the marriage his wife is still his *nuba* . . . ," and then comes the startling conclusion: "The terms *nuba* (etc.), which are applied to large numbers of persons, are not terms for relatives by marriage." True, they are not *distinctive* terms but, precisely for that reason, is not the whole category of *nuba* tinged with affinity? Or should we say that the connections of *nuba* with marriage referred to above are not part of the meaning of the term, on the level on which Professor Radcliffe-Brown considers it?

In general, Professor Radcliffe-Brown objects to widening the concept of affinity. He is satisfied with the current meaning of the word, i.e. with a common-sense category of our own society which has not undergone any transformation or adaptation before being applied to different societies, in particular to societies with positive marriage regulations. I submit that this is untenable. If there are prescribed or preferred mates, what does it mean, if not that affinity in a way precedes the actual marriage, that an individual has potential affines before he acquires actual in-laws by marriage, that affinity in a wider sense is inherited just as our "blood" relationships are?

I can assure Professor Radcliffe-Brown that I have only tried to do justice to my field data by adapting my ideas to them. I do not for a moment equate terminology with the whole of kinship. Of the latter in some South Indian groups I would in fact claim that it is not possible to get a satisfactory picture without widening our notion of affinity. Whether or not, by doing so, I succeed in giving a relatively simple and well connected account, as he instructed us to do, Professor Radcliffe-Brown will judge from an article to be published.

Louis Dumont

Comment (1981)

It certainly cannot be said that the above analysis of thirty years ago has been in the meantime generally accepted, even in its main lines, by specialists in the region. Yet I feel neither that the objections to it are well founded, nor that it has been superseded. I rather think that it has hardly been understood, in part, no doubt, because of the shortcomings of the paper. A few formulations have been corrected in the above (see the notes). What this comment will in the main try to do is to dispel the misunderstandings by making more explicit the presuppositions and the method, in the hope that the main articulations of the argument and the real bearing of disagreements will appear more clearly.

We are concerned here only with the vocabulary as a subsystem of the kinship system at large (cf. Dumont 1971, 22–28). The desirability and usefulness of isolating it as such is the first object of disagreement. Instructed by experience, I should not today generalize from the present case regarding either the importance of the vocabulary subsystem in relation to the other aspects of kinship or its nature and the mode of analysis appropriate to it. In particular, I have learned to my cost that the North Indian (Hindi) vocabulary is of a different type and is not liable to a similar analysis (Dumont 1975*b*, 198). At any rate, and however it may be in other cases, we have before us here a *clearly bounded, simply patterned, indigenous system of categories* (see fig. 1). This being so, I make two contentions. First, here are the terms in which the people actually think their kinship relationships, and they are for us more important, and above all more certain, than the "over-arching cultural categories" detached from practice cherished by symbolic or cultural analysts, because the terms in which the people actually think are more important than what they say—in answer to questions or otherwise—about the terms in which they think that they are thinking. Moreover, seeing the crystalline beauty of the scheme, its regularity and economy and, to single out one feature, the perfect symmetry between the two sexes—which transcribes in terms of equality the segregation of the sexes in social life—we might call it a superb invention, or a cultural gem, but certainly not suppose that it is the chance result of a complicated process by which the meaning of each kinship word has been extended from one particular relative to others, nor think that it can be understood in that fashion. This is my second contention: that the scheme is the form of a unitary thought, or principle, and that it can therefore be understood as a whole and is not to be taken as a chance combination of elements.

The Dravidian vocabulary is not the only one presenting an immediately apparent or simple basic structure. Surprisingly perhaps the same is true, in the rough, of the modern Western vocabulary, be it common French or English or "Yankee." I take the occasion to remark upon a subtle but significant difference in analytical procedures. Following an idea of Goodenough, Wallace and Atkins have offered an analysis of the American vocabulary based on the same perception as a sketch of mine, namely the perception of a "dimension of contrast" in the region of lineal-collateral. Once a first category was defined as lineal "ancestors or descendants of Ego" (c1), there remained to distinguish between siblings and cousins. This was done as between those "whose ancestors include, or are included in, all the ancestors of Ego" (first called co-lineals) (c2), and the others (c3) (Wallace and Atkins 1960). Goodenough introduced a further refinement. Unhappy about separating in such a manner brother and sister from father, mother, etc., as this seemed to go against the feel of the culture, he resorted to a more complicated scheme (Goodenough 1965, 260 ff.).

As against this mode of proceeding, we might be content with looking at the configuration as it is: "The difference between the father and the uncle, the mother and the aunt, the brother (or sister) and the cousin, the son (or daughter) and the nephew (or niece) is one and the same" (Dumont 1962, 32 ff.). Clearly those words should go into two columns (and not three), and *we have to define the two broad implicit categories accordingly*. The choice of labels is secondary as against the recognition of the configuration as it is. In such a truly structural procedure, there is no risk of alienating the feel of the culture, for we have, up to now, introduced nothing that might be foreign to it. Even if we later on come to label the categories arbitrarily, we shall at any rate have properly isolated or constructed our object.

The mistake of these American authors is easy to locate: where Ego says, in short, "people of my own line," they introduce lineality in their sense of the term "ascendants and descendants," thus excluding siblings and missing the fact that siblingship is at this point encompassed in filiation as against the other relatives.

For clarity, I restate here the principles of the analysis, which were all too briefly mentioned in the original paper. Certain words of the native language are used as labels for the categories or classes of (types of) relatives. The purpose of the analysis is to get at the categories through the words that label them. Those words, which designate relatives by classifying them, are both part of the language at large and part of the kinship vocabulary as a restricted part of the language. The problem is whether we may, and how we can, isolate the latter within the former. The hypothesis is that we may and can do so provided the kinship vocabulary can be seen as a clearly bounded configuration of separate categories (without any overlap between them), for then we can assume that the *kinship meaning* of a word, as opposed to its general meaning(s) in the language at large, results only from its place in the configuration of categories, in other words that in the linguistic form of the word only those aspects are relevant to the analysis that distinguish one category from the others. That is to say, at this fundamental level words as labels have only to be radically different in order to differentiate categories of relatives. For the rest, their concrete linguistic form is irrelevant (as clearly recognized in Conklin 1969, 43§1.1). To put it otherwise, we distinguish here two degrees of linguistic distinction: words differ from each other either radically, i.e. primarily, or barely through affixes, i.e. secondarily. *Son* and *daughter* are two (fundamentally) distinct kinship words, while the French equivalents *fils* and *fille* are actually only one, i.e. designate only one category, within which a secondary distinction is effected through gender affixes. Similarly, *father, grandfather, father-in-law, stepfather,* etc., are clearly not independent of each other on that (fundamental) level: they are only parts of a wide category made up of them all and subdivided— on a secondary level which does not interest us here—through affixes (including the affix zero). (Goodenough 1965 gives his reasons for considering *grandfather* as a term per se; see p. 268 and note 10.) Strangely enough this important distinction, which was used by Morgan (Dumont 1962, 10), is almost universally disregarded nowadays, with the result that the contours of the basic kinship distinctions are blurred by being confused with less important ones. For instance, we find here itself—and it could be shown on other examples, beyond India as well as within India—that the difference in this regard in the treatment of sex is generally significant: whether sex is expressed by a mere affix (between relatives that are brother and sister or spouses, see Dumont 1975*b*, 208) or by a radical difference is meaningful in relation to the whole configuration.

The principle entails some complications. I had initially supposed that linguistic resemblances might occur between words far apart in the configuration without hindering the distinction, but this does not seem to be the case. Moreover it is *for the speakers themselves* that the words have to be radically distinct, and whether they are so for them may not always be easy to ascertain. It is essential, as already mentioned, that there should be no overlap—or rather "neither overlap nor inclusion" (Wallace and Atkins 1969, 354)—between categories: two (radically) different words should designate either two entirely different sets of individual relationships, or the same set (as alternative designations). Strictly, all the words used for the designation of a given set or category, taken together, constitute for us *the* (complex) kinship *term* corresponding to the category. Linguists may frown at this admission of synonymy. It is enough here to insist that we are dealing only with the primordial level of distinction of kinship words as such.

Harold Conklin has noted these requirements. When they are met, they allow us to isolate what he calls a "paradigm" as opposed to a "hierarchy" or taxonomy (Conklin 1969, 52§3). In view of a discussion to come, it is important to note that we have before us in Dravidian a "paradigm" in Conklin's sense, a configuration in which no hierarchical distinction of levels is found (but which can itself be part of a taxonomy as one level of it).

Regarding the hierarchical disposition, there is one point on which we can go a little further. Conklin took the example of "*animal* and *man* in the following partial contrastive sets: *animal*[1] vs. *plant, animal*[2] vs. *man*[1], *man*[2] vs. *woman*," and was led by the need to clearly distinguish "successive levels" in a hierarchy to consider *animal*[1] and *animal*[2], *man*[1] and *man*[2] as homonymous lexemes (Conklin 1969, 50). If we stress the hierarchical relation instead of the absolute distinction of levels, we can regroup animal[1] and animal[2], or man[1] and man[2] (cf. man and woman in Dumont 1980, 240), and both together as cases of successive linguistic *encompassing* where the hierarchical relation is precisely expressed in the double meaning of the words (see fig. 5).

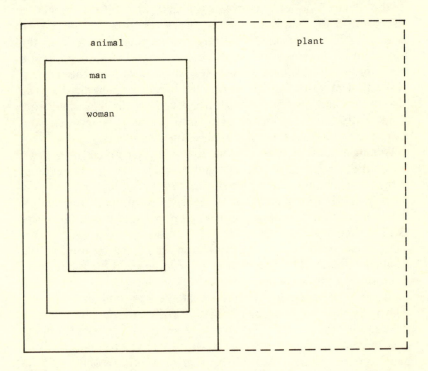

Fig. 5.

The point is of some interest here, because such encompassing is sometimes found, and usually not easily treated, in kinship vocabularies. Actually we have an example at hand in North India with, in Hindi, *bhāī* "brother" being on one level opposed to *sālā* "wife's brother" while it encompasses it on the immediately superior level, *sālā* being a *bhāī* as against other relatives (and it is not the end of *bhāī's* encompassing capacity, cf. Dumont 1975b). I recalled this example because the clear contrast with South Indian usage goes to show that there is in the South a clearly "paradigmatic" (in Conklin's sense) nature of kinship as a separate domain, contrary to recent attempts to equate the relation between caste and kinship in the South with that which prevails in the North (see below, chapter 4).

Once we are in possession of the fundamental categories and terms, we can construct or map, as it were, their configuration, as was done above (fig. 1). At first sight there is something arbitrary in the disposition of the boxes in that figure (this aspect is discussed in the Kariera analysis below, chapter 5). The global feature to be emphasized is surely the perfect similitude in the treatment of the sexes on the three central levels, *in conjunction with the axial distinction:* we see that wherever the *radical* distinction of sexes is maintained, it is accompanied by the axial distinction, and wherever female relatives are distinguished from male relatives only by an affix, i.e. in the extreme generations and that of the children, the axial distinction disappears.

To single out one aspect of the equivalent treatment of the two sexes: the relationships "father" and "mother" are treated exactly in the same manner. Therefore it is natural to put the "mother" on the same side of the axis as the "father." This point is essential. It is the main shortcoming of the original paper that it was not made explicit there.

We come now to the main question: the interpretation of the axial distinction. The fact that it is accompanied by a complete separation of the sexes directs us to reckon the relationships within each sex separately: fig. 1 shows that we may connect a female relative in, say, box C neither with her brother (as the chart does in the children's generation), nor with her spouse or brother (as in the grandparents' generation). This is why I refused to read from the figure anything like a mother's brother or a father's sister. At the same time, if we define "affines" as persons of the same sex linked by an intermarriage, we see that every box on the left can be taken as having globally an affinity relationship (real in some cases, virtual in others) with its symmetrical counterpart on the left. Thus one's own father and one's own mother's brother are brothers-in-law, and the configuration by itself tells us that they are classified here as such.

This interpretation is confirmed by the native speakers themselves, for they distinguish male relatives into two categories, differently labeled in different groups and languages, which correspond to the axial distinction on our figure 1 and which we may therefore translate as "consanguines" and "affines," it being understood that in doing so we give these words a meaning slightly different from our own.

It can be recalled also that, if we step out of the vocabulary itself and look at kinship as a whole, we find that the terminological dichotomy is highly meaningful in relation to the latter (below, chapter 2).

To return to the overarching categories that divide into two all the male relatives of the three central generations and age groups: they are not just "cultural categories" detached from kinship (Carter 1974, col. 41*b*); they are in fact collective kinship categories that are currently used as such in the discussion of relationships, of intermarriage, etc. Moreover, they are now abundantly testified to in the literature. It is therefore in vain that Scheffler has tried, by using the linguistic form and the other meanings of the particular words used by the people I studied, to show that the distinction is of a different nature and does not immediately relate to the axial, affinal, dichotomy (Scheffler 1977, 874–75).

This is not all. As we saw, the mother, being treated exactly as the father, must be located on the same side of the chart, that of consanguines, which results in putting the "father's sister" or "cross-aunt" on the affinal side and led me to extend to females the general classification used in the language for males only. With one proviso, though, which should have been stated more clearly than I perhaps did, namely that, affinity holding strictly only between persons of the same sex, FZ and her likes are affines primarily for females and secondarily for a male Ego, through his mother (or sister in Ego's generation). This extension to females of the native distinction for males has scandalized some of my colleagues. They introduced into their protest considerations of birthplace or descent, which are out of place here, as descent is virtually present in the scheme only as a particular, restricted form of consanguinity.

Thus Kathleen Gough, maintaining that "these categories relate always to unilineal groups," opposed to affines "lineal *or pseudo-lineal*" relatives (my emphasis) and insisted that in the case at hand it was "most logical to classify women with their natal descent group," thus reversing the positions of M and FZ stated here (Gough 1959*c*; *Current Anthropology* 1966, 334–35; Gough 1979, 273). Which means, I think, refusing both to think in terms of oppositions and to consider the vocabulary in itself. (I was not as clear as I should have been in rejoining on the last point: Dumont 1961, 87; 1964, 79). A point that comes out clearly in the 1966 discussion is that K. Gough thinks it is not possible to abstract a common model from all the variety of vocabularies and institutions (*Current Anthropology* 1966, 334–35, cf. Gough 1979; in this regard, see also S. Tyler, *Current Anthropology* 1966, 341, 343).

I shall now consider at some length a relatively recent, elaborate, and closely argued criticism, even though some of the relevant points have been made above. In a review article, Harold Scheffler has outspokenly rejected my approach, and more specifically this analysis (Scheffler 1977, 869–75 for what concerns us here; regarding Australia, see postscript below in chapter 5). He stated that the analysis was based on "the demonstrably false assumption that polysemy by extension (or generalization) is *not* a feature of Dravidian . . . kinship terms," and that it suffered "from two major internal contradictions, either of which is sufficient to invalidate the theory" (p. 870). One of those two imputed contradictions was alluded to above. It bears on the designation in the native language of the two overarching categories that I translate as consanguines and affines. Scheffler argues that, contrary to my stated principle, I do here " 'read' terminological structure from group structure" (p. 874). Actually Scheffler's "polysemy" plays a role here also, and the argument is involved (pp. 874–75). To cut it short, let me simply restate that, when the native speakers distinguish all male relatives into A and B in accordance with the dichotomy of the vocabulary, whatever may be the meanings of A and B in other contexts, and whatever the words designating A and B are—and there are now in the literature a whole series of examples from different groups—they impose this dichotomy to our consideration as the global feature of their classification. Scheffler himself hardly confronts this dichotomy at all. Indeed, his one-page discussion on the topic bears on its linguistic form only and results in pushing the dichotomy itself under the carpet (see pp. 874–75).

The other and main contradiction with which I am charged relates to "polysemy." For the critic, kinship terms are always "polysemic." Previously, in a brief indictment of the approach (Scheffler 1971, note 2), he had made two strictures: that it took the terms as monosemic, and that it interpreted the cross categories as affinal while they are—axiomatically—basically consanguineal. It is noteworthy that the latter stricture has dropped from the present criticism and that the former has been modified. Maybe the two points are interconnected. It is stated now that "Dumont does not deny that many Tamil terms are polysemous" (p. 871), and that the difference lies in the interpretation. I go from the wider to the narrower meaning ("polysemy by narrowing or specialization"; ibid.). Surprisingly Scheffler now admits that this is right in some cases, or rather that "polysemy by specialization is . . . a feature of some of these terms" (p. 874). Might this acknowledgement constitute the link between the two changes noted above? Yet he maintains that "polysemy" by generalization or extension, i.e. from narrow primary meaning to wider meaning, predominates. Hence the new formulation of the charge: that I do not recognize the existence of "polysemy by extension" while this kind of "polysemy" is actually presupposed in my argument, as Scheffler purports to demonstrate on several examples. Let us here notice a difference: Scheffler projects his viewpoint into the datum ("polysemy is a feature of . . . terms") including "extension" or "specialization," while I do nothing of the sort but only construct, or rather recognize, from the configuration as a whole, the (major) categories within each of which a number of narrower meanings are contained and a number of words (Scheffler's "terms") used as designations.

I note in passing that the critic found it fit to make abundant use in his initial pages (pp. 869–72) of an early text in which I was still groping for the solution of the problem, and which should be taken as superseded by those here reproduced. (I made it clear in both 1953a and 1957a, cf. here itself chapter 1—where the early interpretation is rejected, and note 5: "a first attempt in the present direction"; chap. 2, note 2: "a preliminary report from the field.") Yet he noted the difference by saying, "Later Dumont expressed himself differently" (p. 872); the author takes precedence against the thesis.

In one of his elaborate attempts at demonstrating my contradiction, the critic involves himself in contradiction in his turn. He writes on page 874: "Normally . . . where an expression has both a broad basic sense and a derivative specialized sense, its occurrence in the specialized sense is lexically marked, as in the case of French *femme* "woman" versus *ma femme* "my wife," and, one page further on, "We may acknowledge that the most inclusive class designated as *appa* is indeed composed of several subclasses, but we may not regard this most inclusive class as the principal or structurally most prior of these classes. Instead, we must say that the class designated as *tagappaN* is the principal or structurally most basic class on which the most inclusive *appa* and its other subclasses . . . are based.''

What Scheffler aims to show is that in my presentation of the categories I actually start from their narrower meaning: "While overtly denying polysemy by extension, Dumont actually posits it" (p. 873). Here is one example. About the opposition consanguines/affines I am made to say that it is "first and foremost the opposition between siblings and siblings-in-law of the same sex" (p. 871). The references are to 1953*a*, 35, and 1957*a*, 25. Actually both passages introduce the categories "father" and "mother's brother" as distinguished and linked by in-lawship, or affinity. In-lawship is no doubt fundamental, but it is one thing to say that the relationship between F and MB is the same as that between ZH and WB and it would be quite another thing to say that a word designating primarily ZH is extended to other relatives. It is true of the Tamils as of ourselves that affinity is generated through marriage. Only, while with us it is present exclusively in that way, with them it is also transmitted in a manner from one generation to the next. Scheffler concludes that my use of " 'transmission' amounts to recognition of polysemy by extension." Taken literally, it is true; taken in Scheffler's sense of the word, it is not, because there is all the difference in the world between an expression, "transmission," that makes sense of the whole configuration in relation to our own conceptions of consanguinity and affinity and a purely analytical expression, "extension," that means nothing at all except for those who turn their back to the configuration as a whole and insist on generating it from its elements.

To stress this point, let me enlarge on what is done in the end through the introduction of "transmission." In Dravidian, affinity is transmitted from one generation to the next as only consanguinity is with us. In Dravidian, affinity and consanguinity have thus equal status, while they have unequal status with us. In Dravidian, they are given in a simple, binary, or "distinctive opposition," i.e. an equistatutory opposition. With us, affinity is ephemeral; it fades into consanguinity for the next generation: my brother-in-law becomes an uncle for my child. In other words, with us affinity is opposed to consanguinity on one level, while on a more global level it is identical with it. This is what I called a hierarchical opposition, where one term is "encompassed" in the other (Dumont 1980, Postface). We have thus come not only to understand the Dravidian system, but to learn something from it about our own.

Scheffler is often led by his preoccupation to take what is in fact a mode of presentation as a statement of principle. For an *understanding* study, which componentialism of Scheffler's variety is not, there is a problem of "translation" of the foreign mode of representation into our familiar one. We all the time juxtapose our native categories (of "father," etc.) with the different ones under study. Thus I speak of F and MB to introduce the real native major (or "most inclusive") categories which are more exactly rendered as "male consanguine of parents' generation" and "male affine of parents' generation." To simply state that the Tamils distinguish in the two or three central generations consanguines and affines does not make sense unless and until it is shown on particular terms and relatives how affinity, which for us is purely synchronic or intragenerational, can be and is thought by them as diachronic or transgenerational.

To notice two more points. To maintain that all other meanings of "father" are derived by extension from one's own father, Scheffler notes that "the other subclasses of the most inclusive *appa* class are lexically marked by forms which signify relative age in relation to one's father" (pp. 873–74). Well, these distinctions take place on a different level, on a secondary level which is not that of the broad categories themselves. In the particular case, the relative age is reckoned in relation to one's own father only for his siblings or agnatic cousins (not in the case, for instance, of a "mother" 's husband). Similarly, the analytical description of a particular relationship (as in English say MZHB) is distinguished from the ascription of a broad categorical status (*sondam* versus *muRei*, cf. my French monograph 1957*b*, p. 273). The discontinuity is clear when the Tamils argue that X is *a* (MZHB) and hence falls into the category of *A* ("father"). This bears on Scheffler, pp. 871–72.

On the whole, the controversy very much resembles a discussion between deaf protagonists, which could only be settled by comparing the results of the two approaches.

To me, it is striking how impervious Scheffler is to the basic issues of the case, especially the global dichotomy. The same is true regarding the equation of relatives that in our own native view and in Scheffler's as well are consanguines on the one hand, affines on the other—say WB = MBS (etc.)—a feature that is basically related to the general dichotomy. It can also be remarked that, whatever his talk about oppositions or relations, Scheffler is all the time harking back to defining *each category in itself,* through "primary focus" and "extensions," through the linguistic form of the term that designates it, etc. To come back to "father" and "mother's brother," what is essential is that a F is *not* a MB, a MB *not* a F. Only because he disregards this can Scheffler write that "there is no way to specify definitions of the broadest kin classes which does not recognize that they are structurally derivative." This is so if each category is considered in itself, that is, independently of the other categories, i.e. of its place in the whole system.

We are thus brought back to the root of the disagreement. Scheffler professes not to object to the "structuralist tenet" but only to its "corruption" into the principle that "no part can be defined other than by its relation to the whole" (p. 875), a principle short of which any "structuralist tenet" is, I hold, empty talk—but perhaps it would better be called the "holistic tenet." In contrast to Scheffler, I am quite ready to admit that we cannot always start from the whole. But here, fortunately, we can.

To leave the last word in this controversy to a historian of ideas: Lovejoy (1973, p. 10) opposes the organismic and the nominalist tempers, and characterizes the latter by "the tendency, almost instinctive with some men, to reduce the meaning of all general notions to an enumeration of the concrete and sensible particulars which fall under those notions."

Also, it may well be the case that the stress on the broad classification, so vivid in South India, and so compelling for its anthropologist, is not experienced in other cultures and is thus foreign to their anthropologists. Perhaps the main difficulty in these studies is to reconcile the systematic classification, which exists by itself, objectively or absolutely, with the fact that in its actual operation it starts from an Ego located at one particular place within it: when we designate a relative we start from one point or person, and yet we step into the systematic configuration of categories. The problem is thus perhaps how this takes place, how Ego puts himself or herself into the grid. The upshot of this analysis would seem to be that in our case it is done essentially through immediate filiation (to parents and children) and through affinity or alliance operating both from Ego and from Ego's siblings and parents. Would this view reconcile the insistence on starting from Ego with the recognition that only the holistic framework or configuration makes sense of the categories it defines?

In closing this comment, let me state again that this analysis claims to deal only with the basic level of distinction in the vocabulary, and to thus deliver the basic cognitive grid through which the people think their kinship relationships. It is incomplete in the sense that the secondary levels of distinction are not explored.

We have dealt here in principle with the vocabulary subsystem alone. The question of its relation to the system at large will be taken up in chapter 4.

2

Hierarchy and Marriage Alliance in South Indian Kinship

To Claude Lévi-Strauss

Introduction

The present study is based upon two years' research in the Tamil-speaking part of South India in 1949–50. The groups with which it deals live in the southernmost part of the area, in the districts of Madura, Tinnevelly, and Ramnad. When comparing these several groups, which are close to one another in the caste hierarchy as well as in space, one is faced with a contradiction. While their social life, broadly considered, gives the impression of being quite homogeneous, yet a certain diversity is found in what the anthropologist usually considers to be the basic features of kinship. Such

This study was first published by the Royal Anthropological Institute, London, 1957 (Occasional Paper no. 12). Reprinted by permission of the Royal Anthropological Institute. The text is reproduced without changes (except for minor verbal alterations and a few passages signaled in the notes). The notes have been modified. Regarding the reception of the paper, the discussion of particular points is when possible accommodated in the notes, while the more general points will be taken up in chapter 4.

a discrepancy may seem, at first sight, to run counter to the "functionalist" postulate of monographic analysis, according to which the institutions of any group are so interdependent that any one feature, for instance descent, cannot change without involving a change in the other features.

This study may be taken as an attempt to remove the contradiction mentioned by showing that it results from too crude a formulation of the data, and that the organization of the groups considered rests on fundamental institutions which are common to all, although they take particular forms in each of them. In point of fact, the comparative approach, which aims at discovering what different groups have in common, has directed the field work itself. It is an adaptation of the general monographic method to Indian conditions, and rests on solid methodological ground. For, limited as their results may otherwise have been, general studies of the caste system have shown that a caste group cannot be considered as a self-contained whole—as a society in itself—but only as a segmentary, or structural, group in the entire system. While one caste can be easily distinguished from another, it is not the caste itself but its subdivisions which become apparent when the internal organization is considered (Senart 1896; Blunt 1931, 6–7). In other words, we can speak of the "caste" if we look at it from outside, but it splits into segments when we consider it from inside. Recently, Professor Hutton (1946, 44–45) has recognized that it is impossible to define the individual caste by itself, i.e. by features inherent in it or by permanent attributes of its essence. A caste is a shifting and elusive reality because its characteristics in each case depend upon the position it occupies in the whole system. Only the system is susceptible of definition, and that, not by the elements which might be said to enter into its composition, but by the principles of their arrangement in the system. Bouglé (1908), as a sociologist, had rightly begun to do this. In brief, the caste system is a structural system.

If this is so, important consequences follow. There is no absolute difference between what happens inside and outside a caste group, and we may expect to find in its internal constitution something of the principles which govern its external relations. This happens with a certain type of hierarchy which is prominent in the caste order and which, as will be shown, occurs within the endogamous units. Hence we see a way of pursuing within each group the common "culture" or the common "set of values" that the different groups are considered by some anthropologists to share in a rather vague way, and the simplest hypothesis we can make is to suppose that this is present in each group under the form of common institutions, susceptible of precise sociological description. The object of the present study is not any one group considered in its individual features, but rather a common "pattern" which appears in particular forms within each group.

Such a comparative approach somewhat complicates the exposition. By studying the subdivisions of the endogamous groups, the existence of a gradation of status can be established. Brief separate descriptions of the individual groups have then to be given, against which it is possible to test certain hypotheses about the way in which the features of descent, residence, marriage regulations, etc. are associated in each case. The comparison, however, reveals as common to all only the principle of unilineality. This is but half of the common pattern. The other half has to do with marriage, and some revision of habitual anthropological categories is necessary in order to define it precisely as "marriage alliance," which in turn allows for a connected description of a number of apparently discrete features.

I have unfortunately found it necessary for clear discussion to give a more restricted definition to certain terms than is found in anthropological usage generally. By "descent" I mean exclusively transmission of membership in the exogamous group. The terms "patrilineal" and "matrilineal" are applied only to descent in that sense, and not to succession and inheritance, of which I speak as being from father to son, etc. While "patrilocal" and "matrilocal" refer as usual to residence, the terms "patrilateral" and "matrilateral" are used solely in connection with marriage, i.e. to distinguish two of the three varieties of cross-cousin marriage. When it is necessary to speak of all the preceding features in a general sense, the adjectives "paternal" and "maternal" will be used. Thus, to say that people are patrilocal means that they have a patrilocal residence rule; to say that they are patrilineal means that they have patrilineal exogamous groups or units. Similarly, the terms "lineage," "patrilineage," and "matrilineage" refer only to such exogamous units as are recognized and named by the people. As distinct from lineage, I call a "line" a grouping in one line, either as a part—isolated by me alone—of a recognized lineage or as a grouping recognized by the people but irrelevant to exogamy.

It is also advisable to make a precise use of the categories of endogamy and exogamy. Apart from individual interdictions (close relatives), the range of permissible marriage is determined by two limits: (1) an outer limit, beyond which marriage is prohibited by the endogamic rule—this limit defines the "unit of endogamy" inside which one may marry everywhere, except within (2) an inner limit, in which marriage is prohibited by the exogamic rule— this limit defines the "unit of exogamy." In other words, compared with the looser sense in which "endogamous" is sometimes used as meaning a group outside which one does not marry, the unit of endogamy is the smallest of the groupings which can be called endogamous in that looser sense. Similarly, the unit of exogamy is the largest grouping which can be called exogamous in the loose sense. For instance, the unit of exogamy may be much larger than the exogamous unit when a number of patrilineages are agnatically related.

Apart from gathering "background" information and making a preliminary survey, the field work was carried out in two phases, the first being devoted to a major inquiry in one group and the second to minor comparative inquiries in several other groups. The major inquiry dealt with a part of the Kallar caste, the subcaste called Pramalai Kallar (*pramalei kallar*),[1] located west of Madura in the northern part of Tirumangalam "taluk" or subdistrict.[2] Two other Kallar groups will be mentioned, the Ambalakkarar (*ambalakkārar*), who live around Melur, east of Madura; and a small group to the south, near Sivaganga, named after their main village Paganeri. The Kondaiyam Kottai Maravar (*kondeiyam kōttei maRavar*), forming the most numerous subcaste of the Maravar caste, are spread irregularly over a vast territory from the vicinity of Ramnad to the western boundary of the Tinnevelly District. Finally the Nangudi Vellalar (*nangudi vellālar*) are located in a few villages of Srivaikuntham taluk (Tinnevelly District). Their status is distinctly higher than that of the Kallar and Maravar. They are rich landowners and are also more educated and progressive but have kept their distinctive organization.

1. Tamil words are transcribed in italics according to Meile 1945 (with some material simplification).
2. I spent about seven months among the Pramalai Kallar, on whom a preliminary report was published from the field (Dumont 1950). For a more elaborate description of that group see Dumont 1957*b* (an English translation is now in preparation).

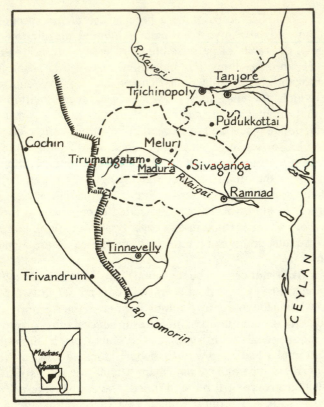

Fig. 6. Map of South India, showing principal places mentioned.

Kallar ("thieves") and Maravar ("killers" or "warriors") have much in common. They are now agriculturists but still tend to consider themselves as the descendants of warriors—including local rulers and their retinues and troops—who traditionally acted as watchmen in the village. Their local groups share, though not equally, in a heritage of violent and warlike propensities. This feature, associated as it is with the idea of power and rule, is not a stigma in traditional Indian society, but meat eating is one, and they are meat eaters. These two characteristics seem to account roughly for their intermediate position in the social scale, halfway between the Brahmans on the one hand and the Untouchables on the other. Most of them are poor and uneducated and live in a state of more or less complete territorial segregation in some of the most barren tracts.

Part I. Hierarchy

Absence of Systematic Subdivision

Some misconceptions might arise from a previous article on one of the groups here considered. Fawcett (1903) rightly reported the existence of matrilineal units, called *kīlei* or branches, among the Kondaiyam Kottai Maravar of the Tinnevelly District. But he also gave a chart showing the subcaste as made up of eighteen such units grouped by threes into six larger groups (*kottu,* "bunch"). This is not, I think, substantiated in fact, and may create a misleading impression that the group is systematically divided.

Fawcett's source is a song in praise of the subcaste, the *maRam pādal* or "kili song", an ancient text which is still sung at certain religious festivals. I have seen one manuscript copy written on palm-leaf in the hands of priests from Vannikonendal (east of Uttumalai). It has also been printed, and, furthermore, Fawcett's classification has been reproduced in a booklet in Tamil entitled *Maravar History,* which is found in many villages (Kulandaiveluc-cami and Udaiyarttevar 1938). All this has largely influenced the ideas of the people, but their actual practice is quite different. Inquiry in Tinnevelly has confirmed the statements of an important Maravar chieftain in Ramnad that no more than eleven *kīlei*—instead of eighteen—are actually found at present, and that nothing like the alleged groups of three *kīlei* exists. According to the same informant, the name *kottu* would apply only, and then but occasionally, to an honorific grouping smaller than the *kīlei.* I did not find it at all in Tinnevelly. It will be seen later that comparison strengthens the probability that the *kottu* was never anything else than a grouping within the *kīlei.*

But if the text quoted by Fawcett represents a rationalization a posteriori of the data, how could it be admitted by the people themselves? The answer lies in the wide dispersal of the subcaste and in the laudatory purpose of the song. It is remarkable enough that the same matrilineal units are found from one end to the other of the large territory over which the group is scattered, but people in one part do not know whether other units are not found elsewhere. One might admit that some *kīlei* have disappeared since the song was composed, but the contrary is probable because, on the one hand, eighteen is a sacred number, and, on the other hand, increasing the number of the units in order to make it a "sacred" total could only increase the prestige of the group in the eyes of its own members. It is probable that the *kottu* has been rationalized in the same way among people, in the Tinnevelly District, who had quite vague ideas about it. Finally, the fine regularity of Fawcett's chart is misleading: it represents an arbitrary secondary formulation, partly in terms of an obvious cultural pattern. We shall presently see, from the example of other groups, that the actual number of exogamous units does not spring from a systematic division of the endogamous group, but is the historical result of a tendency to fission akin to that which is found in the caste system at large.

Gradation of Status

It is well known that the endogamous subcastes of which an individual caste is as a rule composed show a tendency to order themselves hierarchically. What I should like to show is that here the tendency to graded statuses does not stop at the boundary of the endogamous group but enters it and finally pervades the whole sphere of kinship, so that South Indian kinship cannot be severed from the caste system.[3] With notable exceptions, the permanence of a group's status in the caste system is based on endogamy, the children of an endogamous marriage reproducing the status of their parents. But the Westerner commonly sees the system as more rigid than it is in fact. If one imagines that all unions not conforming to the endogamic rule automatically lead to excommunication, and that the excommunicated member is not only expelled from his own endogamous group and his own caste but also falls down to the level of the Untouchables, then it seems that no difference of status can arise within the endogamous group as a result of differences in marriage. But things are not so clear-cut, at any rate among the groups I am going to consider, and indeed on the whole there is ample reason for thinking that the caste system

3. The expression in the text, that kinship and caste "cannot be severed," is wrong. Having found in North India a more intimate combination of the two domains, I proposed to speak of "overlap" in the South, of "compenetration" in the North (Dumont 1975a, 143; cf. 1966, 114). This language is still insufficient, for it evokes material objects in space. Granted that we cannot *materially* separate kinship and caste by drawing a neat boundary between all their manifestations, we still can in the present case distinguish two systems of *conceptions*, although they may both be present in the same place or have their imprint on the same object. This is important in view of a discussion to come (chap. 4, second part).

was much more pliable than that. We can gain an insight into the question from the mere inspection of the units into which a few groups are split.

Pramalai Kallar

The Pramalai Kallar constitute what is generally called a subcaste: they distinguish themselves from other groups belonging to the Kallar caste, from which they are widely distant in space and with whom they do not intermarry. They say that their ancestors separated from another group of Kallar, the Ambalakkarar, some thirty miles to the east. These ancestors were "junior" people, i.e. children of secondary, possibly not endogamous, unions. Some of the customs of the Pramalai Kallar suggest that they still acknowledge the superiority of their neighbors and caste-fellows.

At first sight the Pramalai Kallar are an endogamous group occupying a certain tract of country, the "Kallar country", with only a slight admixture of other castes. They are patrilocal and patrilineal. Actually there are, inside the Kallar country, families, grouped in villages, into which no decent person will marry. These people are called *pulukkar* and are considered as the descendants of irregular unions; they had no rights in land. For an outsider they are Kallar; for an ordinary Kallar they are almost strangers. They constitute, theoretically at least, an endogamous section.

If what may be called the Pulukkar section is left aside, the rest of the Pramalai Kallar is really a unit of endogamy as defined above. Being patrilocal and occupying, practically alone, a continuous tract of country, they have territorial divisions. But here a striking fact confronts us: these territorial divisions are of two kinds. It is a stock phrase to say that the (Pramalai) Kallar country is made up of eight countries or provinces (*nādu*) and twenty-four secondary villages (*upagrāmam*). (A more complete formula would add the Pulukkar settlements and two kinds of intermediary units which I omit here.) The difference between "provinces" and "secondary villages" is not, as the translation might suggest, a difference in territorial dimension, although the first may be slightly bigger than the second. It is a difference in social status. It was very difficult to get an explanation of the phrase mentioned above, which every Kallar repeats. Finally it emerged that the secondary villages were founded by people of less pure descent, sons of chiefs and their concubines; but intermarriage has been going on, and at present the difference has almost faded out. Again, in one of the eight "provinces," or main or noble territories, the accounts of origin show men of pure descent readmitting, under certain circumstances, "junior" brothers (sons of irregular unions) into their midst.

This account of the origin of the depressed status of certain units is confirmed by what could be learned about the limits of excommunication and the rights, limited but real, of bastards. It should be added that all this largely belongs to the past. At present—in contrast to polygyny, which, although relatively rare, is still found—the practice of keeping concubines seems quite uncommon, and most of the differences of status I have mentioned, or at least their causes, are unsuspected except by a few old and knowledgeable men.

To sum up, we find among the Pramalai Kallar three kinds of local groups (two being territorial units and the third a merely residential group),[4] the unequal status of which is based, theoretically, on the difference of status between sons of orthodox endogamous marriages and sons of secondary unions. In other words, the latter were not automatically expelled, and if they were, they might be reintegrated later. Such persons were also, sometimes at least, accommodated in inferior positions within the group. Their final rank, and that of their descendants, depended very largely on individual circumstances, but the conditions of their birth introduced the principle of a lower rank. The situation may perhaps be generalized in a hypothetical form as follows: everything looks as if the caste order was concerned first of all with maintaining the status of the family, or of the main line, or of whatever it may be. Once this is assured, e.g. by the birth of sons of full right, what happens next does not matter so much in itself; if excommunication is resorted to, it is rather to prevent the lapse of one individual from endangering the status of the group. When such a fear is not too great (as probably in the conditions of territorial isolation of the Pramalai Kallar), the way is open to compromises which, while maintaining the principle of a difference of status, will not sever all links with the illegitimate offspring.

Kallar of Paganeri

This is a small group living in and round the village of Paganeri, near Sivaganga in the Ramnad District. They are the southernmost

4. Precision added.

group of Kallar east of Madura, and there are Maravar settlements close to the south. They have matrilineal exogamous units, which they call *kilei* or branches, just as the Maravar do. My inquiries among them were extremely brief, but the following picture emerged almost immediately, a fact which is, I think, characteristic.

There are five exogamous matrilineal units, but only four of them, which bear women's names, are ancient and fundamental; the fifth is considered as recent and secondary. It is called *aRiyāN*, which may mean either "unknown" or "who does not know," indicating that the people belonging to this group do not know the name of their ancestress. They, or rather their forefathers, did not belong to any of the four main units, because they were born of non-Kallar women. Until recently, no intermarriage took place between this fifth unit and the four main units, as the pedigree of both bride and bridegroom had to be produced before any marriage could take place. Now it is different, but some people still object to intermarriage. We see here a situation which recalls that of the Pulukkar in the foregoing section but which has developed differently, as is expressed in the fact that the name of *kilei* is applied to the lower group. This is not all, for still another distinction parallels one of the Pramalai Kallar.

At a funeral, a piece of cloth, twenty cubits long, styled a *sīlei*, i.e. sari or woman's garment, is given by the mourner to the two chiefs of the *kilei* of the deceased person. They then grant permission to fetch water for bathing the corpse. After the funeral pyre has been lighted, the cloth is divided between the members of the *kilei*, each of whom afterward presents his share to the husbands of his sisters.[5] The distribution is made by successive divisions on a genealogical basis, but a smaller share is given to certain lines on account of ancient sins, mainly, it is said, sexual intercourse outside the caste. We see here that among the four fundamental *kilei* there are lines of lesser status. These are called *kottu*. Still more facts go to show that, if great stress is put on endogamous marriage and sexual morality, at the same time the culprit's offspring are not expelled but integrated into the group at one of two different lower levels—either in the fifth *kilei* if the

5. The gift of a cloth by the heir to the men of the deceased's *kilei*, etc., among the "Sivaganga Kallar" is recorded by Stuart (1891, 215, quoted in Thurston & Rangachari 1909, 3:73); see also Jagor 1914, 82 ff.

mother is "unknown," or in disparaged lines (possibly when the father is a stranger or for lesser offenses).

Notwithstanding all the obvious differences, the hierarchical scheme is very much like that of the Pramalai Kallar (see fig. 2): both result from a recognition of three different main statuses within the group, a lowest level with which marriage tends to cease and two others which intermarry, the first level only having a full status and the second being considered as depressed.

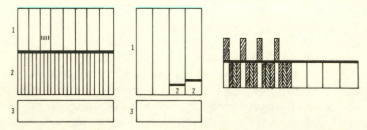

PRAMALAI KALLAR   KALLAR OF PAGANERI   NANGUDI VELLALAR

Fig. 7. Gradation of status of constituent units in three groups: Pramalai Kallar: (1) first-rank territorial units (with a trace of stratification); (2) second-rank territorial units; (3) "impure people." Kallar of Paganeri: (1) four fundamental matrilineal units; (2) "disparaged" lines at bottom; (3) fifth unit (until recently no intermarriage). Nangudi Vellalar: subdivisions of four of the matrilineal units into four sections, some of which rank higher than others.

Nangudi Vellalar

In the two preceding examples, the differentiation developed toward the bottom, from the inferior status of descendants of nonorthodox, nonendogamous unions. A third group will provide an example of differentiation at the top, thus leading us to a more general formula.

The Nangudi Vellalar are matrilineal and matrilocal. Their matrilineal exogamous groups are again called *kĭlei*. The group had in the past a powerful chieftain, who seems to have been the owner of all their lands. The succession to the office was from father to son. The authority has sharply declined, and at present the succession is not even settled. As shown in fig. 7, the rule of patrilateral cross-cousin marriage was strictly followed in the chief's line, which means that successive generations of chiefs alternately resided in two different places only; in fact, the chief had two residences but he could choose to remain always in the same one.

Now, the Nangudi Vellalar not only have eight or more matrilineal local groups (*kilei*), but these groups themselves have subdivisions called *pidir*, about which the evidence seemed at first quite confusing. Their function was not clear: there appeared to be either eight *kilei* and sixteen *pidir*, each *kilei* being divided into two *pidir*, or, as some literate informants suggested, the *pidir* might be a patrilineal descent group (Sanskrit *pitr*, "father") cutting across the matrilineal ones. (The same tendency appeared in an effort to identify the matrilineal *kilei* with the Brahmanical—and hence fashionable—*gotra*, which is patrilineal). Better information from the chief's family and the study of an extensive genealogy shows that, in fact, only four of the *kilei* are subdivided, each of them in four sections or *pidir* (probably for *piridu*, "division"), which do not regulate exogamy. The extract from the genealogy (fig. 7) readily shows that the male line of the chiefs is entirely composed of two intermarrying matrilines. My informant said that these matrilines (to which others should be added if the marriages of the chief's sisters were included) consider themselves as nobles when compared with commoners, i.e. with the mass of the respective *kilei* to which they belong, and that this corresponds to the subdivision into *pidir*, accounts for it, and explains why other *kilei*, unrelated to the chiefly ones, are not subdivided.

In other words, there is here a tendency, among the people connected with chieftainship, to express or attain a higher status by setting themselves a higher degree of endogamy than is generally required, or by expressing in terms of social units the higher degree of endogamy that corresponds to a strict observance of the marriage regulation. In the two preceding examples, a lesser degree of endogamy led to the addition of units to stress inferiority, here a greater degree of endogamy leads to subdivision of the units to stress superiority. There is another difference: in the first case the difference of status sprang directly from difference regarding endogamy, here the higher status results in the last analysis from the chief's prestige, and it is extended to, or used by, groups by means of a higher endogamic standard.[6]

6. It is wrong to speak of "endogamy," as I did here, on the level of facts. It should be reserved to the level of norms, lest one introduces confusion. Rather than of a "higher endogamic standard" I should have spoken of a greater restriction of the field of factual intermarriage. See the note 7.

General

To sum up, we have seen three examples which show a tendency to the "hierarchization" of subdivisions inside the endogamous group, these subdivisions being local groups among the Pramalai Kallar and matrilineages and their segments among the Kallar of Paganeri and the Nangudi Vellalar. I say "a tendency" to account for the unequal realization, the probable presence of counterbalancing factors. In recent times the differentiation seems to be checked either by general or by special conditions. As an example of general conditions I may mention the fact that the name "Pulukkar" has almost become taboo among certain groups, and that this is connected by them with the modern political tendency towards equalitarianism. A special condition among the Nangudi Vellalar is the almost complete loss of prestige by the chiefs dispossessed of their exclusive rights in land.

If the result has been to stabilize the organization in recent times, the fact nevertheless remains that these groups and their subdivisions have a history, i.e. that, particularly in the past, the mere fact of their existing and functioning led to distinctions, segregations, subdivisions—in brief, to changes in the number and arrangement of their constituent units.[7]

This is rather far removed from the systematic division of society which the Kondaiyam Kottai poem quoted by Fawcett seemed to indicate. True, I have not been able to adduce any example from that specific group, but comparison with other groups throws some light on their case. In particular, the subdivisions of the *kilei* (*kottu* in Paganeri, *pidir* with the Nangudi) go to

---

7. On this point, a criticism of M. A. Shah is particularly welcome (*Current Anthropology* 1966, 340*b*). He wrote that I did not "go far enough," that the "gradation of status is continuous," that "it is impossible to find definite boundaries." This is true in great measure. That is why all my efforts went to relativize endogamy and how I came to conclude, at about the same time that Shah wrote, that "endogamy is a corollary of hierarchy, rather than a primary principle" (*Homo Hier.* §52, Dumont 1980, 113). Is this not the conclusion that comes upon us forcefully here itself?

This is said on the level of caste. On the level of kinship there is a factor which tends to concentrate intermarriage within a limited group or circle, namely, the tendency to marry a close relative. To call it a tendency to endogamy would be to stretch the meaning of the word and to introduce confusion, but it is a tendency consonant with endogamy and which works in favor of, rather than against, the existence of (relatively small) endogamous groups.

confirm that the Maravar *kottu* may have been a subdivision of the *kilei* rather than a group of several *kilei*. Yet the Kondaiyam Kottai also have their Pulukkar or "impure people." I came across some of them, but their relation to the main group was not clear—although intermarriage is of course out of the question—whether on account of the modern tendency I mentioned, or for other reasons like the fact that they did not reside in their region of origin.

The category of Pulukkar is not limited to those castes. It is met also among the Shanar or Nadar, toddy-tappers, where it forms the fifth and lowest division of the caste, being properly speaking, according to the *Tinnevelly Gazetteer,* the domestic servants of the four others (Pate 1917, 130; cf. Thurston-Rangachari 1909, s.v. Shanar). According to the same source (p. 132) Maravar zamindars, or local chieftains, had Pulukkar servants. Every caste thus had its Pulukkar. The word is probably akin to Malayalam *pula,* "pollution," which evokes the relation between general ceremonial impurity and the so to speak specialized impurity attaching to certain groups. As Aiyappan wrote (1944, 166–67): "The pollution created by death is called *pula,* a word which means impurity. Service castes are called Pulayas in certain parts of Malabar, obviously with reference to their impurity in the social sense. The persons under pollution on account of a death (of a relative in the father's line) are called *pulakkar.*"

The same notion can be followed in great detail among the Coorgs, under the equivalent Kannada form, *pole,* thanks to Srinivas (Srinivas 1952, chap. 4). There are similar names for groups: *poleya* (Coorg), "Holeya" (Kannada).

Moreover, the Agambadiyar caste (Thurston-Rangachari 1909, s.v.) may have developed in a similar way from the Maravar caste. In this case the "junior" sons, beginning with menial tasks in the chiefs' households, would, by educating themselves and adopting upper-class, Brahmanical customs, have been able to raise themselves above their "senior" brothers, traditionally satisfied with their warriors' pride. In this whole environment, the accomplishment of more or less degrading domestic tasks, as the removal of the leaves on which people have eaten and which are viewed as polluted by their saliva (*eccu-ilei* "saliva leaf"—in literary Tamil *eccil* designates those polluted remnants) characterize people of lower status and especially bastard sons. The name of the caste is thus understood as *agam-adi*-yar "those who stand within." The view is hypothetical but widely admitted among Maravar. The Pramalai Kallar have traces of a similar status in the past with the servants called Panikkar (cf. Dumont 1957*b*, 286, etc.).[8]

Senior and Junior

The difference of status attaching to the offspring of the different kinds of union is reflected even in the kinship terminology itself. An all-pervading distinction between older and younger, senior and junior, great and little (brothers etc.) is common to all four written Dravidian languages. On the level of kinship taken in isolation it indicates a difference in age, and the very strong stress which is laid upon it may seem excessive. But it does not only express mere difference of age; it is also indicative to some degree of a difference of status. For instance, in Tamil, the opposition between *periya*, "great" and *ciNNa*, "little," may express either: (1) distinction of age between two sons of the same father and mother, (2) distinction between the son of a man and his first wife and the son of the same man and another woman or, as they put it, between the son of the "older" (*mūtta*) mother or union (*tāram*), and the son of a "younger" (*ileiya*) mother or union. Here several cases may be distinguished, the two mothers being either: (*a*) women of the same status, equal to that of the father, and his lawful wives, e.g. real older and younger sisters as first and second wives—the most common type of polygyny; (*b*) women of different status, both regularly married (no example forthcoming), or (*c*) the principal wife on one side and a concubine, generally from a lower caste, on the other. (I have many examples of the latter's being referred to, perhaps euphemistically or politely, simply as "younger mother.")[9]

The different kinds of subsidiary sons as listed above may rank

8. The foregoing section is more developed than in the original version.
9. Niggemeyer 1933 has given a long list of castes constituted of two divisions—"great" and "little," "pure" and "mixed"—and has rightly insisted on the hierarchical content (pp. 419–21). The distinction goes far beyond South India; thus, speaking of tribes of the Northwest Frontier area Baden-Powell mentioned "the sons of an older wife . . . distinguished from the sons of a younger wife or of a concubine" (1896, 237). Hocart insisted on the point with respect not only to India (1938, 90 ff.) but also to Fiji (1938, 182 ff.; 1952, 27 ff., 33, etc.). The distinction is thus found more widely than caste, with which it is linked in our case.

differently, but the basic fact is the distinction between them all, on the one hand, and the full-fledged son, i.e. the eldest son of the first or principal wife, on the other. We should translate *periya* and *ciNNa* as "senior" and "junior" to keep in mind the ambiguous character of the distinction, which may refer to age or to the mother's status as a wife (through her birth or through the type of union with the father). The two categories of social status and age are fused in that opposition.[10]

Mixed Unions in the Law Books

It seemed from the analysis that the main thing was the maintenance of status through the first-born son, all others being subsidiary and ranking somewhere below him. This is quite in accordance with e.g. the tenth chapter of the Laws of Manu discussing mixed unions (Bühler 1886; cf. Jolly 1896, 61–62, 82; Mayne 1938, §§175–84), where it is explained how a number of social groups equivalent to castes came into existence from different possible unions between two members of the four fundamental classes (Sanskrit *varna*) of society (Brahmans, Kshatriyas, Vaishyas, Shudras). This has been considered, probably rightly, as an attempt to trace the origin of the actual castes (Sanskrit *jāti*) to the four classes (Sanskrit *varna*) of the society of old. Western scholars are inclined to attribute it to the speculative fantasy and classificatory mania of the Brahmanic pandits of the past, which is perhaps an incomplete truth.

It should first be recalled, as seems generally admitted, that according to the ideas of the authors of the Law Books all these mixed unions were secondary, the main union or (principal) marriage being always between a man and a woman of the same group. Now we may ask whether the authors of the Shastras could have imagined interclass unions if they had had no knowledge at all of some kind of intergroup unions. Could they have invented these secondary unions giving rise to more or less debased groups if they had known in actual life only marriages between persons of the

---

10. To say this is not quite enough. There are special distinctions, bearing on age alone: older and younger (see text) and *annaN/tambi*, "older brother/younger brother" (there is no name for brother in general), but the opposition *periya/ciNNa*, "great/little" is quite general and, as applied here, it *encompasses* age in status (it even tinges the proper age distinctions). We should say "superior and inferior."

same status? Here the situations now prevailing in some obscure groups of South India seem to provide a help for the understanding of ancient texts: if we leave aside for a moment the question of the groups concerned—classes, castes, or subcastes—and if we consider only the principle of a gradation of status between the sons of the same man, we find in Manu the same fact as among our groups, namely that a son par excellence, the product of orthodox endogamous marriage, ranks above a hierarchy of sons born from secondary unions between persons of unequal status. The authors of the Law Books are unlikely to have invented this, but they may very well have carried it over from the level of the actual groups to the level of the theoretical *varna* in order to be able to derive the actual castes from the *varna* archetypes. In such a perspective, it seems that even a part of the difficulties in those texts, their contradictions, and their hesitations about the possibility of regaining the previous status by a series of marriage of the same type, can be understood if we remember that, while the principle of hierarchy is stable, the actual distance between the groups—especially if it is measured by reference to other castes—depends upon the conditions prevailing at a given time in a given environment.

Part II. Main Kinship Features

Features in Common

From a general point of view, the groups under study have much in common. First they share with many others a common language, a common religion, and a common culture. Thus we might perhaps, by taking culture or civilization as the sum of phenomena common to different societies, consider each of our groups as a society sharing with others a common civilization. I think this would be insufficient. Each group here is part and parcel of the caste order, in which Kallar and Maravar occupy almost identical positions and had in the past similar functions. Their social life and psychology give a uniform impression, dominated by the frequency of quarrels, litigation and even murder, the stress on prestige and conflict, and the individual's extreme aggressiveness. It is difficult indeed to consider each of these groups as a separate society in which social phenomena could be assumed to be only internally interrelated.

On the other hand, this common social pattern stands in sharp contrast to the wide diversities in kinship organization, and the contrast confronts us with a general methodological problem: is it possible that in such societies there is no relation between the two spheres, except the hierarchical pattern already described? Is one group taken separately a legitimate object of study? Are there perhaps two distinct levels, irrelevant to each other, on which the interconnection of features could be studied, namely the caste system on the one hand, and the endogamous group on the other? As already stated, my contention is that there is only one level in the sense that the organization of each group can be considered as a particular form of a general pattern, which constitutes the first legitimate object of study. If this is true, then there must be, beneath all the apparent differences in the kinship makeup, something in common. It is this "something in common" that we now attempt to discover. Restricting ourselves to the fundamental features of kinship, we shall have to compare the different groups in their diversities. Before doing so, however, it is possible to point out a few features that they have in common.

First of all, authority is everywhere vested in men and transmitted from father to son, and nowhere, even in the matrilineal groups, from mother's brother to sister's son. This is so in the family, it is so in the lineage when it has a chief and when in such a case election is not resorted to, and it is so for political offices where they exist: succession is always in the male line. The authority of the father, the distance between him and his sons, and his privileges in regard to them are strongly marked. Participation in a yearly cult in a certain temple is also uniformly transmitted from father to son.

The individual family is, at least at the present day, general. I came across only one village with joint families in the Mudukkulattur taluk, among Maravar of low status whom the Kondaiyam Kottai regard as *pulukkar*.

Everywhere there is a prohibition against marrying close parallel relatives, and a preference for cross-cousin marriage qualified by a dislike for the double cross-cousin variety. It is not that examples of such marriages are not occasionally found in genealogies, but they are rare and condemned everywhere in the same terms: *kundamunda sambandam*, "ball-ball marriage," meaning a muddled, tangled, or confusing marriage. It is alleged in particular that such a marriage formula is unpractical, because if two men exchange sisters and one pair divorces, the other will do the same in retaliation.

All groups also condemn the uncle-niece marriage. In general, marriages outside one's generation, although rare, are found, and this does not matter very much if the two persons are only distantly related, but the marriage of (real) mother's brother and sister's daughter is absolutely excluded. This feature distinguishes very sharply our groups (together with others which share it) from upper castes of Tamil society which practice and favor such a type of marriage. The prohibition is self-evident in matrilineal groups, where uncle and niece belong to the same exogamous unit, but it is also found among the patrilineal Pramalai Kallar (see below). These also share, not merely with our groups, but apparently with all Tamil-speaking groups, another feature which seems to point to the ancient general prevalence of patrilateral cross-cousin marriage. The grandson is called *pēraN,* "he (who bears the) name (of his grandfather)," and this expression corresponds to a widespread practice. Now, if double cross-cousin marriage is excluded, the patrilateral formula alone can account for this. So far with similarities. We have now to consider differences, and for this purpose I shall give summary individual pictures.

Individual Groups

Pramalai Kallar
In one way, the Pramalai Kallar stand at one end of the series, since among them everything is transmitted from father to son: membership in the exogamous group (transmitted of course also to daughters), residence, and property. The preferred cross-cousin marriage is matrilateral; the preference is an obligation for the eldest son, provided that the age of his prescribed cousin fits with his own, and unless an indemnity is paid, which is equal to the customary amount of the first and most important marriage payment.

All these features would make this group very much like castes at higher levels, e.g. Brahmans, were it not for the complete prohibition among the Kallar of uncle-niece marriage which is current among such higher castes. (In fact many other features, which are not considered here, would differentiate them—divorce, remarriage of widows, etc.) The Pramalai Kallar base their prohibition solely upon the necessity of marrying in one's generation, a rule which is by no means as absolute as the prohibition is.

Patrilocal residence gives to the patrilineal units a quite solid and permanent character, but it is noteworthy that each patrilineage is not directly identified with or attached to a particular territory. The territorial unit is generally made up of several lineages, either all "brothers"—then the territorial unit is exogamous—or including an affinal relationship, in which case people marry inside the territory as well as outside it.

Nangudi Vellalar

The Nangudi Vellalar are a small group, caste or subcaste, located in a few villages near Srivaikuntham, in the Tinnevelly District, along the lower course of the Tambraparni River (cf. Pate 1917, 140–41; Thurston and Rangachari 1909, 5:246–47). They are agriculturists and rank slightly higher and are more literate and progressive than the other groups. Their organization offers an almost perfect contrast to that of the Pramalai Kallar, as they are matrilineal and matrilocal with a patrilateral cross-cousin marriage rule. A part of the property is held by women—half of the fields in their main village, Sevalai, where this feature is the most developed—and transmitted mainly from mother to daughter as dowry. The houses are females' property everywhere. At the same time this group had a powerful (male) chief—previously, I was told, the owner of all fields—and chieftainship was transmitted from father to son.

It is necessary to make a qualification in regard to residence. Whereas in all other groups, which are patrilocal, the married couple live for a time in the household of the man's parents and only after a time get a separate house, here on the contrary it is prescribed that the wife's parents should provide a house for the new couple from the beginning. This means that the husband does not live as a stranger in the house of his parents-in-law, as the young wife generally does in India; although he comes to reside near them, he has his separate home. The necessary independence of the husband, as chief of the new household, of his parents-in-law explains, I think, the stress put on their duty to provide a house, and this stands in clear contrast to the position of men in matrilineal and matrilocal communities on the West Coast. Here a contradiction appears between male authority and matrilocal residence, which we may follow further. I have instances of a man's returning to his birthplace and leaving to his daughter on her marriage the house in which he had lived since his own marriage, so that at that stage residence becomes patrilocal. For example, a man born in M. goes to S. as a husband, and, on the marriage of his daughter, he returns, taking his wife with him, to M., where, his parents having died, he replaces them in his native house. This oscillation between the two villages of S. and M., or their association into a kind of residential unit, is found in the line of the chiefs, where it is clearly linked up with patrilateral cross-cousin marriage.

I give an extract from the genealogy of the chiefs, as it provides a remarkable example of application of the patrilateral marriage rule (fig. 8). The result is that two intermarrying matrilines suffice to make up the male line of the chiefs for six generations. In terms of locality, this would mean theoretically that the generations of chiefs alternated between M. and S., but in fact, by a kind of coalescence of the two groups, the matrilocal residence rule, which otherwise might have been felt cumbrous, was put aside, and the line of the chiefs had a permanent, if double, residence. In such a way what is emphasized in fig. 8—and not by me alone—is a closed aspect of the system which then appears very like the double cross-cousin formula. This is obtained by focusing attention on a male line while leaving out the marriages of the female siblings, which, because they have no influence on the matriline of the chief's wife, are not relevant. It does not contradict what has been already demonstrated, namely that at least three intermarrying groups are necessary (Lévi-Strauss 1949, chap. 27), but here we must distinguish between the lineage and its parts. While the unit of exogamy is here the matrilineage, intermarriage takes place between smaller groups. It is true that in a small settlement we find representatives of at least three intermarrying groups, namely, apart from the local matriline, husbands from two other matrilines. It is possible, however, for these two matrilines to belong to one single matrilineage, so that on the whole there may be only two matrilineages represented in a small settlement. In fig. 8, for instance, if we call A and B the two matrilineages parts of which are present in that genealogy, the chief's sister in A is not necessarily married in a third matrilineage, she may very well be so in another part of B, or in a different formal subdivision of it, as it has been shown that here such subdivisions actually exist. This happens in fact with 5, and we see that two generations further down—as the prescribed cousin is lacking—the marriage of the chief is with a girl of that same subdivision of his spouse's normal matrilineage. In other words, one marries outside one's own lineage, not, as it were, into another, but in effect into a certain part of another lineage. Intermarriage and exogamy do not operate at the same level. The unit which appears as one in terms of exogamy is split in terms of intermarriage. This seems general.

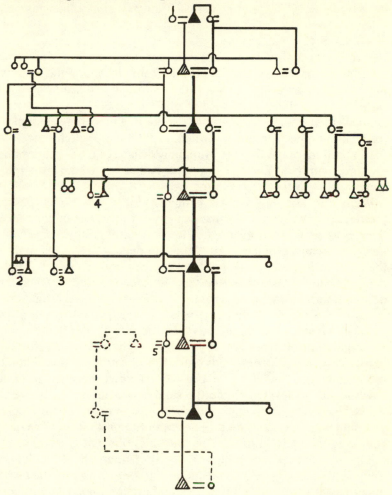

Fig. 8. Marriage of the Nangudi Vellalar chief and his brothers during the last seven generations. The chiefs are in the center, and the order of birth is disregarded. There are two matrilines linked by patrilateral cross-cousin marriage. The marriages of twenty-one individuals are considered; fifteen are patrilateral—twelve of them with the cousin, two with her mother (2 and 3), and one with her daughter (1). The link is reversed only in 4, which is included for that reason (matrilateral marriage).

To sum up, it is clear that under conditions of matrilineality and absolute patrilateral cross-cousin marriage, a male line is made up of individuals belonging alternately to two matrilines. If matrilocality is added, a small local settlement contains representatives of at least three matrilines, but possibly of only two matrilineages.

Kondaiyam Kottai Maravar

Reference has already been made to the fact that the same exogamous matrilineal units are found from one end to the other of the extended area over which this subcaste is scattered (see Fawcett 1903; Thurston and Rangachari 1909, 5:33 ff.). Its organization is intermediate between that of the two preceding examples; for if these Maravar are matrilineal and have a preference for patrilateral marriage like the Nangudi Vellalar, on the other hand they are patrilocal like the Pramalai Kallar, of whom in certain localities they very much remind us.

While the matrilineal unit, being nonlocal, has no corporate existence of any kind and is used solely for purposes of exogamy, there is as a rule no exogamy in the paternal line. For our present purpose, an interesting feature of the Kondaiyam Kottai is found in the local variety and in the limits of the paternal groupings. There being no central institution and very little connection between the different parts of the area, with no intermarriage apart from some cases in the chiefs' families, it was to be expected that a great variety of institutions should have developed. This is best seen in the regulation of cross-cousin marriage. The preference for the patrilateral cousin varies from outright obligation in Mudukkulattur (Ramnad) to indifference between the two cousins in some localities in Tinnevelly. While the double-cousin variety is everywhere disapproved, a slight patrilateral preference is most common and was, it is said, more marked in the past, since nowadays people care only for money. The change in this matter as in others seems to have set in relatively early among the Maravar of Tinnevelly, possibly as a consequence either of closer contact with upper castes or of the fact that certain families among commoners have become wealthy.

Arupangu Maravar. The *āRupaṅgu* or "six-shares" Maravar are a section of the Kondaiyam Kottai, or rather a cluster of Kondaiyam Kottai local groups surrounding Nanguneri (Tinnevelly). If the individuality of the group is recognized in the language, the Arupangu are not theoretically a unit of endogamy, though they are very much so in practice, marriages with outsiders being rare.

The unity of the group had in the past not only a local but also an economic basis. The tradition is that its ancestors came to settle as watchmen of the large estates of the important Vaishnava temple and foundation in Nanguneri, and divided their duties and income into six shares corresponding to six settlements of which only five at present remain. The original charge disappeared after the watchmanship institution was abolished by the government.

At present, the "shares" correspond to no more than settlements. The main village, Marugalkuricci, is locally divided as follows. There are two divisions of the first order: (1) the major part of the village as occupied by the descendants of the original settlement; (2) the northern part, where the people from the sixth and abandoned settlement, the name of which they bear, are found. The first part alone is subdivided into "shares" named according to their situation—Middle Street, West Street—and these themselves are sometimes further subdivided. Every division and subdivision of each order has its temple among its houses. Each group is mainly but not exclusively paternal, as a son-in-law may always come and settle near his father-in-law, without, it is stated, taking part in worship. Correspondingly, these groups are not exogamous, and marriages within the main division of the first order are almost as frequent as they are outside it. Once close parallel relatives are avoided, the only rule is to marry outside one's matrilineage. Moreover, some of the people have become wealthy, and the search for a rich bride has jeopardized the preference, still stated, for the patrilateral cousin.

In short, we find here the agglomeration of houses segmented into predominantly patrilocal groups which correspond, though incompletely, to corporate religious units, but which are not exogamous. Incidentally, it is interesting to note that the members of those groups (*pangu*, "share") are called *pangāli*, "sharers," a word which is generally used for parallel relatives, specially agnatic relatives, as opposed to cross-relatives, and which for this reason will be translated in such contexts as "brother." It is here seen clearly that the original content of the category is in the nature more of a socioeconomic relationship than of kinship proper.

Cokkampatti. This is a village in Tenkasi taluk (Tinnevelly) which offers a different and still more characteristic picture. It was the residence of a chieftain or zamindar, the ruins of whose mansion are still to be seen. Here, under a name used elsewhere (Pramalai Kallar) for lineages (*kūttam,* "group," "assembly"), people distinguish various clusters of houses inside the village, which bear the name of a man either living or recently dead. These are not permanent groups, but temporary aggregates where agnatic ties are the main but not the only bonds, which gather round a man of influence and may attract distant paternal relatives as well as relatives by marriage. Moreover, two of these local groups take their names from a former relationship with the chief's house. One, adjoining the "palace," is called the bridegrooms' or rather affinal relatives' group, as the chief is said to have taken wives from that group. Another is "the Feverish," from an ancestor who pretended to have fever in order not to accompany the chief on a hunting trip. Again, these groups are not purely agnatic, nor is a well identified patriline recognized as predominant among them. In brief, in order to recognize sections within the village, one resorts to kinship as well as to a particular relationship with the chieftain. The annual worship in a certain temple, either near the village or farther off, is inherited from father to son, but this produces only a periodical congregation at the place of worship and not a corporate group with permanent existence. This last feature is very widespread in Tinnevelly.

We can safely generalize on the basis of these two examples: the patrilocal groups among the Kondaiyam Kottai Maravar of Tinnevelly have a shifting character depending first of all upon local social and economic conditions; they do not exclude other relatives, and they never come to an outright expression on the level of kinship as exogamous patrilineal groups. Such a point should be remembered for its theoretical importance. Apparently there was room here for a patrilineal patrilocal corporate group—as the matrilineal unit is neither—and its place remains vacant. In the face of this, it is difficult to speak of South Indian kinship as based on a balance between matrilineal and patrilineal principles. But it might perhaps be argued that the organization in Tinnevelly has been altered and that we should turn to the probable original home of the Kondaiyam Kottai, the Ramnad District, if we want to study their original customs.

Mudukkulattur Taluk (Ramnad). The picture here looks very traditional. First, these people are at present the only members of the sub-caste who can be labeled as "criminal." Compared with them, the much feared Arupangu are now just difficult children, and the Pramalai Kallar, except in a few localities, may be said to have progressed far in the acknowledgment of commonly admitted ethics. (This stands in direct relation to the economic situation, Mudukkulattur being economically one of the most ill-favored areas.)

Here as elsewhere there are matrilineal exogamous units, authority is vested in men, residence is patrilocal and inheritance is in the male line. The most spectacular feature is the stringency of the rule prescribing patrilateral cross-cousin marriage. It is the only case I found in which the rule is systematically applied in a classificatory way, or rather as a rule of intermarriage between two matrilines: not only has a man to marry his father's sister's daughter if one of convenient age is available but, if there is none, the obligation also extends to classificatory relatives of the same category one or even two degrees more remote, mainly to the father's mother's sister's daughter's daughter and to the father's mother's mother's sister's daughter's daughter's daughter. This is not mere theory; it is abundantly verified by genealogies (see fig. 17). If no such relative is available, one may not marry before permission has been obtained from the father's sister (or her equivalent) through a customary present.

Another distinctive feature lies in the existence of well-defined patrilocal groups. In a small village near Kamuthi, Kundukulam, there are three of them. The first two have arisen from a split in one single group, S, and are called "Senior S" and "Junior S"; the third has come as an affine to both. Each group, locally distinguished within the agglomeration, has its temple where it worships once a year or so, but it does not act corporately on other occasions, as in the village assembly, and it has no chief. There is no absolute prohibition against marrying inside each group, but in practice one does not do so, and all three groups intermarry. In particular, Senior S and Junior S intermarry although they are recognized as "distant brothers."

Here is a critical point for the understanding of the evidence in relation to a discussion to come. Are we to consider Senior S and Junior S as exogamous groups, as they are very much so in practice, although they are not so in theory and although they intermarry while being agnatically related? First, a detailed genealogy of Junior S shows that it is not quite homogeneous, a few families not being related to the rest in the paternal line. Apart from this fact, let us remember that it is everywhere forbidden to marry close parallel relatives, and let us admit that the split between Senior S and Junior S indicates here the point where agnation ceases to be in any degree a bar to intermarriage. I submit that the very existence of such a point makes it impossible to speak of exogamy. On the other hand, it is easy to understand the situation as an extension of the interdiction of marrying close parallel relatives, as such an extension is natural in conditions of stricter patrilocal neighborhood, when compared with the groups mentioned in Tinnevelly. It would be misleading, strictly speaking, to see here an "exogamous tendency" in the father's line (see below): on the contrary it is necessary to distinguish clearly from exogamy proper what does happen in this case.

It should be noted that the situation does not seem to be universal in the group. In Appanur, for instance, a village which possesses several small tanks, one finds, attached to each of them, a paternal group which recalls by its socioeconomic nature the "shares" of the Arupangu (see above) and which bears the same name, *karei,* or "bank," as do similar groups among the Ambalakkarar.

Kallar called Ambalakkarar

As against the "West country Kallar" or Pramalai Kallar, who bear, as do many others, the title of Tevar, the "East country Kallar" live east of Madurai, around Melur and more to the east.[11] I shall designate them by their title, Ambalakkarar, which actually is not reserved to them (it applies for instance to the small group of Kallar in Paganeri mentioned above). These Ambalakkarar say that they inhabit four territories or provinces (*nādu*), the Western province, the Central province (Melur), and to the East those of Sirugudi and Vellalur. In some cases those provinces intermarry, in others they seem to be units of endogamy. Given the complicated territorial segmentation of the caste, it is difficult here to speak of subcaste. This may be due to the fact that I could only very briefly visit those people at the end of the fieldwork, which will oblige me to remain circumspect in what follows.

---

11. Literature: Turnbull 1895, 5–12; Nelson 1868, 44 ff.; Francis 1914, 88–96; Thurston and Rangachari 1909, 53–91. The text in this section has been revised and slightly expanded.

Each village is divided, for social, economic and religious purposes, into units called *karei* or "banks." In the multicaste villages, there are Kallar *karei* and *karei* of other castes. Among the Kallar these are mainly but not exclusive patrilocal units, similar to the "shares" of the Arupangu Maravar (above).

The Ambalakkarar do not seem to have exogamous units. That there are no exogamous matrilineages called *kilei* or otherwise, and that there is nothing resembling the exogamous patrilineage of the Pramalai Kallar is in fact pretty certain.

Another feature, equally interesting for comparative purposes, is the existence, in different localities, of two different marriage preferences. The patrilateral preference is the more widespread, but it is replaced by matrilateral preference in a group of villages of the Western province. Here we can construct a historical or genetic sequence. It stands fast that the Pramalai Kallar, or a part of them, have detached themselves from the Ambalakkarar (Dumont 1957*b*, II A 2a). Precisely the villages which are most often given as their places of origin are those where we find today the matrilateral preference, and this same preference is general among Pramalai Kallar. We may thus presume that the change has occurred in those Ambalakkarar villages and that the Pramalai Kallar have carried it along to their new habitat.

Moreover, the Ambalakkarar describe very clearly the different properties of those two kinds of marriage and thus offer a quasi-experimental confirmation of the theory (Lévi-Strauss 1949, chap. 18 and passim). They state that in the patrilateral system the dowry (see below) given in one generation comes back in the next generation, while in the matrilateral formula one lines goes on, from generation to generation, giving to another without receiving back anything in exchange. They link the change of custom to those characteristics: in the former case the return of the dowry depends on circumstances that make it hypothetical: for instance the sister given in marriage must later on have a daughter of suitable age, etc. As the dowry, in this case, tends to be high, its return is the more desired. People may prefer the latter method, where the gifts are more modest and one is not led to speculate about the future. Surely, all that is exact, but we may doubt that such was really the cause of the change. It is impossible not to bring together a series of changes in the *logical* series of the groups studied:

1) The exogamous matrilineal unit disappears in the Ambalak-

karar settlement in general (by comparison to the other groups, except the Pramalai Kallar).

2) The marriage rule is inverted in a small part of the Ambalakkarar area.

3) The exogamous patrilineal unit appears with the Pramalai Kallar who had inherited the inverted marriage rule.

We are going to see what logical relation it is possible to find in that series of changes. One might be tempted to take it whole as a series of historical changes. To my mind that is not necessary, and it would be hazardous, as we do not know for sure whether the Ambalakkarar have ever had institutions similar to those of the Maravar, for instance. Therefore we shall be content with a logical comparison which relates to history only with respect to the last two changes in the series.

Interrelation of Features

Faced with such diverse features, we can try to test their interdependence in terms of Professor Lévi-Strauss's analysis. This author states (Lévi-Strauss 1949, 270) that wherever everything is transmitted along the same line, either paternal or maternal, i.e. in "harmonic systems," there will be a matrilateral marriage rule, and that there will be on the contrary a double cross-cousin marriage rule wherever both lines play a role in descent, residence, etc., i.e. in "disharmonic systems." Here, as the double formula is excluded, we may replace it by the patrilateral formula, which is very similar in that respect (ibid. chap. 27). In fig. 9, paternal features are marked with a minus sign (−) and maternal features with a plus sign (+). Succession and inheritance, descent and residence are successively considered. The occurrence of both signs (−) and (+) in these categories is summed up as an "index," which is followed by the sign of the marriage rule with which it is to be compared. The groups have been arranged in the order of logical transition, with the opposites at both ends. A subsidiary sign has been added to account for opposite features (female inheritance among Nangudi etc.)

It can readily be seen that on the whole the assumed interrelation is confirmed. For instance, the change in residence between 1 and 2 has no consequence, as the minus sign was already present. The change from Kondaiyam Kottai (2–3) to Pramalai Kallar 6 seems to be remarkably consistent with the theory, were it not for some uncertainty in 5. First, the disharmonic element in descent disap-

Institution	1 Nangudi Vellalar	Kondaiyam Kottai Maravar			Kallar	
		2 Mudukkulattur	3 Tinnevelly	4 Paganeri	5 Ambalakkarar	6 Pramalai Kallar
Succession } Inheritance	– +	–	–	–	–	–
Descent	+	+ (–)	+	+	O (?)	–
Residence	+	–	–	–	–	–
Index	– +	– +	– +	– +	– – (?)	– –
Marriage	–	–	– (+)	–	+ / –	+

Fig. 9. Interrelation of kinship features: – indicates paternal and + maternal features.

pears in 5, followed in a part of the area by a reversal in marriage. Then, in accordance with the new "harmonic" pattern, patrilineal descent appears in 6.

The relative lack of a preferred marriage in 3 may be recent; otherwise it would seem to mean that, whereas a strong disharmony arises either between succession and residence, as was actually found in 1, or within descent 2, disharmony on the contrary between succession-and-residence on the one hand and descent on the other is weak 3.[12] This can be stated in another way. On the whole, the general interrelation as found here can be expressed in a more particular form. Against a background comprising paternal features, marriage would be correlated with descent: patrilineal descent would go with matrilateral marriage and vice versa. This appeared in the field under a slightly different form: a male Ego tends to marry that one of his cross-cousins who automatically and always belongs to the exogamous group of one of his parents. For instance, if I must marry outside my father's (patrilineal) group, I marry by preference my matrilateral cousin, who always belongs to my mother's (patrilineal) group. This means building a male line out of two groups only; it is equivalent to the symmetrical or "closed" formula if only one male line is considered. In its turn this supposes a stress on the male line, as is found with the Nangudi Vellalar. If we turn from them to the Kondaiyam Kottai of Tinnevelly 3, the male line becomes local, and the stress on it seems relaxed, as is seen from the looseness of patrilocal formations. Hence, perhaps, the indifference in marriage choice. In Mudukkulattur 2 the male stress reappears with well-defined, quasi-exogamous, patrilocal units, and the disharmonic marriage

12. In fact what the chart shows in the first place is that the concepts used are insufficient for really grasping the differences between groups 1, 2, and 3. The notions of harmony and disharmony, although they were here made more operative than in their original source (cf. Dumont 1971, 102–4), cease to operate efficiently beyond a certain point. (But see the similar attempt by Kathleen Gough in Current Anthropology 1966, 332–34). Keeping to the variables mentioned, one would propose that the dimensions to be distinguished should be on the one hand that of marriage (including descent as defined here), on the other that of authority cum locality (rights). The comparison shows that the relation between those two dimensions can vary from a relative independence (case 3) to a strict combination (case 1: "disharmony"; case 6: "harmony"), only the latter corresponding to a clear marriage preference, patrilateral in (1), matrilateral in (6).

rule is again enforced. Similarly, it seems that only in the case of double (unilineal) descent would the formula of double cross-cousin marriage be favored. We can venture the following hypothesis: the general prevalence in South India of the (single) unilineal principle accounts for the condemnation of double cross-cousin marriage.

Unilineality

Here it is necessary to discuss the opinion of some scholars who have held not merely that double unilineal descent was found in South India but that it constituted the general principle of kinship organization in all groups, i.e. precisely the underlying element which we are trying to discover. Professor Emeneau (1941, 174–75) finds that "the generalized South-Indian culture background includes exogamous patrilineal sibs with marriage forbidden also within the matrilineal line to degrees that vary from community to community" and he adds: "There is no record of fully developed exogamous matrilineal sibs in the large area until we reach the Malabar region on the southwest coast of India" but "the exogamous tendencies of the matrilineal line . . . work in varying degrees in all South Indian communities (cf. Held 1935, 53, 63, quoted in Lévi-Strauss 1949, 502–3). The assumption here seems to be that the prohibition of marrying close parallel relatives outside one's exogamous group—which is real—is an index of a second underlying exogamic principle, and finally that exogamy would be the only principle of all marriage prohibitions. This can hardly be admitted, as it would follow, for instance, that the prohibition of incest with the mother in a patrilineal society would have to be taken as an index of matrilineal exogamy. There are clearly two sets of prohibitions of a different nature: exogamy, attached to a group, is one, while the prohibition of marriage between close relatives attaches to each individual and is another. Here parallel cousins are terminologically "brothers" and "sisters" as opposed to cross cousins, and the fact that one may not marry a close "sister" has nothing to do with descent but only with cognatic— agnatic as well as uterine—kinship at large. The same author seemed to be on safer ground when he wrote earlier (Emeneau 1937, 104): "No man can marry . . . any woman who is related to him through a wholly male line or through a wholly female line. This is the system which is generally followed by the castes and communities of Hindu South India." The rule is not so stringent in general, but such is in fact its spirit, except that we need not suppose a "line" behind every parallel relationship.

Now, the existence of both the patrilineal and the matrilineal principles of descent in South India is one thing, and their presence and combination in the same group is another. We have clearly seen that either of these principles may be found but that one will generally exclude the other. As has been shown in the crucial case of Mudukkulattur, we have to do with unilineal descent. Furthermore, this can be assumed to hold in general unless contrary evidence is adduced. On the whole it may be concluded that: (1) double unilineal descent cannot be considered as the common underlying principle of South Indian kinship; and (2) both unilineal principles are found separately, while paternal and maternal features may interplay in one given group in a great variety of ways.

There is, however, an element of truth in the statements we have just criticized, namely that two principles balance each other in all these groups. The question is this: if (single) unilineality has to be recognized, then what is the element, complementary to it, the presence of which is felt in South India?

Marriage: Rules and Practice

We come closer to that element by considering marriage. But in starting from the marriage rules, we should first find out how and why it is that different regulations fail to develop long-range differences between the groups. The theory of the consequences brought about by marriage regulations of the kind here considered (Lévi-Strauss 1949, chap. 16 and passim) rests on two basic assumptions: (1) that it is the units of exogamy themselves which "exchange" women; and (2) that this exchange can be considered as existing as a whole at the level of the group. The first assumption supposes that the rule is carried out in a classificatory spirit, i.e. that failing the prescribed cousin, she will be replaced by a classificatory equivalent belonging to the same unit. This is true only in Mudukkulattur, but as the matrilineages there are nonlocal and have otherwise no social existence at all, this has no consequence on any other level. Elsewhere the obligation is purely individual, the Pramalai Kallar limit it to the firstborn son and allow it to be dispensed with by paying an indemnity. Moreover, the lineage and its larger subdivisions have no say in it. It is exclusively a matter of a small line of the lineage, as is shown by

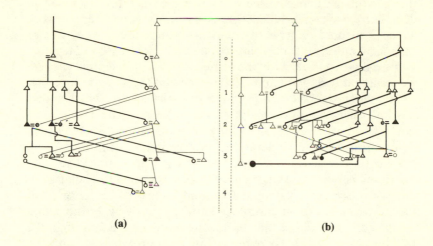

(a)   (b)

AYENARKULAM   TENGALAPATTI   TENGALAPATTI   MELAKKUDI

Fig. 10. Intermarriage under matrilateral rule (Pramalai Kallar). The two charts are extracted from genealogies of both lines involved. All elements irrelevant to the interrelation of those lines are omitted, and order of birth is disregarded. Black signs indicate reversal from the individual's point of view (patrilateral marriage). (a) The initial relationship between lines is reproduced six times and reversed five times. Generations 2 and 3 tend toward reciprocal exchange, as is shown by a (real) double cross-cousin marriage in generation 4. Generation 4 may seem more regular, but in fact the system collapses in a multiplication of disagreements which is responsible for the occurrence of an absolutely irregular marriage (with a classificatory "daughter" as a substitute). (b) The initial relationship between lines is reproduced ten times and reversed four times. But of the latter four marriages, three follow regularly (matrilaterally) from the one in generation 2. Three marriages appear as reversed in terms of the individual relationship (patrilateral marriages), of which one only—again generation 2—does not conform to the general relationship between lines; the last one is irregular in terms of generations. On the whole, M keeps "giving" girls to T, but a part of M begins also "taking" girls from T.

the fact that several closely related lines have conducted their marriage alliances in the last generations in quite different ways (see fig. 10). Again, as has already been observed of the Nangudi Vellalar, a line in lineage A may have independent marriage alliances going on with several lines of another lineage B. Among the Pramalai Kallar with their matrilateral asymmetrical regulation this might appear as a symmetrical relationship between the two lineages, but such a formulation would be misleading, as it is not at the level of the lineages that intermarriage operates. The system does not exist as a whole; it consists in a complicated network which is focused on as many centers as there are lines of two or three generations (cf. in a similar direction Leach 1951, 24, 28).

If we now consider how the regulations are applied in practice, we shall find wide variations within one and the same group. Fig. 10 gives an instance taken from the Pramalai Kallar, which shows how intermarriage develops in successful cases over the generations. Two paternal cousins belonging to the Kacciti sublineage in Tengalapatti start in Generation (o) marrying a girl in Melakkudi (b) and in Ayenarkulam (a). The charts show all subsequent marriages between the lines concerned. According to Kallar standards, (b) is a very good example, and (a) a very bad case. That there is actually a great difference between the two is borne out by a detailed inspection of the charts. But let us notice first of all the fact that even in (b) the reversed relationship appears, with the result that in the course of the development the theoretical asymmetrical relationship tends toward symmetry. If genealogies from the different groups could be compared, they would appear much more alike than their different rules suggest, for two reasons. As we just saw on Fig. 10, matrilateral marriage, which could theoretically exclude the patrilateral, does not do so in fact. As to patrilateral marriage, it contains within itself a secondary matrilateral element, for when the rule is followed the prescribed cousin is at the same time a second degree matrilateral cousin, as can be seen on figs. 8 and 17. We can thus formulate a quasi-statistical principle as underlying the different rules: apart from a variable proportion of "foreign" marriages, one mostly marries a person who is related to one at the same time, though in different degrees, patrilaterally and matrilaterally, mainly as a real or classificatory cross-cousin. If in one group there is a patrilateral preference, the patrilateral link is likely to be closer.

On the whole, all this amounts to a restatement under a more complex form of the discarded "closed exchange" formula combined with a unilateral preference which may be more stressed or less stressed in each case. This is quite in accordance with Professor Lévi-Strauss's broad view of South Indian kinship. The interest of the above formula is that it points to a basic similarity which underlies the differences, and it suggests that the common element, complementary to unilineality, which we are searching for, may be found in marriage or be related to it.

Part III. The Marriage Alliance

To introduce an institution which is shared by all groups referred to here and, I believe, by many others, some criticism of current anthropological categories is first necessary.

Marriage Regulations and Affinity

A (positive) marriage regulation like "a man should marry his mother's brother's daughter" might be a native statement indicating whom a given individual should marry. But, in anthropological thought, it takes on a slightly different meaning. There it appears as a rule for deriving a man's marriage from a relationship excluding any idea of marriage or affinity, i.e. from a relationship of consanguinity. It is implied that consanguinity is preexistent to the marriage, since I must be born before I marry. The marriage regulation is in fact used as a tool for deducing a secondary category (a certain marriage) from a primary category (a certain relationship of consanguinity). After marriage is so introduced, it brings with it relationships of a secondary kind (affinal relationships) which are never considered as full kinship relationships, because they are individual and above all temporary—they disappear with the married person and are not transmitted to his or her descendants as such but only under the form of a consanguinity relationship.

I submit that all this is wrong and needs revision for the following reasons: (1) it rests only on undue generalization of our commonsense categories, and does not do justice to the facts because in our societies marriage is an individual affair, not positively regulated; (2) it is contradictory for, as I shall show, the very existence of the marriage regulation implies that affinity is transmitted from one generation to the next just as consanguinity ties are. We have thus to give a proper definition of marriage regulation on the one hand and to widen our concept of affinity on the other.

First, it is almost unnecessary to recall that marriage cannot in general be considered as a secondary product of other institutions such as descent, which are then taken as being primary; there is rather an interrelation in the complete makeup. Still less is it possible to reduce the content of the marriage regulation to the codification of an individual affair, which marriage is not. Consequently, the regulation should not be considered as consisting of a relation between consanguineous ties and affinity, but as a feature of affinity itself. It is possible to do so, by pointing out that the regulation determines one's marriage by reference to one's ascendants' marriages: in a patrilineal, patrilocal society, marrying the matrilateral cross-cousin means reproducing the marriage of one's father, while in the patrilateral formula one reproduces one's grandfather's marriage, and so on. In general, the regulation determines a cycle of repetition of a marriage of a certain sort. If we say that "one marries one's cross-cousin," we merely state a condition to be observed in order to maintain a certain pattern of intermarriage.

In other words, the regulation causes marriage to be transmitted much as membership in the descent group is transmitted. With it, marriage acquires a diachronic dimension, it becomes an institution enduring from generation to generation, which I therefore call "marriage alliance," or simply "alliance."

In the matter of affinity, we generally admit too readily that, while the relationship between a man and his brother-in-law is affinal, the relationship between their sons (cross cousins) has no longer any affinal content, but is a mere consanguineous relationship. This is certainly not so in South India, where to call E and A cross cousins—as in fig. 11(b)—instead of "sons of affines"—as in fig. 11(a)—is quite deceptive. Being sons of affines, they are ipso facto affines, at least in a virtual or rather a general sense, before or without becoming so individually, as when E marries A's sister. We are now out of the vicious circle and we can look at it with amusement: "marrying a cross-cousin"[13] is nothing but marrying an affine, i.e. the person who is the closest affine by virtue of the transmission of affinity ties from one generation to the next.

I submit that, in societies where there are (positive) marriage

---

13. Briffault (1927, 1:563 ff.) rightly uses the Tamil term for cross cousin, *"machuna"* (for *maccuNaN*), to stress the affinal content of the category; he speaks of a "marriage agreement between two groups." Aiyappan (1944, 68) classifies the sister' son among the *bandhukkal* or affines, but contradicts it in a footnote.

My figure has been taken up in a slightly different form and without acknowledgment in Robin Fox, *Kinship and Marriage* (1967). What is more, his chapter 8 reproduces the fundamental ideas expounded here without any reference to their source, whether in the text or in the bibliography of the book.

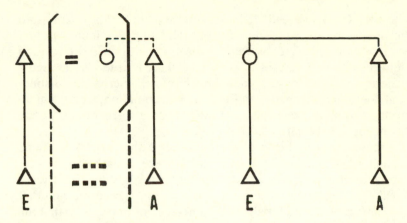

Fig. 11. Cross cousins or affines. (a) A as an "affine" of E; (b) A as a "cross cousin" of E.

regulations: (1) marriage should be considered as a part of a marriage alliance institution running through generations; (2) the concept of affinity should be extended so as to include not only immediate, individual relationships (affines in the ordinary sense) but also the people who inherit such a relationship from their parents, those who share it as siblings of the individual affines, etc.; (3) there is likely to be an affinal content in terms which are generally considered to connote consanguinity or "genealogical" relationships (such as "mother's brother" etc.). This is obviously so when there are no special terms for affines, for otherwise we should have to admit that in such cases affinity is not expressed at all.

Terminological Dichotomy: Kin and Affines

Structure of Terminology
All our groups share with many others a structurally identical terminology which in its broad features has been recorded from all four written Dravidian languages. Here I shall summarize a separate study (Dumont 1953a; see above, section 1).

The two sexes should be taken separately. With certain exceptions there is one term for all males in the grandfather's generation, but two terms in the father's generation. The latter terms, generally translated as "father" and "mother's brother," denote two classes, the members of which are respectively brothers-in-law to one another. Or, if we call "alliance relationship" this relationship between two persons of the same sex, and represent it by $\triangle$ [=] $\triangle$, standing for $\triangle = \bar{\bigcirc \triangle}$ as well as for $\overline{\triangle \bigcirc} = \triangle$ etc., the relation between the two classes is $\triangle$ [=] $\triangle$. This is true also in Ego's generation (for older and younger relatives), whereas the distinction does not fully operate in Ego's son's generation, where a mere prefix is used, and disappears in the grandson's generation. Terms for males are recapitulated in fig. 12(a).

Among females, the "mother" and the "father's sister" may be distinguished exactly as above. Now if we remark (1) that the terms for grandmother and granddaughter are not distinct, except for the ending, from those for grandfather and grandson, and that the same root is used for all in the son's generation; and (2) that the principle of distinction is the same for males and for females, we can represent the whole by a symmetrical scheme in which the identity of terms is expressed by superpositions of signs—see fig. 12(b). One sees that the distinction of sex and the alliance distinction go together, and that the system might be called "bifurcate-merging" in a new sense, that is, bifurcate in the central and merging in the extreme generations. One sees also how simple and regular the system looks once one ceases to remove alliance artificially from the content of kinship terms. It consists in distinguishing, in three generations or age groups, two kinds of relatives of each sex: those related to Ego by a link excluding alliance, or "kin link" (on the left), and those related to the first by alliance (on the right). From the basic structure of the system we have on one side the "fathers," on the other the "fathers' affines," and on one side the "mothers," on the other the "mothers' affines"; and nowhere such beings as mother's brother or father's sister, who are just particular cases of fathers' affines and mothers' affines. Obviously, too, the system implies a marriage regulation, namely that one marries an affine in one's generation, the nearest of these in terms of individual relationship being a cross cousin.

Definitions
The whole of the kinship terminology is split into two halves, "kin" terms and "alliance" or "affinity" terms. By thus stating that kinship = kin + affinity, we escape an ambiguity found in anthropological writings, where "kin" or "kinship" is sometimes opposed to affinity and sometimes taken as embracing it. We prefer to speak of kin and affines rather than of parallel and cross-

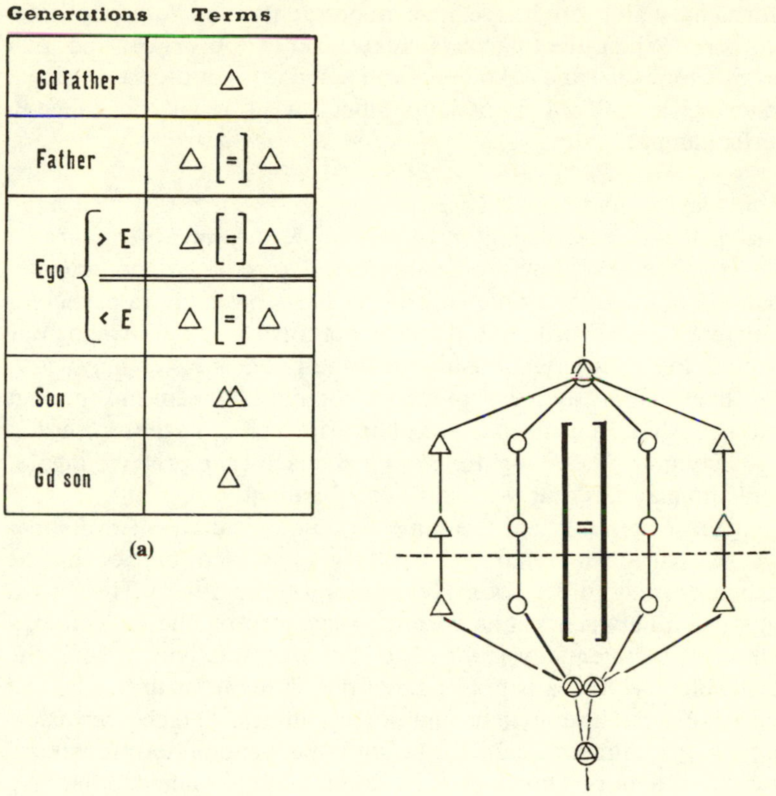

Generations		Terms
Gd father		△
Father		△ [=] △
Ego	> E	△ [=] △
	< E	△ [=] △
Son		△△
Gd son		△

(a)

(b)

Fig. 12. Structure of the system of kinship terms, (a) terms for males only, five generations; (b) terms for both sexes, five generations. The superposition of signs shows identity of terms, apart from word endings.

relatives. We should not however forget that these are only categories abstracted by us from the form of the terminological system. To avoid any confusion when actual kinship configurations are studied, we should designate them as "terminological kin" and "terminological affines." Moreover, as the latter expression has been obtained by extending the meaning of the word "affine", we should distinguish between (a) immediate or synchronic affines, i.e. affines in the ordinary sense, in-laws, and (b) genealogical or diachronic affines, who inherit, so to speak, an affinal tie which originated in a upper generation (e.g. mother's brother). When the marriage regulation is observed, the two subcategories (*a*) and (*b*) merge, and a person is at the same time a genealogical and an immediate affine, what might be called a perfect affine.

How the Terminology is Applied

The system as analysed hitherto is no more than an abstract frame of reference, no doubt pointing to alliance as a fundamental institution, but one to which each social group will give a particular concrete form according to its particular institutions.[14] Among our groups, the actual relationship with the father's sister may vary, but there will always be found as a common background the fact that she is different from a "mother," first of all in the sense that Ego may marry her daughter even if she is not the preferred mate, while he may not marry a "mother's" daughter.

Again, within one and the same terminological class the distinction of particular relatives, whether expressed or not in the language, may differ from one group to another. The broad opposition between kin and affines suggested by the terminology will itself be unequally realized for different relatives: among the terminological kin, a part is singled out as really or fully kin, and the same happens among terminological affines. The choice varies, but all the different choices fit into the general terminological frame, no doubt because they fit into a common alliance pattern. Another general difference is found in the degree to which relationships are extended from the groups of siblings to extensive sociopolitical groups. A comparison will show how the terminological categories are given different shapes by different institutions.

---

14. At the end of the preceding paragraph, (*a*) and (*b*) were wrongly called "categories," and S. Tyler criticized the distinction (*Current Anthropology* 1966, 341*b*). It should be clear that the distinction is purely analytical.

I have deleted here from the original text a speculative remark about the possibility of a reversal of consanguinity and affinity as bearing on the closest relatives. It was absolutely wrong, and possible only because the analysis had remained incomplete on one basic point. As emphasized above (chap. 1), the basic fact about father and mother is that they are treated exactly the same way, apart from the distinction of sex. What the vocabulary acknowledges is (immediate) filiation in the sense of the parent-child relationship (between Ego and Ego's father and mother). Therefore father and mother are—as should have been expected—always consanguines in the terminological sense.

The Pramalai Kallar are patrilineal and patrilocal. In one locality there is as a rule only one or a few patrilineages. Hence:

1. The category of "brothers" is split into two: on the one hand all my paternal "brothers" (sons of my father's brothers, etc.) are members of my local descent group, on the other hand my maternal "brothers" (sons of my mother's sisters, etc.) are spread over different groups and places. On the paternal side each individual link is made to endure through generations by becoming an element among all other similar elements in the continuous fabric of the local group, clearly defined as against others by the exogamic rule. On the maternal side, each individual relationship, being isolated—see however 2 below—is liable to be rapidly forgotten. While the paternal half is stressed to the point of becoming almost equivalent to the whole, the maternal half appears, except in special cases, as temporary, subsidiary, almost conventional.

2. The opposition between kin and affines takes on a spatial aspect; there are kin places and affinal places, and as one marries mostly in the neighborhood, this might be represented ideally in the form of concentric circles, a territorial unit made up of kin, A, being surrounded by affinal places, B. As these in their turn intermarry with other places, there arises a third circle, C, made up of people who are affines to B, and hence "brothers" to A, as the affine of my affine is kin to me. (In these C places will be found some of the maternal brothers mentioned above.) The matter is of course not so simple in fact, but on the whole, when seen from one point, there is a picture of the division of the not-too-far-removed localities into the two fundamental categories. It will be readily grasped that this apparent dichotomy in space results from the working of the organization and has nothing to do with a systematic division or a dual organization of the society. Nevertheless it represents a maximum in the extension to groups of the basic terminological categories.

3. Let us now compare the position of the mother's brother with that of the father's sister. The mother's brother is not only terminologically opposed to the father, who is here kin par excellence, but he also lives in an affinal place. He is an affine pure and simple, in fact the closest, at least until one marries. On the contrary, the father's sister, born in one's local descent group, becomes only with her marriage a member of an affinal group, just as the mother, born in an affinal group, has become kin first as

mother, at the same time thrusting, so to speak, the father's sister into the affinal category. The terminology here directs us to look at the father's sister as already married and as mother of affinal cousins. Nevertheless she is at the same time to some extent kin, and it follows that she is less clearly and unambiguously an affine than the mother's brother. If we then suppose, as will be confirmed, that affinal relatives are in charge of ceremonial functions, we may expect the mother's brother to precede the father's sister in those functions.

The picture is quite different for the matrilineal, patrilocal Kondaiyam Kottai Maravar. With them descent and locality work in opposite directions, with the result that individual kinship relationships are not backed by corresponding relationships between groups. Here the sons of two brothers on the one hand and of two sisters on the other are recognized as "brothers" in two different ways and the two kinds of relationship are stressed in quite different conditions, the first in a context of locality and the second in a context of alliance or of special ceremonial circumstances. On one side, a remote relationship between patrilocal brothers does not in general exclude alliance, so that the category in the long run is stripped of any kin content, being mainly a matter of socioeconomic neighborliness. On the other side, it is between sisters (and not brothers) and their descendants that the matrilineal kin relationship endures. The descent group has no tangible reality. What is stressed here is a matriline scattered in different localities, shifting from place to place and from house to house in each generation. In every locality a number of matrilineal exogamous units are represented, and a man may marry into any of them, except his own. In one's own village the terminological categories are fully realized only for three kinds of people: a smaller or larger circle of patrilocal brothers, a number of matrilineal brothers, and the affines of the first two. At the same time, a great number of people are undifferentiated: they may be at the same time brothers in a loose, merely local sense, and virtual affines, and it is only the nexus of individual alliances and their classificatory extensions which decides the question.

The opposition between father and mother's brother is seen here in different ways. From the matrilineal point of view the situation would be reversed, the mother's brother could be considered as kin and the father as an affine, but nevertheless the mother's brother's children will be terminological affines. We see that it is the mother's brother who receives the ambiguous character which attaches to the father's sister among Pramalai Kallar. In contradistinction to them, the foremost affine here is the father's sister, because locality is not exclusive of alliance and because matrilineality stresses the kin link with the mother. This will be confirmed later, when we study the ceremonial functions.

If the two preceding examples are compared, the difference in the affinal value of the mother's brother and of the father's sister can perhaps be summed up by saying that when paternal features (authority, locality) are present, the foremost affinal relative in the upper generation is the affine of the lineally-stressed parent, i.e. the mother's brother in patrilineality and the father's sister in matrilineality. This is only another expression of harmony and disharmony (fig. 13; cf. "Unilineality" above). It is hoped that this brief comparison has shown how we may speak of a common underlying alliance pattern which, when combined with different institutions, assumes different concrete forms.

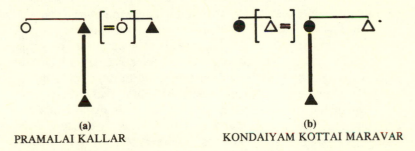

(a)
PRAMALAI KALLAR

(b)
KONDAIYAM KOTTAI MARAVAR

Fig. 13. Emphasis on one affine in relation to descent.

Inheritance and Gifts

The most conspicuous feature of alliance as an enduring marriage institution that defines and links the two kinds of relatives consists in ceremonial gifts and functions. This perspective can be indirectly justified. If ceremonial gifts are essentially affinal and if they are important, it should follow that, in societies with male predominance, property is transmitted from one generation to the next under two forms: by inheritance in the male line, and also by gifts to in-laws, namely from father-in-law to son-in-law. This is precisely what happens. In the groups with which we are immediately concerned, apart from the Nangudi Vellalar among whom female property is important, daughters have no formal share in their father's property, but they are entitled to maintenance and to the expenses necessary for their marriage and establishment.

Moreover, this is a case for generalization. The same rule, if it is not absolute and universal, has a widespread validity in Indian customary law, where it makes itself felt even when it is contradicted (Jolly 1896, 83; Mayne 1938, §§436, 421, 431, 488, etc.). The marriage expenses should not be taken as including only the cost of the necessary feasting and display, but also that of gifts to the in-laws on the occasion of marriage itself and later on as well. If the details vary, the broad institution is general, at least in the Tamil country, even among well-to-do people. This double transmission of property confirms the opposition between kin and alliance. It indicates that a review of ceremonial gifts must begin with marriage.

Marriage Gifts

What is the most salient feature of the marriage ceremonies among the groups referred to? Sacramental acts like uniting hands or circumambulating the fire are not found. The tying of a string, with or without the well-known marriage badge or *tāli,* round the bride's neck has certainly a sacramental value, especially for the bride. But it is not witnessed by all relatives, because the ceremonies take place partly in the bride's and partly in the bridegroom's house, and only a few people go from one to the other. This explains why the tying of the *tāli* was sometimes repeated (Pramalai Kallar). A common meeting of the relatives of both sides is conspicuously absent. As a sign of union between the two families, I think we may say that it is replaced by the long series of alternate shiftings of the couple from one place to the other and back and again, which takes place from the marriage onward and is accompanied by gifts in one direction and increased gifts in return. This chain of gifts, or "prestations" and "counterprestations," symbolizes the alliance tie and is the most important feature of marriage ceremonies from the point of view of the relation between the two families.

The Pramalai Kallar state with particular emphasis that "gifts sent to the bride's house return increased twofold or threefold." Among them, the man's family (which I shall designate as M) gives first a sum of money, *parisam,* to the woman's family (designated as F) which has to spend at least twice as much for the bride's jewels. Then with the ceremony proper begins the series of visits to and stays with F, the couple being every time accompanied by a number of baskets (sīr), containing foodstuffs and other articles for consumption, from M to F and, increased, back from F to M. Prestations from F dominate more and more as time goes on until finally—it may be two or three years after the marriage ceremony—the young couple establish a separate household near M, and receive the necessary pots and pans from F without any return gift. This is the "sīr of going apart."

Such are the main prestations, which I call external prestations in order to distinguish them from the following. During the marriage ceremony, in both houses, money is collected among the bridegroom's relatives on the one hand and the bride's relatives on the other. This is called moy; its effect is to make the relatives contribute to the expenses of the family; it may be called an internal prestation. These two kinds of prestations are found in most other groups, internal prestations being likewise called moy, whereas there is no general term for external prestations, sometimes called surul if they consist of gifts in money and sīr if in kind. Linguistically, while moy indicates a mere collection ("crowd," "multitude"), surul connotes a circular movement, a rolling up, perhaps a circular accumulation. Among the Nangudi all prestations are external, and people say that the moy has been replaced by collections where the two groups of relatives are mixed (iNām, a solemn word for "gift"). The moy is not found in connection with marriage in Mudukkulattur, where it is known on other ceremonial occasions, i.e. girl's puberty and funerals. In Paganeri, internal prestations comprise a contribution in rice brought by all taking part in the feast (which may well be more widespread) and also a collection of money similar to the moy, bearing the name of rēvei or rēgei, "list", and accompanied by small gifts of thanks in return. Among the Arupangu, the two moy are associated with a series of small external gifts.

In considering the external prestations, it is necessary to single out the matrilineal and matrilocal Nangudi who do not make reciprocal gifts. The pattern is definitely different: M's prestations are very slight on a ceremonial level; there is no parisam, no gift of tāli or sari; the idea of competition is absent; the cost of the feasts is shared afterwards between the two families. The parents of the bride make a point of providing everything except a foodstuff allowance, the same in all cases, which has to be regularly delivered by M to the new household. Moreover, the emphasis is here on the dowry, strictly the wife's property. In Paganeri also the reciprocity in gifts is weaker, but there a part of the usual prestations from M is found.

Otherwise the comparison shows that, while there are all possible variations for each element in particular, the whole is more uniform than its parts, and still more so is the form of small cycles inside the whole cycle. Leaving aside once for all the Nangudi Vellalar, we see that the *tāli* is everywhere paid by M. The gift of one or two saris to the bride by M is lacking among the Pramalai, so is the *parisam* in Paganeri and among the Arupangu, while it is present in Mudukkulattur, and present but small among the Ambalakkarar. As a counterpart, the importance of jewels and dowry varies. Land is given among the Ambalakkarar and in Paganeri. Jewels are important in those two groups, but on the contrary their value is hardly mentioned at all in Mudukkulattur. This is obviously related to the economic situation, for the Maravar of Mudukkulattur are very poor and the Arupangu occupy an intermediary position between them and Paganeri or the Nangudi.

The masculine *sīr* brought for the ceremony is found everywhere, Nangudi excepted. Among the Arupangu, it is like that of the Pramalai, with one sari added. In Mudukkulattur, where it is preceded by another one for the betrothal, it includes rice. This also is seen, with more rice, in Paganeri and among the Ambalakkarar. In return the gift is multiplied thrice in Mudukkulattur, while in Paganeri the increase is marked in a different way, by the addition of pots and pans. The return gift is lacking among the Ambalakkarar and the Arupangu. In the latter group, it is probably only delayed on the one hand (*sīr* of the first visit to F) and, on the other, there is another form of reciprocity, that of *suru*l, as will be seen below.

Regarding subsequent *sīr* gifts, the difference between the groups bears on the choice of the most important dates. The household equipment will be offered, here on the Pongal festival (in January), there on the first visit to F; the gifts of the month of *ādi* will be more or less important, etc. The *suru*l or external gifts in money are found among the Arupangu (1) from F to M as a return for clothes, (2) from F to M and back (individualized, as in Paganeri, where the *suru*l is a small gift from the wife's father to the husband and from the husband's mother to the wife).

The common mechanism of the gifts appears clearly if one

isolates small cycles based on reciprocity. There are three types. In the first of these, there is an exact reciprocity, as in Paganeri when clothes are given by M to F and then equivalent clothes by F to M; among the Arupangu the clothes presented by M to F are compensated for by a reverse gift in money (*surul*) which must be at least equal to their value. In a second type, the initial gift is not only reciprocated, but multiplied in return, as among the *P*ramalai. A third type has a reduced reciprocity, marked sometimes by a mere symbolical counter-gift. This is true among the Pramalai and in Paganeri for the *moy;* among the Arupangu the *surul* which has just been mentioned is in its turn followed by a symbolical return. It can also be shown how one given object receives a particular ceremonial value from its situation in the whole. This is so with rice among the Pramalai, where it does not occur in internal prestations nor in the masculine, but only in the feminine *sīr* as a sign of their substantial importance, i.e. of the "increase" which characterizes them. On the contrary, rice is to be found everywhere in Paganeri and, to express the pre-eminence of the feminine *sīr,* one resorts to another element, namely the pots and pans which elsewhere appear only later.

The foregoing comparison will have shown how much stress is laid on the chain of prestations in all its details, and also in what sense it may be said to be common in spite of all variations. It is clearly impossible to single out one of the marriage "payments", the *parisam,* and to call it "bride-price."[15] It represents, at least in the examples cited here, the contribution of the husband's family to the buying of jewels which will be worn by the wife but normally become the property of the household, as can be ascertained from their treatment in case of divorce. That terms like "bride-price" are inaccurate here is also obvious if one considers that, on the whole, and to varying degrees, it is the wife's family that gives more. The *parisam* appears rather as a kind of earnest-money which is destined to come back increased. It would be almost equally misleading to reduce the whole to "dowry," in cases when something of the kind actually appears. These are rather extreme

---

15. For a contrary view, see Srinivas 1942, chap. 2 (prestations are not analyzed). Mousset and Dupuis (1928) wisely translated *parisam* by the French *arrhes*. An exchange of gifts similar to those found here, but with mercantile features, has been described among the Nattukkottai Chettiar (Thurston and Rangachari 1909, 5:263 ff.).

cases among the rich and when patrilateral marriage promises a return in the next generation. The transfer of meaning of the classical word for dowry (Sanskrit *strīdhana,* "wife's property") among the Pramalai Kallar is characteristic, since they call *srī-daNam, sīdaNam* all gifts due by the wife's family, including the future gifts of her brother to his sister's children. Obviously the meaning of the protracted exchange of gifts with which we are dealing, if it includes the final result in terms of plus and minus, goes far beyond this. On the whole, the final result is a gift which accompanies the gift of the girl. A relevant question here would be to ask why a transaction which finally amounts to a gift has to take the form of an exchange. I would say that it corresponds to the individual marriage's (i.e. gift's) being conceived of as a part of the whole nexus of intermarriages and their consequences as seen from the point of view of a single family (i.e. exchange). When the Pramalai Kallar state that "gifts sent to the bride's house return increased," this is roughly true of one individual present, but it is still truer of the whole series, or rather it is true in the sense that it accounts for each exchange as seen in the light of the whole. There is certainty about increase, because increase is the law of the whole cycle. One knows very well that masculine gifts will decrease as time goes on, while feminine gifts will increase; the latter are substantial, the former initiatory and provocative. Generosity lies on the girl's side, but it has to be set in motion; a pledge to protracted, manifold, and mainly unilateral gifts is obtained by a formal exchange.

Indeed, this may be taken as a formula of Kallar marriage if one accepts the view that these prestations—and not the "ritual" elements on which attention has been mainly focused—constitute the main part of marriage ceremonies. In favor of this view, the first argument is that prestations in fact do not stop at the point we have somewhat arbitrarily chosen. Those which follow may be called "alliance prestations" and I shall trace them in all ceremonial circumstances of the individual's life. Marriage does not consist only in the consecration of conjugal union and the establishment of a new family, for this family is as inseparable from the alliance prestations as it is from the local lineage affiliation.

That affinal ceremonial prestations in general constitute something like the core of family ceremonies is shown not only by their description, but also by the fact that it is possible for the people to dissociate what might be called the mere rite and the accompaniment of prestations which overshadow it. This is true of marriage among the Maravar (Thurston and Rangachari 1909, 37–38) and of funerals (see below), on which occasions the prestations may be postponed. It is true also of circumcision, as two striking instances will show. Among the Pramalai Kallar, the circumcision of a boy is a source of income for the family. Therefore, two brothers are never circumcised together when their age would permit it. Further, old parents who are said to be anxious to see the circumcision while they are alive may have the ceremony performed several years in advance, but the operation itself will take place later and without any ceremony. The Ambalakkarar had for girls a ceremony parallel to the circumcision of boys, but with no technical counterpart. This had nothing to do with the common girl's puberty ceremony, although the two have been sometimes confused (Francis 1914, 94). An informant states that this ceremony originated because parents who had no sons but only daughters wished to celebrate it as well as the others.

The alliance prestations are of two kinds: some are symmetrical or reversible and some are asymmetrical or oriented. If, after the marriage has been celebrated, a death occurs in the bride's family, the bridegroom's family, together with the other affines, will bring food presents. These I call "reversible" gifts because the bride's family would do the same if a death occurred in the bridegroom's. This reversible relationship we find reflected in the transport of gifts which accompany the young couple both ways after marriage. It is the most general and undifferentiated expression of alliance in gifts. The birth of a child in the new family will create a different situation which has no counterpart in the bride's family. This is an "oriented" situation, where the Kallar will stress the gifts and functions of the maternal uncle. It should be added that one and the same ceremonial occasion calls for the two kinds of responses and gifts from different people. Whereas many people come and give the ordinary, reversible, affinal gift, one particular relative, who may be the maternal uncle, is singled out with particular, oriented gifts and functions: the oriented relationship stands against a background of reversible relationships. Both kinds of relationships are initiated (or renewed) in marriage, and this corresponds to the double aspect of exchange and gift in the marriage prestations: "gifts sent to the bride's house return increased."

We are thus reminded of the result of the analysis of the working of marriage rules, where we had also found a background of symmetry behind the particular preferences. It looks as if each marriage, while it is oriented as a *gift,* was seen as a part of the network of the alliances of a particular family or line, a network symmetrical as a whole (as an *exchange*).[16]

We can now study examples of affinal prestations of the two kinds. In order to follow up immediately the series opened with marriage, I shall begin with oriented gifts and the maternal uncle, the reversible gifts being considered later.

The Maternal Uncle

There is a certain amount of theoretical interest in studying in some detail the ceremonial role of the maternal uncle, since it has been discussed in the past by Rivers and others and is generally considered as a thing quite apart. Moreover, it stands out clearly among the Pramalai Kallar, who stress it more than others and provide some valuable details. I shall consequently discuss here only data taken from that group. But in dealing with such an extreme case, I have in view a general point: if it is possible to demonstrate that the role of the maternal uncle is of an affinal nature, the same should be true a fortiori for other, less prominent relatives like the father's sister. In fact, the demonstration lies almost at hand, for it is sufficient to follow up the series of oriented prestations initiated by the marriage to review at the same time the ceremonial functions of the maternal uncle.

Ceremonial Role

Among the Pramalai Kallar, in all ceremonies connected with the growth of a child, from birth to marriage, the maternal uncle has an important role. True, he is not isolated, but he is the first and

---

16. As to the theory of marriage alliance in general, the text here suggests a conclusion it does not draw. Not only the application of marriage rules and the analysis of prestations but also the vocabulary itself show a symmetrical pattern as common to all our groups while marriage preferences vary and seem, from the example of the maternal uncle that follows, to be essentially related to ceremonial roles. That is why I wrote in 1971: "I have no doubt failed to stress more systematically the hierarchy of the two levels I distinguished: the *imperative* level of the common (sub-)regional culture with its symmetrical pattern, and the *subordinate* level of the particular group with its particular preference" (1971, 131, note). This is an application of the distinction between prescription and preference introduced by Rodney Needham.

foremost of a series of present-giving relatives. However, the present purpose may be served even if that aspect is left aside and the role studied in itself.

Two cases can be distinguished. Let us first suppose that in my family only marriages with unrelated persons take place. In such a case I marry an unrelated girl. If, two years after my marriage, I decide to leave my parents' household and establish a separate one, my father-in-law will conclude the series of marriage gifts (a part of which has gone, not to myself, but to my parents) by sending to me, as the head of the new household, the necessary pots and pans. Then, if a child is subsequently born to me, we are told that it will be presented with gifts by its maternal uncle on each ceremonial occasion. What has happened? I was the gift-receiver and now it is my child which is considered as—and in fact is—the main gift-receiver. This means that the function of gift-receiving has come down one generation. At the same time, my father-in-law is replaced as gift-giver by his son (my brother-in-law, the child's maternal uncle), i.e. the function of gift-giving has also come down one generation. On the whole, the (child's) mother's brother succeeds to (my) father-in-law when a new generation appears (fig. 14a, b). This is quite natural as providing for continuity, but we see that, if it is literally true that the mother's brother appears with the birth of the sister's child, the relationship itself in fact merely continues the relationship that the marriage had initiated. This is still clearer in Tamil, for the father-in-law is *māmaN* and the mother's brother *tāy-māmaN* (or simply *māmaN*).

When the child has grown up, and has been presented with jewels and so on and assisted by the maternal uncle on several occasions (circumcision if it is a boy, puberty if it is a girl), there comes the marriage. Again the maternal uncle comes to the fore (see below). As we have supposed that this family intermarries only with strangers, the child's father-in-law will be an unrelated person. He will give the customary presents; the first cycle, opened by my marriage, has ended, a new cycle is opened—fig. 14(c), the gift relationship has lasted from my marriage to my child's marriage, embracing successively me and my child as receivers and my father-in-law and the child's maternal uncle as givers. Of course this is only how the gift relationship adapts itself to the flow of generations. It does not mean that all ties are cut off in one generation when the next appears, or that I do not know my mother's brother any more when once I have a father-in-law, as they may, for instance, enter into competition if I am affected by a death (see "Funerals" below). But it means that it is in marriage that new ties appear and that it would be misleading to consider the mother's brother as something different (a "cognatic" relative) from the father-in-law (an "affine") as far as their giving functions are concerned.

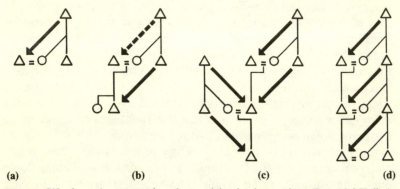

(a)   (b)   (c)   (d)

Fig. 14. Gifts from the maternal uncle as originating in marriage (Pramalai Kallar). (a) marriage—father-in-law gives to son-in-law; (b) birth etc.—mother's brother gives to sister's children; (c) foreign marriage—a new relationship relieves the old one; (d) matrilateral marriage—the same relationship continues.

Let us now consider the alternative situation and suppose that in my family the marriage regulation is observed (as it should be if I am the firstborn son), and see what happens. I marry my matrilateral cross cousin, my father-in-law is my mother's brother, which means that instead of my marriage's initiating a new cycle it merely continues, or renews, the permanent one—fig. 14(d). One patriline keeps giving girls and presents (if we leave out of account the reciprocal and reversible gifts) to another. Incidentally, is it possible to mistake this for a remnant of matrilineal descent? In such a continuous chain of gifts, it is the birth of a child in my family which brings the giver down one generation. (If my child is a boy, the relationship goes on with his marriage. If it is a girl, her mother's brother helps to marry her in another family, to my sister's son, to whom I shall be the giver in the above sense.)

To sum up, in both cases we see that it is the type of marriage which decides whether a gift relationship is maintained or replaced, whether the mother's brother is completely identified with the father-in-law or just succeeds him, the direct effect of the marriage regulation being the maintenance of the relationship and of the identification. I think it would be useless to comment on every detail of the consequences of this, as it is obvious that it demonstrates my point and at the same time justifies my initial assumptions about the relation between regulation on the one hand and affinity on the other.

Replacement

More light is thrown upon the ceremonial functions of the maternal uncle from the Kallar theory and practice of his replacement. That the replacement is possible in itself shows that the role is more important than the actor. First, it should be clear that the relative concerned is the real mother's brother, and not any man of the same classificatory category. This is emphasized by calling him, not simply *māmaN*, i.e. "father's affine" in our sense, or classificatory maternal uncle in the ordinary view, but *tāy-māmaN*, literally "mother-*māmaN*," which I understand as "that particular *māmaN* who is the mother's brother." The *tāy-māmaN*, the ceremonial mother's brother, is the mother's eldest brother, but if there are several brothers they will normally share the expenses. If the eldest brother dies, his role will pass to his younger brother, and if he has no brothers, his son will inherit his obligations. In certain circumstances, his son may even replace him while he is alive. In such cases the people may very well refer to the son, as if not he but his father was present, as the "mother's brother."

The marriage ceremonies give a first example of replacement of the maternal uncle which would have enlightened Rivers. Apart from bringing gifts, the role here consists in introducing one's nephew or niece to the marriage dais as a preliminary ceremony. In the case of a bridegroom this introduction is performed in his house, before he goes to the bride's for the actual marriage. Now, if the bridegroom marries the daughter of his mother's brother, the latter will be at the same time his father-in-law. In such a case, he will not in general go to the bridegroom's house, but he will send his younger brother to act as mother's brother in the introduction ceremony, while he himself will stay at home in the father-in-law's role. We see here clearly distinguished: (*a*) the introduction ceremony, where the man who is, by virtue of a marriage in the upper generation, the mother's brother of the bridegroom has a role; and (*b*) the marriage itself, with the presence of the father-in-law. On one side the old cycle and on the other the new one, the mother's brother bringing his nephew or niece to the marriage booth where another alliance starts or where the same alliance is renewed.

But, one may ask, what happens if the mother has no brother at all? In such an event the role may be taken up by her patrilineal kin (or parallel) cousin, i.e. her father's brother's son. This is an example of how an individual relationship is liable to a classificatory extension in agreement with the principle of descent. But the case is interesting for another reason. Failing a maternal uncle, the mother's father's brother's son, M (fig. 15), may assume his role entirely, provided he agrees to do so. His agreement is necessary because the role entails considerable expense and, if he does not receive a compensation for this but is on good terms with the family, he may very well confine himself to the merely ceremonial functions and refuse to indulge in the present-giving part of the role. It was mentioned at the beginning of the section on gifts that

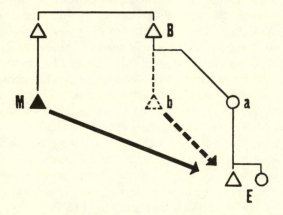

Fig. 15. Replacing the maternal uncle: M as a substitute for b.

normally a man inherits his father's property with the charge of establishing his sister, that is, in fact, with the charge not only of the marriage gifts but also of the subsequent oriented gifts, including the presents to be given to the sister's children. These are provided or compensated for by the fact that the sister had no formal share in the heritage, her share consisting precisely in such presents. Now, if she has no brother and if no special arrangement is made, a woman will exceptionally inherit her father's property, but, as a negative counterpart, nobody will be there to make the customary gifts to her children. If, then, she wishes her cousin to assume the role of a brother, she has to give away to him precisely the same property (or at least a part of it) as would have gone to her brother if she had had one. This is said to happen especially on the occasion of the marriage of a girl, when the mother's brother can scarcely be dispensed with without loss of honor, and if at the same time the mother's father, who could replace the mother's brother, is dead. Then, rather than face the opprobrium of having herself to lead her daughter round the marriage booth, the mother is likely to consent to alienate wealth for her cousin to act as a brother and introduce her daughter to the marriage. This can also be provided for by the sonless father, by leaving his property to a brother's son (M) on condition that he should act as a son would have done for the establishment of his daughter (a). On the whole we can conclude that: (1) the mother's brother's gifts to his sister's children cannot be severed from the expenses of her marriage ceremonies, which are normally in charge of her father; (2) if the role of the maternal uncle is more important than the person, it is on the other hand bound up with his economic position and will not be fully assumed except by somebody who is made to enjoy the same position.

This may also help to define the particular characteristics of the mother's brother-sister's children relationship as among other affinal relationships. Compared with the relationship between affinal cousins, it includes a difference in generation. This fact does not alter its basic affinal nature; nevertheless it is important because it makes the relation not only asymmetrical but projective (from the upper to the lower generation)—it tinges it with filiation, if this word may be used to evoke, not descent, but the recognition of a transmission from one generation to the next. That there is a transmission of property under the form of gifts, and that further, if the father-in-law also gives, it is only the maternal uncle who exerts important ceremonial functions, suggests that the maternal uncle's role, if it is based on affinity, owes its importance to the fact that it shows affinity under a genealogical form. It manifests not only alliance as a synchronic principle, but alliance with its diachronic dimension, it combines in one single relationship alliance together with its transmission. With it a parental aspect is given to alliance; a link receives the form of a filiation. A study of attitudes would confirm this in showing how, for a Kallar, it reconciles authority with affection.

Conclusion

It may be worth while to try and contrast the present approach with others which are still encountered now and then in the Indian field. The maternal uncle–nephew relationship has been considered either as a remnant of dual organization, or of matrilineality, or as a consequence of cross-cousin marriage.[17] Apart from dual organization, which it may not be necessary to discuss nowadays, both other views, though incorrect as a whole, contain some truth which we can now properly acknowledge. The assumption of a connection with cross-cousin marriage is no doubt wrong if conceived mechanically, as when it is argued that the maternal uncle gives presents to his young niece in order to secure her as a wife either for himself or for his son. But the same assumption is partly justified in the sense that the maternal uncle's role as well as cross-cousin marriage appear here as projective forms of alliance, the latter, as a regulation, also giving to the alliance its diachronic dimension. This of course applies only to the compatibility and likeness of the two institutions and it does not mean that they are interdependent so that the one should appear wherever the other is found.[18]

The idea of a connection with matrilineality is perhaps more open to objection if one wishes to form a clear idea of both institutions. I have shown that the maternal uncle's role is a part of the alliance pattern, and that there is a fundamental difference

17. Rivers discussed the possibility of a survival of mother-right, and concluded that the maternal uncle's role is rather linked with (matrilateral) cross-cousin marriage (Rivers 1907, 611 ff., see also Lévi-Strauss 1949, 533).
18. It appears possible, in the light of our comparison, to make a little more precise the relation between the avuncular role and matrilateral marriage (see n. 17). In *South Indian conditions*, we see that the maternal uncle's role is stressed where marriage is matrilateral (Pramalai Kallar). We had seen before (fig. 13) that "the foremost affinal relative in the upper generation is the affine of the lineally-stressed parent, i.e. the mother's brother in patrilineality." Similarly, and again in South Indian conditions, we were able to say earlier that *patri*lineal descent went with *matri*lateral marriage, and vice versa. These two determinations combine; the marriage preference bears on the daughter of the foremost affine in the upper generation, as we shall find again later on in a different form regarding prestations: the main donor, the bearer of oriented functions, is the one of the affines who should in principle give his daughter (or his sister) in marriage to Ego. This is in keeping with the general hindu ideology of marriage as *gift*, the gift being here the alliance *in actu*.

between such links and those which constitute descent groups. This is so true that, far from being a remnant of matrilineality, the role would be found to be much weaker in matrilineal groups, where the father's sister would be more in evidence in the affinal role. What is true in the old idea is that there is a principle which balances patrilineality, which has at the same time a projective or filiation aspect and at first sight a maternal one, and which for these reasons was confused, naturally enough, with descent. But, if the complementary principle is bound to make use of relatives who are not integrated in the descent group, it does not integrate them in turn in another descent group. There is a balance of forces, but the forces are not of the same nature. The descent group ties are counterbalanced by a system of ties which do not link mechanically whole descent groups but regulate and at the same time generalize individual ties. For a classification of relatives in the way in which they appear to the individual as carrying these two opposed forces, we are brought back in the first place to the terminology.

Funeral Gifts
So far we have followed the oriented gift relationship from marriage in one generation to marriage in the next. This concerns the continuity of the genealogical line but leaves aside an important occasion when affinal ties are manifested, i.e. death. In funerals, as in other ceremonies, not only oriented gifts, but also reversible gifts are made. I shall give two examples of these, the first being chosen for its extreme clarity and the second for its extreme complication in reversible gifts coupled with its simplicity in oriented gifts.

If we read in Thurston and Rangachari's compilation the long descriptions of family ceremonies and of funerals in particular, it seems as if most people were concerned first of all with Brahmanical ritual, either performed by a Brahman or imitated from him by someone else. This is, I think, a wrong impression which may be due both to the questionnaire method used by the inquirers and also to the tendency of the caste people to pass themselves off as being as Brahmanical as possible. Intensive research gives a quite different picture: impurity looms large indeed, but apart from it, and considering ritual details mostly not directly connected with impurity, funerals appear much more as social events and much less as religious ones. They are first of all the occasion on which several spectacular gifts are brought by certain relatives, and to a slight extent reciprocated. Characteristic is the fact that the end of mourning is marked, not so much by a Brahmanical purification of the house, as by the "tying of the turban" or the gift of a cloth to the chief mourner, or to several mourners, by prescribed relatives. This is a very general feature, going far beyond the circle of castes here considered and present even among more orthodox ones, in association with the Brahmanical features. At the same time, this institution is rarely mentioned in the literature among a welter of Brahmanical detail. The importance of these features is already obvious from the fact that, for instance, among the Pramalai Kallar, the death of unmarried persons is not ceremonialized, and that it is possible to bury the dead person and postpone the ceremonies until a more convenient period, e.g. after the paddy harvest. They are then concentrated so as to occupy only a short time (one day), but all the gifts are presented in the normal order.

Example No. I. Pramalai Kallar
In this example the affinal nature of the giving relationship is demonstrated by the fact that almost all givers are only in-laws, not genealogically related to the person to whom they give. This is a particular situation arising partly from the fact that the marriage regulation has not been followed, the chief mourner, his sisters, and his classificatory brothers having all, with only one exception, married unrelated persons. Fig. 16(*a*) shows who gave a present of food (raw rice etc.) on the first day, and who gave a cloth to or tied a turban on the head of the chief mourner, the son of the deceased, on the last day of mourning. The turban gifts to subsidiary mourners are represented in fig. 16(*b*). These are only extracts from a complete genealogy of the group, which makes it fairly certain that the persons who appear on the charts are not related in any other way.

To take first fig. 16 (*a*), it will be seen that most givers are brothers-in-law (one is a father-in-law and one a classificatory son-in-law). Three examples show how the relationship spreads from the individual affine, who gives twice, to his real or classificatory brother, who gives only once. To speak of "classificatory" equivalents is not quite enough, for they are related through men only. In other words, while this particular chart can be read without reference to the marriage regulation, it cannot be read without reference to descent and locality. These people are not merely

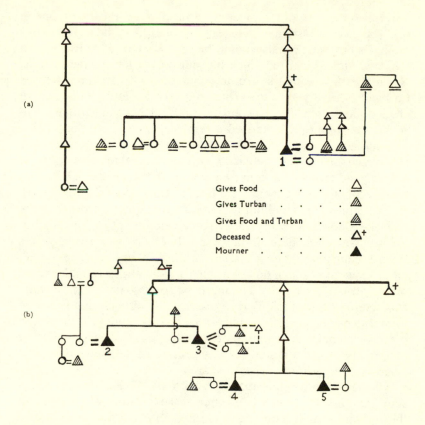

Fig. 16. Funeral gifts. Example no. 1. Pramalai Kallar, Death of Ramattevar in Tengalapatti, September 1949. **(a)** Gifts of food articles, gifts of turban to chief mourner; **(b)** turban to subsidiary mourners.

classificatory equivalents, they belong in all three cases to the same local patrilineal group.

In the same way the quality of mourner spreads—only in this particular circumstance—from the chief mourner to his father's brother's sons and their sons. These, on the last day of mourning, stand in a row with him, and, after him, also receive turbans from their own affines—fig. 16 (b). A few details may be noticed. The three marriages of Mourner 3 are successive, following death or divorce. No polygamy appears here, although one of the brothers-in-law in fig. 16 (a) has another wife. Mourners 1 and 3 married two sisters, so that one of the givers to 3 in (b) is identical with one in (a). The case of Mourner 2 is a special one. First, he says that his mother's brother's family should be represented, were it not for a long and violent quarrel which has cut off the normal ties with it. Not only the mother's brother, but also the father's sister's husband normally tie the turban (or give a cloth). It is due to chance alone that they are entirely absent here. The chart also shows that Mourner 2 married a related person, a second-degree paternal aunt's daughter. The reason why his wife's brothers are absent and, so to speak, replaced by two other relatives is that he is not on good terms with them. He claims that they are indebted to him, because he gave them a cloth on a similar occasion of a death in their family. They did not reciprocate this time in order to show their ill-feeling, but two related people who do not participate in it did so. One is a father-in-law's brother. The other is a wife's sister's daughter standing for her brother or her maternal uncle, but, as married women do not officially give, she gave in the name of her (absent) husband.[19] The importance of quarrels here is quite characteristic. We should also note that the gifts are reciprocated from one occasion to the other; in fact an account is kept for the purpose, it being a matter of reversible gifts. This principle of reciprocity answers more than any precise rule the question as to when the obligation to give ceases.

We may contrast this example with the Kallar theory which states that it is the mother's brother of the mourner who should tie the turban, as first among the cloth-givers. In fact, it would be rather his son, as there is a preference for the giver's belonging to the same generation as the receiver, as shown by the frequency of the brother-in-law, instead of the father-in-law, in the chart. But, as we have seen, "mother's brother" in such contexts designates more a role than a person, and here his son would be so called as standing for his father. There is no doubt, if the mourner is unmarried, that his mother's brother is his closest affine. If he is married, the mother's brother nevertheless represents the traditional, genealogical alliance, whereas the father-in-law, as distinct

---

19. I am thankful to Kathleen Gough for correcting a mistake (cf. *Current Anthropology* 1966, 335 n. 3): I had written that this (second) giver of a turban to Mourner no. 2 was, irregularly, a "son." In fact he is shown to be, quite regularly, a "son-in-law."

from him, represents only an individual incipient alliance. At any rate the rule is not easy to verify in the examples I have where there is, for various reasons, not much room for competition.

Example No. 2. Kondaiyam Kottai Maravar
Money Presents. In general, things are not as clear-cut as in the preceding example, because the givers are normally not only immediate affines but also genealogical affines, and sometimes both at the same time. Moreover, it has been shown in a previous section ("How the Terminology Is Applied") that, if the institutions of the Pramalai Kallar favor the absolute distinction of all relatives in two categories, as appears in the analysis of the terminology, other institutions, like those of the Kondaiyam Kottai Maravar, tend on the contrary to restrict it to a certain circle and to blur it outside this circle. The same subcaste provides a second instance of greater complication. Here the two kinds of gifts which were taken together in the first example will be considered separately. We begin with presents in money roughly analogous to the previous food presents; the turban will be treated afterward. A remarkable circumstance is that the mourning lasted only one day instead of seven as with the Pramalai Kallar, or more orthodoxically for these castes sixteen or even thirty days. This shows how far removed we are here from orthodox Brahmanism when only conditions of isolation and poverty are given. The family of the deceased were presented with gifts in money toward the end of the mourning at about the time of the turban ceremony. These presents are called *moy.* They are not solemnized as are the presents of food among the Pramalai Kallar, and in fact we are here nearer the ordinary collection of small amounts of money called *podupanam* (common money) which is governed only by the rule of reciprocity, and this partly explains the differences.

The chart (fig. 17) has been extracted from more complete genealogies for the purpose of tracing the relationships between the givers and the deceased (not as previously the mourner). In doing so, three groups have come to the fore: (i) upper center, the deceased's local patriline; (ii) left, and (iii) right, two (exogamous) matrilines. The combination of ii and iii in three generations of the deceased's patriline recall the Nangudi genealogy (fig. 8), and we have here the same strong emphasis on patrilateral cross-cousin marriage, but with the addition of a drastic extension: failing such a cousin, one should look for her equivalent, i.e. a father's mother's

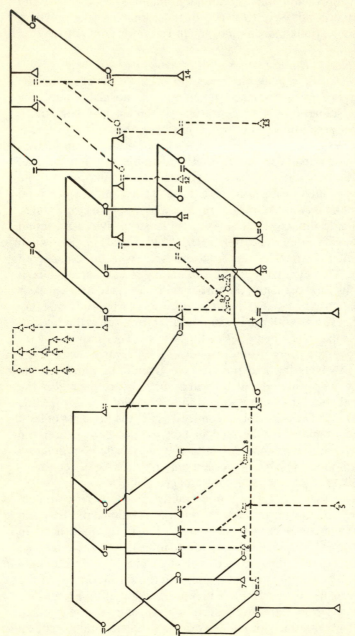

Fig. 17. Funeral gifts. Example no. 2 Kondaiyam Kottai Maravar. Death of Muttukkumarattevar in Kundukulam, October 1950. Money presents. Relationships between the givers numbered from 1 to 14, and the deceased. As far as possible, patrilocality is indicated by vertical lines. Two matrilines are indicated by continuous lines (heavier and lighter) and other genealogical relationships by a broken line.

sister's daughter's daughter, or again one degree more remote. It is this feature, together with other circumstances—the deceased's father and grandfather had no sister—which is responsible for the aspect of the chart that the reader at first sight may be tempted to interpret in terms of cognatic relationships. I shall not discuss it in detail but only emphasize the main features in accordance with the witnesses' statements.

As usual, people distinguish the two categories of kin (or parallel relatives) and affines (or cross relatives) under the names of *pangāli,* "sharers," mainly agnatic classificatory brothers (cf. "Kondaiyam Kottai Maravar," above), and *maccuNaN,* affine of Ego's generation, or cross cousin. As a rule, the givers belong to the second category but, we are told, "distant *pangāli* may also give," this applying in particular to the upper center of the chart, where 1 is an old neighbor and intimate friend of the deceased, 2 lives with his father-in-law in an affinal group, and 3 is a rich member of the patrilocal group, although not an agnatic relative. (This exception is mentioned above, group Junior S.) Direct, immediate affines to the deceased are 10, 15, and 9 (exceptionally a woman). The case of 10 is interesting: the deceased married, one generation up, a (classificatory) father's sister instead of her daughter, with the result that his brother-in-law, 10, is a "father." But 10 would never give as a "father," he gives as a brother-in-law, and, together with him, his classificatory equivalents in the matriline 11 and 14. We see here a new affinal relationship superseding the genealogical tie. The same applies to 12, and consequently to 13, for 12 is to the deceased a father's affine (or classificatory mother's brother) in terms of genealogy, as well as father-in-law of the deceased's brother. He could give as such, and still it is stated that he gives rather as a wife's (classificatory) sister's husband (fig. 18), i.e. a particular kind of "brother." This, moreover, is strengthened by the fact that in ceremonies his daughter was identified with the deceased's daughter.

Mere genealogical affines (cross relatives) are 4 and 6 (mother's brother's sons). They are the people to whom the deceased's sister should have been married. Instead she was given to a (classificatory) mother's brother. Incidentally the conspicuous absence of the latter is due to emigration. In this group again 5, 7, and 8 fall into the category of kin (or parallel) relatives. Still 7 gives as 6's brother-in-law, 5 gives as 4's son-in-law (or sister's son), and 8 perhaps for his father-in-law. (There is some uncertainty in this part of the chart in the sense that another relationship may exist for 7 and 8). On the whole, what happens here in the case of 7 and 5, also 12, and probably 8, is this: one gives together with one's affine to one's affine's affine, i.e. to a terminological kin relative. This would be impossible with the Pramalai Kallar. It shows at the same time both the limit beyond which the abstract terminological scheme is not followed and the emphasis on marriage—in that sense it is probably very general in South India. It gives a transition from affines to kin which is also expressed as "friendship" accounting not only for 2, and partly for 3, but for three more givers who are unrelated people and two of whom do not belong to the caste. As in the previous example, all these are reversible gifts, of which an account is written down for future reciprocation when a death occurs in the family of the present givers.

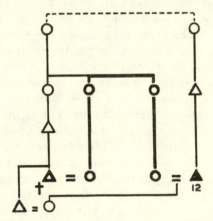

Fig. 18. Funeral gifts. Detail from fig. 17. Emphasis is laid on one relationship between the deceased and the giver no. 12.

Tying the Turban. In contradistinction to the preceding gifts, we are here provided with a simple and clear-cut picture on which to test our hypotheses. This is due first of all to the extreme poverty of the people and to the fact that many of them have emigrated. In better conditions or in rich families, this present-giving would extend as far as the preceding one in our case. Nevertheless, as we have to do with a real ceremony, oriented relationships appear and there is a hierarchical order of the nearest relatives.

The mourner, Ego, is a boy, the deceased's eldest son. Certain relatives of his generation are to help him in the performance of certain mourning duties (so emphasizing in fact affinal ties as is not done among Kallar), and they are also to tie the turban on his head, or give him the equivalent cloth, to mark the end of the mourning. In the example (fig. 1g) the helper and tier was A, Ego's father's sister's son in the second degree (*oNNu vittu atteimagaN,* "one left father's sister's son"). In the turban ceremony, Ego's maternal uncle's son, B, although present, had a subsidiary role. If we observe that Ego's father's sister's son, α, cannot be present because he emigrated with his parents, we find that the case conforms to the local rule which orders the relatives for the purpose as follows: (1) father's sister's son (α, absent); (2) classificatory equivalents (namely A and others who have also left the country); (3) mother's brother's son (B); (4) wife's brother (if Ego was married, and married somewhere else). It is seen at first sight that the rule reproduces the marriage rule in such a way that the preferred givers are the brothers of the preferred wives. After them, (1) and (2), comes the matrilateral male cross-cousin preceding, as is natural where the marriage rule is stringent, a possible individual affine.

In this case the precedence of the patrilateral over the matrilateral is expressed by the people as precedence of the "brother-in-law who took a woman" over the "brother-in-law who gave a woman," *pen edutta maccuNaN* before *pen kodutta maccuNaN.* The

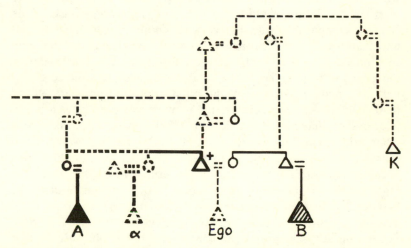

Fig. 19. Funeral gifts. Example no. 2 (continued). Tying the turban.

expression, quite common among these groups, refers here to the father's generation and opposes the sister's husband to the wife's brother. For us it is important as it shows that it is as the son of Ego's father's affine that A ties the turban on Ego's head. The point we made about the transmission of affinal ties will be remembered here: it is precisely such statements which force one to consider that the son of a brother-in-law is not a mere "sister's son." The patrilateral preference with its extension is shown by one more giver, who would be the father of a "father's sister's daughter in the third degree," that is K, who has contributed the cost of a turban. Incidentally we see here that, because Ego's father has made a patrilateral marriage, Ego's maternal uncle is at the same time a (more distant) patrilateral relative. This shows that, when the patrilateral preference is conceived classificatorily, there is no more pure matrilateral relationship to be opposed to it, the latter being contained in the former. Apart from its theoretical impact, the fact may justify our quasi-statistical definition of the type of marriage as consisting in marrying somebody related, if unequally, on both sides (see "Marriage: Rules and Practice," above).

To sum up, the example shows: (1) that the ceremonial function of tying the turban is conceived as springing from previous marriages, as expressing affinal relationships as we defined them here throughout; (2) that the first and foremost affine is the man who, by virtue of transmitted alliance and according to the marriage regulation, should give his sister in marriage to Ego. This is quite comparable with the general emphasis on the maternal uncle among the Pramalai Kallar: in both cases the oriented giving relationship, crowned with ceremonial duties, goes together with the giving of a wife. The same relatives as are expected to give a wife to a male Ego give him the most important presents, either materially or ceremonially. This is why we may speak of an underlying alliance pattern despite all the changes it undergoes when other institutions differ. In fact, in the present example, the Maravar in funerals are not satisfied with stressing the affinal ties between males. The mourner's daughters, with classificatory extensions, have accessory ceremonial duties in which they are assisted by their affines (or female cross cousins). It would seem that these again are oriented in accordance with the marriage rule, but the matter is slightly complicated and is left out here on that account.

Conclusion

In the quest for a common South Indian kinship pattern, a review of the basic features among a handful of groups exhibited mostly differences in descent, residence, etc. as well as differences, correlated with the former, in marriage regulations. But underneath the latter it was already possible to descry something common in the actual application of the marriage rules. Then an analysis of the terminology showed that it rested upon a complementary opposition between two underlying categories, "kin" and "alliance," which define each other reciprocally, and that the idea of "affinal relative" had to be extended to cover all the so-called cross relatives as opposed to the parallel relatives, who are "kin" in a general terminological sense. Ceremonial gifts as studied in different series are primarily attached to that affinal category.[20] Their cycle originates in marriage, and the obligations of the maternal uncle are best considered as a particular case of this alliance pattern. The transmission of property is regulated in fact in two ways: a part of it is inherited by the sons, while another part is disposed of under the form of gifts (and ceremonial expenses), mainly as affinal gifts to the daughters' households and children.

We can now return to Professor Emeneau's statement: he was right in assuming that unilineal descent was complemented by another principle. Only this complementary principle is not to be found in descent. It is alliance as opposed to kin, but this time in a concrete aspect: alliance under the form of a particular pattern of marriage rules and ceremonial gifts and functions is complementary to a particular combination of one given unilineal principle with rules of residence etc. But whereas the principle of descent and the other features shift and change, the principle of alliance is found everywhere in slightly different forms. In that sense it is already the fundamental principle of South Indian kinship. But it is

20. There are some grounds for inquiring whether the basic meaning of the Malayalam *inangu* is not "affinity" in the widest sense, and whether there is another way of accounting for the conflicting data given by Aiyappan for three different castes, Nayar (Aiyappan 1932), Nayadi (Aiyappan 1937, 32–33, 66–67, 69, 71), and Irava (Aiyappan 1944, see Index). The Coorg *aruva* corresponds to Mayalam *inangan* (see Srinivas 1952, 56, 124 *et passim*). [See now chapter 3 hereafter].

certainly also fundamental in another respect, i.e. in relation to caste, as the reflection of the hierarchical principle from without to within the endogamous group has shown. Endogamous marriage is there the main factor of status, without which one cannot maintain it. This is another matter altogether, but it is characteristic that the analysis of kinship leads us to emphasize an institution which is of the highest importance in caste. That marriage is crucial on both levels of caste and kinship, and that it constitutes in a sense their articulation, is quite in accordance with the obvious and well-known stress that Indian society lays upon it.

3

Nayar Marriages as Indian Facts

The purpose of this paper is to pick up the question of the sociological interpretation of Nayar marriages at the point where it was left by the latest and most modern of the exegetes. Dr. E. Kathleen Gough, after a long stay in Kerala, analyzed kinship and marriage among the Nayar in three successive articles, from different viewpoints (Gough 1952, 1955, 1959a). In the second, she concluded that her study of the *tāli* marriage, or rite, in relation to the Nayar kinship system had not led to understanding its necessity; and she turned to a psychoanalytical interpretation (1955, 45). This is where we shall take over, to attempt to give a sociological answer to a sociological question. To do so, we shall resort to comparison; we shall consider the Nayar no more as constituting a society by themselves, but as an Indian caste sharing with others certain conceptions and institutions. The analysis will be more limited than that of Kathleen Gough; it will leave out questions of ritual symbolism, and will deal with only one of the four groups she studied in 1955. We shall consider only the Nayar of Central

The original, French version of this chapter appeared in *L'Homme* 1, no. 1 (1961): 11–36. Translated by permission of the Ecole des Hautes Etudes en Sciences Sociales. 1981 additions to the text are between brackets.

Kerala, the least problematic for her and the most typical; the Nayar of North Kerala, and the Tiyar in the north and the center, will be dealt with in the appendix to this chapter.

My original intention was to base my interpretation exclusively on Gough's description. But she has been less concerned with giving a general description than with treating, in each case with great analytical sophistication, a particular problem on the basis of only those data that appeared relevant to her. To my mind, the description remains incomplete, and the facts are not always as firmly established as one might wish. The risks involved are reduced if we limit ourselves to a question that is central for her— namely, the Nayar distinction between, and association of, two different forms of marriage or union (1955, 53)—and if we take the liberty of discussing some points by calling upon other sources. Yet our interpretation will in large measure remain dependent upon Gough, profiting from her descriptions and data; on the other hand, it will remain temporary to a degree, pending a more complete description and a comparative and critical inventory of the sources.

Let me briefly mark the differences in approach and the intention of this essay. Kathleen Gough is not unaware that there is an Indian civilization; but, to all appearances, she seems to have thought that the similarities one can find between the groups she studied and other Indian groups are of a cultural nature and therefore of no avail for a sociological analysis. If, on the contrary, one thinks—as I do—that the India of caste is sociologically one (*Contributions to Indian Sociology* 1:9 ff; Dumont 1957*b*, ii–iii), then, as the Nayar are in the first approximation a caste, the Indian environment should afford adequate ideas for the understanding of their institutions. It is a matter of reading these institutions in the sociological language of India, and of South India in particular. Conversely, if our endeavor succeeds in this reputedly exceptional case, it will perhaps be granted that the thesis of the sociological unity of India will have been confirmed.

The Two Kinds of Nayar Marriages (Central Kerala)

The social conditions among the Nayar (*nāyar*) that we shall be dealing with no longer exist. However, to simplify the discussion we shall use the ethnographic present.

The western slope of the southernmost part of the Deccan has recently been politically unified, and forms the state of Kerala. We can thus express geographical distinctions in a simple way. We shall speak of the Northern Nayar or the Nayar of North Kerala (corresponding to the north of the Malabar district, in Gough's work) and of the Central Nayar or the Nayar of central Kerala (corresponding in Gough's writings to the south of the Malabar district plus the Cochin kingdom). South Kerala (former Travancore kingdom) is not considered.

Two main points must be stressed: first, the symbiosis between the Nayar and the Nambudiri Brahmans (*nambudiri*). Nayar institutions are not, as is sometimes imagined, a "primitive" remnant surviving by a sort of miracle in the midst of the general Indian environment; they exist, in fact, in close association with a set of Brahmans who are among the most orthodox in India. This point will be taken up later. The second point is that both the *tāli kettu kalyānam* and the *sambandham* are marriages here (Gough 1959*a*, 31). Every girl is first ritually married before reaching puberty—the "auspicious ceremony of tying the *tāli*," which is followed by cohabitation (real or feigned) for three days, which is in turn followed or not followed by formal divorce. Later on, before or after puberty (Gough 1955, 48), she contracts a much less solemn marriage with a man of suitable status who visits her by night. This is what is called the *sambandham,* and several *sambandham* may go on simultaneously. The author clearly states that the institution centers on the distinction between the two types of marriage, "the separation of the tāli-rite (the ritual marriage) from the later *sambandham* unions (initiated without rites)"[1] (1955, 53). This distinction immediately evokes the distinction, which is general in India, between primary and secondary marriage. To understand the nature of that distinction, it must be clearly separated from another that is also present in India: that between legitimate and illegitimate unions and children. For instance, where a married man can have concubines, the sons of the latter have no formal right to inherit from their father.

---

1. I have some reservation about the absence of rites, or "religious rites" (Gough 1955, 48, §2) in the inauguration of *sambandham*. It is true that most of the ceremonies mentioned in the literature are those of Northern Nayar; but even in Central Kerala the circumstance is solemnized (Fawcett 1901: 232–35; Thurston & Rangachari 1909, 5:328 ff.; Anantakrishna Iyer 1912, 30 ff.).

Radcliffe-Brown had varied in his interpretation of *samband-ham,* sometimes saying that it united "lovers" (1935, in 1952, 37; also 1953 [this volume, p. 19]) but elsewhere regarding it as marriage (1950, 71–6). Similarly, Gough was long tempted to regard *sambandham* as concubinage pure and simple. Fortunately she has given up that interpretation, for two facts go against it: first, concubinage differs from legitimate unions in that it is not under the control of the protagonists' kin, instead depending only upon personal choice (Dumont 1957*b*, 182); among the Nayar, the *sambandham* is inaugurated and solemnized by the persons in authority in the woman's *tarvād*. Second, the children born of the *sambandham* are legitimate children—indeed, all Nayar originated thus—from which we conclude that the distinction here is not that of illegitimacy versus legitimacy.

The Indian Distinction between Primary and Secondary Marriage

Let me clarify some points and some terms: We are dealing here with the India of castes (and not with tribes). I call "pan-Indian" a feature which, as far as we know, is present in all cases where a sufficient description is available. I call "general" a feature which, although widespread, is lacking in some cases; and I call "universal" a pan-Indian feature which is necessarily implied by the caste system. (I may of course be wrong, especially regarding the precise identification, or formulation, of the feature in question.) Indian castes generally have patrilineal descent,[2] patrilocal residence, with inheritance and succession going from father to son. To sum up all these features, we shall speak of "transmission in the father's line," or "paternal transmission," or even say that those groups are "paternal" from that point of view. In opposition to this, the Central Nayar have matrilineal descent, matrilocal residence, transmission of goods and attributes in the mother's line; in brief, they have maternal transmission, they are "maternal."

I shall use the term "status" exclusively to designate a relative hierarchical position—whether of a group, a person, or even a form of marriage. In the world of caste, everything tends to be ranked or hierarchized more or less strictly; and this feature must be singled

2. Descent = transmission of membership in exogamous group.

out. While personal status is formally transmitted in one line (paternal or maternal), we observe that its continuance from one generation to the next depends on the parent who is not relevant in the transmission at large—namely, the mother in general, the father(s) in the Nayar case. Actually this formula is still not sufficient, and we shall presently make it more complete; but for the time being, let us keep in mind the idea of a certain complementarity between transmission and the status of the spouse. It is implicit in a passage of Gough's last article:

All rights are acquired *through* the mother but . . . a relationship must be established between the mother and one or more other persons [=husbands] in order for these matrilineal rights to be ratified [1959*a*, 33].

We note in passing that this view is important in Gough's evolution; having started from what I would call a substantialist juridism, here she managed to go beyond it and to reach what is at least the principle of a structural view of kinship.[3]

We posit that all Indian castes distinguish, from the point of view of status or prestige, between two kinds of marriage: on the one hand, *primary* or *main* marriage; on the other, *secondary* or *subsidiary* marriages (or unions).[4] The distinction has many aspects, and there are variations from one group to another; but in all groups, people recognize a type of perfect marriage, a marriage *par excellence*, which is in general more strictly regulated, more solemn, and more costly, which offers the greatest prestige possible within that particular group—and which is most often the precondition for the existence of less reputable marriages or unions. These latter in their turn divide into two types: (1) a type of secondary marriage, a legitimate union less prestigious than the primary marriage; (2) the nonlegitimate union, inferior to the

3. In order to fully appreciate the import of Gough's admission, one should compare it with the declarations of a member of the same school of thought (which, by ironic chance, appeared quite near by: *Journal of the Royal Anthropological Institute* 89/1 (1959):65). Regarding South India, of which he had no experience, Jack Goody asked a priori: "In dealing with such societies, is there any need to regard the concepts of affinity and kinship as necessarily exclusive?"

4. For a brief statement and an example from North India, see Dumont 1960. An observation by Leach led to distinguishing more clearly, in what follows, between legitimacy and status.

secondary marriage—"concubinage" in the above-mentioned sense (in general, it is in this case that commensality is excluded if the status of the woman is too low).

Note that the central distinction is not contradicted in groups where marriage cannot be dissolved and the remarriage of widows is forbidden. This is merely the borderline case where no secondary marriage exists, so that a woman can undergo only primary marriage.

The situation could be looked at in another way. Given the three forms of union—primary marriage, secondary marriage, and concubinage—as found together mainly in royal castes (for instance, in the case of a Rajput king), one could posit on the one hand a distinction between principal and subsidiary marriage, on the other a distinction between those marriages (taken together) and concubinage. It could be said that the first distinction relates to a difference in "rank" (a hierarchical difference within the endogamous group) between the two kinds of wives and between their sons, while the second distinction is a matter of "status" (a hierarchical difference between groups), which entails the juridical disabilities mentioned above. But endogamy applies universally only to the main marriage, and the limit between "rank" and "status" thus defined is not precise and depends on circumstances. Therefore, rather than linking the distinction between unions with the endogamous group, and superimposing "status" and legitimacy, I prefer to single out *the principles* of two distinctions (distinction of status in the wider sense, and "juridical" distinction) that are always present but are combined here and there in various ways. For instance, it is true in general that a son who does not indisputably belong to the caste of his father has no right to inherit from him; but the distinction relating to inheritance can also be at play on a different level—as we shall see with the Nambudiri, where only the oldest of the legitimate sons inherits. [Actually, "inherits" is inaccurate; see note 8.]

Another objection could be offered: the status distinction between marriages takes on diverse forms, and we shall have to consider it both from the viewpoint of a male subject and of the transmission of status in the father's line (we shall use the terms *main* marriage as opposed to *subsidiary* marriages or unions) and from the viewpoint of a female subject (using the terms *primary* marriage as opposed to *secondary* marriages or unions). Are we not thus actually dealing with a number of different distinctions, which may be similar but should nevertheless be separated? I believe not. It is of course an empirical matter: the chosen approach must be judged, in the end, according to whether or not it throws light on the particular data at hand—in this case, the Nayar data. To that end, then, we must preserve what appears to us as the spirit of the system: we may transcend or encompass it, but we may not ignore it. It is clear from the very beginning that there is such a spirit. As so often in India, it is initially a matter of a carefully codified ideal—which here ensures that a maximum of status is maintained through the generations. After that, practices at variance with that ideal are not absolutely rejected, but are only judged inferior. Speaking broadly, we can say that there is a more or less brahmanical model, together with a tolerance for less orthodox customs being added to it—without ever replacing it. Thus, in general the status of a son depends not only on that of his father and that of his mother but also on the status of the union between them, of which he was born.[5]

Dravidian-speaking India offers remarkable examples of the status distinction applied to marriages and to their products with reference to males. Elsewhere I studied how, in some Tamil castes, the distinction between main marriage and subsidiary marriage or union combines with the distinction between older and younger. Not only are the sons of a main marriage "older" in relation to those of the subsidiary marriage; the eldest son among those "older" ones figures as "main" son in relation to his younger brothers;[6] thus the possibility arises that only the eldest

---

5. On the three forms of union among the Pramalai Kallar, see Dumont 1957b: 269–70: "[from the viewpoint of a male subject, there are] principal marriage, secondary marriages, concubinage. . . . There can be neither concubinage nor secondary marriage if there has not been first principal marriage. In that sense, whatever the differences between the two inferior forms of union, both are opposed to the principal marriage. Now the principal marriage unites spouses of equal status, . . . and it is only once this condition has been met that a given individual may enter unions where the status of the man is more or less superior to that of the woman." Hence the general proposition (this volume, chap. 2): "Everything looks as if the caste order was concerned first of all with maintaining the status of the family, or of the main line. . . . Once this is assured, i.e. by the birth of sons of full right, what happens next does not matter so much in itself."

6. Among the Kallar and others, "the different kinds of subsidiary sons . . . may rank differently, but the basic fact is the distinction between them all, on the one hand, and the full-fledged son, i.e. the eldest son of the first or principal

(main) son will have a main marriage, while the younger (subsidiary) sons will have only subsidiary marriages or unions. In other words, the distinction between marriage types will apply not to each male individual but to a whole group of brothers. We encounter something of that sort in the case of the Pramalai Kallar, but only on the level of kinship: the eldest son alone is obliged (in principle) to make a marriage of the preferred kind—that is, with his mother's brother's daughter. In passing, it must be pointed out that in this group, though the eldest son is differentiated with respect to *status,* with respect to *inheritance* all the (legitimate) "younger" sons have equal rights with him.

Among Nambudiri Brahmans, the combination is complete. Transmission being paternal with them—as is the case among most castes—only the eldest son has a main marriage: he marries, with all the required rites and display, a Nambudiri girl who, provided she gives him a son, will be (or so we may suppose) his main wife. After this main marriage, he may marry other Nambudiri girls (there will always be some available in such a system).[7] He may also contract *sambandham* unions with Nayar women, whose children will be Nayar (the Nayar being "maternal"). This is in conformity with the general case insofar as the offspring of such nonlegitimate unions rank, as Nayar, below the legitimate Nambudiri offspring; what is peculiar is their automatic absorption in another caste. As for a younger Nambudiri, he cannot make a marriage; he cannot marry a Nambudiri girl; he can only have *sambandham* union with Nayar girls, and their offspring will be treated as in the above-mentioned case. In the same way, inheri-

---

wife, on the other. . . . The distinction . . . may refer to age or to the mother's status as a wife (through her birth or through the type of union with the father)" (Dumont 1957a, 11–12; this volume, chap. 2). From a different point of view, regarding the substitution of one kind of son for another who is lacking, the literature of dharma contrasts the principal *(mukhya)* son or son "of the breast" *(aurāsa)* with eleven or twelve kinds of secondary *(gauna)* sons. (see Kane 1946, 3/2:641 ff.)

7. The example shows a difference, which is general, between the male and the female viewpoints: provided she gives him children, the first wife of a man becomes his main or principal wife, as distinguished from his subsequent wives. But his marriage to the latter is (or, elsewhere, may be) a primary marriage for each of the wives. In other words, the ritual of primary marriage can be repeated for a male Ego; the distinction between main and subsidiary applies to the wives as mothers, and to their children.

tance is reserved for the eldest son—to the exclusion of all younger sons, who are entitled only to maintenance on the familial patrimony.[8] (It seems probable that all offspring from a secondary marriage of the eldest brother are treated as "younger," so that each eldest brother has only one heir.) What is peculiar here is that the senior line has not only the prestige but the whole inheritance as well (with the obligation to maintain the juniors); the younger sons of a main marriage are treated here almost as bastard sons would be elsewhere. More precisely, they are both excluded from inheritance and refused a regular marriage. This is not in contradiction to the treatises of Hindu law, for in essence the official doctrine links the transmission of property with the perpetuation of the line and the performance of the necessary rites for the deceased; as the juniors cannot have proper sons, they are in effect excluded in advance from perpetuating the lineage. On this point, Thurston quoted a verse from Manu: "The one through whom a man pays his debt [to his ancestors] and attains immortality is the son born of the law, all others are said to be born of pleasure."[9] The drastic Nambudiri system has the advantage of preventing the fragmentation of property. At the same time, it is an integral part of the symbiosis between Nambudiri and Nayar, representing the Nambudiri aspect of the reciprocal adaptation of the two castes; we shall return to that aspect.

It is in the case of a female subject that the distinction between the two kinds of marriage is the clearest: a girl must always be first married according to the full and solemn formula; where "remarriage" is allowed, either upon widowhood or after divorce (where divorce exists), it will be a marriage of a different character—less

---

8. A correction is needed. "Inheritance" here is both inaccurate and misleading. Inaccurate: in a nuclear family context, the son inherits his father's possessions; but the Nambudiri eldest son *succeeds* in the full rights of his father as head of the joint family and manager of its estate. Misleading: very generally, I believe, economic assets are shared equally among the heirs, but political or politico-economic functions are transmitted to one son only.

9. My translation maintains the parallel between *dharmaja* "born of the law" or "for the law" and *kāmaja:*

> yasmin rnam sannayati yena cānantyam aśnetu
> sa eva dharmajah putrah kāmajānitaran viduh (Manu IX, 107)

The preceding verse seems to indicate that the oldest son deserves all the estate (*sarvam arhati*). The same text also approves of equal partition among all full-right sons (ibid. IX, 104).

solemn, less costly, and less prestigious. The example from Uttar Pradesh summed up elsewhere (see note 4 above) is remarkable in that while it stresses the difference in the ceremonies, it makes no difference in status between the sons of the two kinds of marriage, so that the distinction is really operative only from the point of view of the woman. I proposed an explanation.

Everywhere, the primary marriage of a girl carries a complete, if somewhat variable, conceptual elaboration underlining its value. Classically, it is the *kanyādān,* the "gift of a girl (or virgin)," which shares to a high degree the meritorious character of "gift" in general. By comparison the secondary marriage is a small affair, a practical arrangement—no doubt legitimate, but devoid of prestige and religious value. In the orthodox view, proper marriage must precede all manifestation of sexuality in the girl; it is one of the reasons given for child marriage. In that case, of course, cohabitation begins only much later, after puberty; yet in the meantime the little girl is considered a married woman, and becomes a widow if the husband dies. I recall those well-known facts because Gough (1955, 50), quoting the Nayar saying "Having had the *tāli* tied, a girl becomes a (married) woman," draws the conclusion that the ceremony was—at least ritually—a defloration;[10] by that account, all child marriages should have been accompanied by defloration. What we tend to translate as "a virgin" (Skt. *kumārī*) actually means "a not-yet-married girl." Among Nayar, let us rather think of the immediate function of the *tāli* rite. In the large Nayar house, where a number of matrilineally related persons live together (as neither the men nor the women leave the house upon marriage), the two sexes are strictly separated. The *tāli* rite marks the beginning of the rules for behavior that isolate the girl from the men of the house, her transition from the category of child to that of woman.

10. The fact of defloration is not established. Radcliffe-Brown had already given it as probable (1935, in 1952, 37). If it has ever existed, the fact is exceptional in India. Barbosa clearly separates it from the *tāli* rite (Gough 1955, 53). According to Innes (1908, 102), cohabitation was not necessary. Among Nambudiri, before the funeral of an unmarried girl, the *tāli* is tied (Thurston 1909, 5:197).

What Is Particular to the Nayar Case

[The above applies to the general "paternal" milieu, and some complication will result from the Nayar "maternal" makeup.]

In some of its aspects the Nayar distinction between *tāli* marriage and *sambandham* recalls the general separation between primary and secondary marriage. In other aspects, it is distinctive. The chronological sequence is the same. Tying the *tāli* has all the solemnity of the primary marriage of a prepuberty girl. The *sambandham* relations established later on between the woman and one or more men of status equal or superior to her own represent secondary marriages, for, as we have seen, such relations are not concubinage but are clearly distinguishable from primary marriage through several features: there is no common residence—and, in some cases, no sharing of food—and the two persons concerned are free to end the relationship as they please (at least according to most sources; cf. Anantakrishna Iyer 1912, 35). One can draw a parallel between the Nayar woman's ability to simultaneously sustain several *sambandham* unions, and, in the paternal castes, the man's ability to have several subsidiary wives (although the man would, at the same time, keep his main spouse). Actually, some features go beyond the degree of freedom allowed elsewhere in secondary or subsidiary marriages. Thus the difference of status between the spouses—between a Nayar woman and a Nambudiri man—and the concomitant nonsharing of food are probably found elsewhere only on the level of concubinage. Yet here these two traits are significant only for the person of upper status; and we have seen that, for the Nambudiri, the relationship is a concubinage.

Above all, starting from the general case, that of the Nayar presents at first sight a reversal. Elsewhere, what is essential is the primary marriage of a woman, the main marriage of a man; any marriage that might follow appears to be a supplementary one, which is freer because less relevant. With the Nayar, on the contrary, it appears that one gets the primary marriage out of the way as a mere "ritual" formality—once and for all—in order for the "real" unions to fall into the category of secondary marriage. For example, we read that, should the man who has tied the *tāli*— let us call him the *tāli*-husband—later wish to visit his *tāli*-wife, he must, just like anyone else (where it is allowed; Gough 1955, 51

§3), establish a *sambandham* with her. It should be noted that the *tāli*-wife and her children often go into mourning at the death of the *tāli*-husband (more precisely, his death makes them temporarily impure; the death of a *sambandham*-husband, on the other hand, entails no impurity): this shows that the *tāli*-husband remains all his life the ritual husband and ritual father to the Nayar. To sum up: on the religious level, the distinction between the two types of marriage is emphasized as much here as it is anywhere else; at the same time, what happens here is that the ritual of (primary) marriage is dissociated as completely as possible from what usually constitutes the substance of conjugal life—that is, permanent sexual union and the sharing of food. To account for the fact, Kathleen Gough—surprisingly—resorted to the notion of "group marriage." In 1955, considering *sambandham* to be promiscuous, she saw in the *tāli* rite a collective marriage in which

> through a chosen representative the local caste group as a whole married the lineage as a whole, and ritually set free the procreative powers of the girl to perpetuate the lineage [p. 53].
> The idea is curious, for the *tāli* rite is essentially individual.

Paradoxically, in 1959, she maintained that interpretation, even though she no longer treated *sambandham* as concubinage. Actually, against the general South Indian background, the Nayar situation would be immediately understandable on only one condition: namely, that the *tāli*-marriage should always be a strictly endogamous marriage; then the woman, having been first regularly married, could later have freer unions. But that condition is not fulfilled, as the *tāli* is often tied by a Nambudiri. This fact compels us to take a closer look at the whole. In the region, marriages are regulated, as to the choice of the spouse, not only at the level of caste or status but also at the level of kinship. Before considering these two levels in detail, let me present a more general observation. When passing from the general case to that of the Nayar, we find a kind of reversal in the relative importance of de facto relationships in the primary and the secondary marriage. It is likely that this reversal is connected with the transition from "paternal" to "maternal" people. More precisely, in the general case, where everything is transmitted from father to son (except that the mother is relevant for status), the man is the principal subject in marriage; with the Nayar, on the contrary, where everything is transmitted through women (except, as we shall see, the relevance of the father for status), it is the woman that is the principal subject in marriage. We have already encountered the point, in concrete forms, above; it will become even more apparent in what follows.

Nayar Marriages and Kinship: The inangan

On the level of kinship, we observe that the preference encountered in South India for marriage between certain closely related persons applies essentially to the main marriage (of a man).[11] In a study of the preference for cross-cousin marriage, I showed that we could understand it most simply by widening our conception of affinity—which here extends from the immediate affines to their respective kin and, more importantly, is transmitted from one generation to the next—and by conceiving of affinity as the logical counterpart of consanguinity. In a comparative note, I suggested that such might well be the essential content of the Malayalam category *inangu*, particularly among the Nayar.[12] Kathleen Gough confirms that (among commoners, at any rate) the *tāli*-husband belongs to a lineage that is *inangan* to that of the woman. It would thus seem that the *tāli*-marriage allows for the marriage preference to be both obeyed and disposed of. Gough preferred another view (group marriage; see above), but she was progressively led to recognize more and more clearly the presence here of affinity. In 1952 (p. 72, col. 1), she stated that each lineage has two or more *inangar* lineages, and she listed the lineage ceremonies in which those *inangar* lineages must be represented; there was "a hereditary relationship of ceremonial neighbourliness and ritual co-operation," a reciprocal relationship. In 1955, in two characteristic paragraphs (pp. 48–49), she again described the "chain" of *inangar* relationships between lineages. To the functions of "ritual co-operation" was added a kind of disciplinary function: the lineage having the duty of denouncing to the assembly of the local group (*tara* or *inangu*) any failure of its *inangar* to keep the "caste law." This seemed to be a new fact, and one would have liked to have it documented through explicit data. In the lines that followed, the author drew a parallel between the ceremonial functions of the Nayar *inangar* and those of certain relatives—mainly affines—in

11. Cf. the case of a man marrying the prescribed cousin and divorcing her at once in order to be able to marry freely (Dumont 1957*b*, 200).
12. Cf. above, chap. 2, note 20, and passim.

patrilineal groups; and she mentioned their function as *tāli*-tiers. Lastly, in 1959 Gough called the relationship one of "perpetual affinity." She added a point, which seems obscure to me, about the relationship between lineages "which though it carried the ceremonial functions of affinity, persisted irrespective of particular *sambandhams* and *tāli*-rites . . . . a particular *tāli*-rite in no way modified the hereditary relationships between male *enangar*" (1959*a*, 28; cf. 1955, 49, lines 5–6). The *tāli* is tied by an *inangan*, and the perpetual relationship of affinity is actually perpetuated through that act; hence it is difficult to see how it could be "modified," and what advantage there would be in separating the "perpetual" relationship from its effective perpetuation. What happens here in a ritual form is that intermarriage is repeated from generation to generation; and this is precisely the formula arrived at in my analysis of cross-cousin marriage, with the difference that here the relationship is between lineages.

Another dimension is present in Dr. Gough's exposition: that of neighborhood, or locality. In an early article, Aiyappan (1932, 337) wrote that the *inangu* formerly was a local group of the subcaste but more recently designated three or four neighboring houses having the following functions: cooking food for the household when it is impure as a consequence of death; providing the funerary priest, who is to be fed lavishly; and tying the *tāli*. The first of these functions is, I believe, comparatively a matter of neighborhood pure and simple; elsewhere even distant agnates will render this service to the mourning family. The second function is quite different: to act as funerary priest entails an impurity and borders on the barber's role. Does Gough consider this function as deriving from neighborhood? I believe, on the contrary, that it is associated with affinity. I cannot go into a full discussion of this point here; but, speaking broadly, it can be said that in South India we often observe—alongside the permanent specialization of castes—a temporary and reciprocal complementarity between relatives which, quite naturally in the environment, attaches to affinity. The role of the barber, particularly, can be taken up or complemented, in some cases, by an affine. Aiyappan (1937, 33) sensed that when he said of the Nayadi, where the *inangan* is both "priest and barber," that this arrangement perhaps represented a first step toward the formation of professional subcastes (though it is difficult to accept this statement literally, because of the difference just mentioned).

If the affinity content of the institution of *inangan* is the same as that of cousin marriage, it follows that only one of the two can have functional value in a given group. This is verified among the Northern Nayar, who have cross-cousin marriage and among whom *inangu* is weak; among the Northern Tiyar, where it seems absent; and among the Central Tiyar, where *inangu* excludes intermarriage. Yet this last fact appears to go against our interpretation. Gough explains it through the function of censorship, which she here again attributes to the *inangu* (1955, 60). Aiyappan, who was born into this group, knows nothing of that; he provides another explanation (1944, 67), which I interpret here somewhat freely. According to him, for the Central Tiyar there is a contradiction between impure functions and affinity—the affines being guests of honor. Why do these people, and they alone, feel this incompatibility? Let us first recall that, to ensure the perpetuation of affinity, they have cross-cousin marriage. Then we may ask ourselves whether the fact of *inangu* excluding intermarriage is not linked with a tendency to marry outside the locality, while the functions in question are confined within it. We are told, in effect, that "the relatives by marriage are guests in the village" (ibid.).[13] Therefore I take the fact as an exceptional development issuing from a Malayali situation in which the *inangan* is both a "perpetual affine" and a neighbor and has ritual functions on both counts—it

---

13. The incompatibility, among Central Tiyar, between impure functions and affinity is very interesting from the standpoint of comparison. For instance, in a hypergamous context the affines may be differentiated into superior and inferior affines to whom honorific and inferior functions will be correspondingly attributed. Thus Crooke long ago noted (1896, 2:60) the role of the maternal uncle as funerary priest, and that of the sister's son as priest pure and simple (1906, 178). Perhaps he was dealing with tribes rather than castes; moreover, I am here extending to North India a notion of affinity that I have established only for the South. If we ask, in a general way, in which conditions a kinship function can supplement or replace a caste function, we may perhaps surmise a priori that two factors are at work: on the one hand an emphasis on affinity relationships which results in the attribution to them of ceremonial roles (for instance, Srinivas 1952, 80: "The bride undergoes . . . a rite analogous to shaving. The bride's brother's wife removes from the bride's head a thin whisp of hair and pares her nails"); on the other hand, a need to find the necessary functions within the caste—whether as a result of relative isolation (quasi-tribal settlement) or because the caste is located near either end of the system so that it is difficult for it to find, locally, either superior or inferior people to fill the roles in question.

being understood that the affinity dimension is more widespread (there being cross-cousin marriage in Tamilnad, for instance), the locality dimension (especially in its elaboration) more geographically restricted.[14]

Let us return to the Central Nayar. Following Gough, we must now distinguish between commoners and aristocratic lineages. Among the former, the woman to whom an *inangan* has tied the *tāli*[15] may subsequently have *sambandham* with men belonging not only to the lineage of the *tāli*-tier but to all other lineages within the subcaste. Thus, the ritual marriage makes permissible secondary unions that are freer in the sense of a wider choice being open. The only prohibition is having *sambandham* with two members of the same lineage segment ("property group" or joint-family) at the same time. That is far from being promiscuity, and fraternal polyandry and sororal polygyny are specifically excluded.

As to aristocratic lineages, it was said in the 1955 article (p. 53) that the *tāli* was tied by a member of a lineage of status superior to that of the woman's lineage, "in place of" an *inangan*. This expression made one wonder whether such a lineage was not also an *inangan*. Happily, the 1959 article fully answers the question; and if it contradicts the earlier formulation, it is all to the good:

14. This sentence, unclear in the original, required emendation.
15. Let us avoid any confusion. I believe that the *tāli* never symbolizes anything but the condition of "married woman" (*contra:* Aiyappan 1944, 161), and that tying the *tāli* is a marriage rite (or, at the very least, an imitation of it). By contrast, the comparison shows that the question as to *who* ties the *tāli* to the girl has only secondary meaning. It may be, as with the Nayar, the bridegroom himself (or at least the men whom the Nayar consider as such, for if he is a Nambudiri he may have a different view; see later in the text). This is probably the case in Tamil Nad generally, as Aiyappan (1944, 161) insists, not without somewhat schematizing (cf. Thurston 1907, 42, 44: Dumont 1957b: 219, 226–27). On the contrary, it is quite otherwise in Kerala. Gough herself cites a number of cases in which the *tāli* is tied by another person, usually a woman: the Nayar mother if the family is poor (1955, 52; cf. Anantakrishna Iyer 1912, 27 and 25); among Northern Tiyar (p. 59) and Central Tiyar (p. 62), a woman helps. But all those cases seem problematic for our author. We can add that among Nambudiri, the *tāli* is tied by the girl's father before the religious ceremony proper (Thurston and Rangachari 1909, 5:207; etc.). Compare the cases of a girl married to an object (see below). Also, in the Brahmanical marriage, the officiant is one person and the bridegroom another; but Gough gives a different impression when she writes, on the Kshatriyas of Cochin, that the marriage was celebrated by a Nambudiri who had to deflower the girl afterward (1955:52).

An aristocratic Nayar lineage had as *enangar* two or more lineages of a sub-caste higher than itself from which its women were wont to draw husbands in the *sambandham* relationship. The linked lineage relationship was in these cases not reciprocal. A chiefly lineage might act as *enangar* for the lineages of one or two village headmen, but had as its own *enangar* one or two chiefly or royal lineages of higher rank than itself. Nambudiri Brahman lineages acted as [N.B.] *enangar* for the highest ranks of chiefs and royalty. . . . Men of the higher ranking *enangar* lineages tied the *tāli* at the pre-puberty marriage of aristocratic girls [1959a, 29].

From the perspective of comparison, this passage confronts us with a difficulty we have already encountered. In South India in general, the primary or main marriage is between persons of equal status; it is only in secondary (or subsidiary) marriage, or in concubinage, that the status of the man may be superior to that of the woman. Here the status difference appears in the primary marriage itself. The hierarchy of statuses invades the realm of kinship; it penetrates within ritual affinity. "Perpetual affinity" ceases to be reciprocal: someone's affine is ipso facto his superior or his inferior according to whether one gives to him or receives from him girls in (ritual) marriage.[16] Instead of "isogamy" resulting from a reciprocal affinity relationship, we have "hypergamy."[17] In the quest for rank, one neglects one's equals, if they exist; and we shall see, moreover, that at the upper levels there are hardly any equals, or a subcaste, but only a few hierarchized lineages. This sort of sliding from kinship to status is clearly marked in the extension, or quasi-extension (in the words "acted as") to Nambudiri of the *inangan* relationship, defined on the level of kinship as certainly a relationship internal to the caste. Perhaps this same "sliding" explains the discrepancy between Gough's two

16. The situation is the same in North India; *Contributions to Indian Sociology* 1 (1957):19.

17. I am using the term "hypergamy" here only with reservation, for hypergamy has been defined in North India, where it is a matter not only of marriage between persons of unequal status but of main or principal marriages in which the status of the children does not depend on that of their mother (provided of course that the latter's status is not beyond a certain limit). It is another matter when a difference in status in secondary marriages is tolerated but remains significant. Moreover, hypergamy thus precisely defined applies to the case in which the father is the main parent as regards transmission, whereas here it is the mother.

successive expositions, for it is conceivable that some of her informants, insisting on the basic meaning of the term *inangan*, should be averse to extending it in such a way, and that the term might have two different values at the two different Nayar levels.

Nayar Marriages and Status

We have just seen status superseding, as it were, kinship. This complex, but characteristically Indian, situation compels us to consider central the place of status—and, as a consequence, of the Nambudiri—in the matrimonial institutions of the Central Nayar. First, the woman, even among commoners, is forbidden to have *sambandham* with a man of inferior status. The status of the children (from a male point of view, the status of the sister's sons or nephews through whom the lineage perpetuates itself) depends not only on that of their lineage but also on that of their "fathers" in the widest sense, both as *tāli*-husbands and *sambandham*-husbands. Then, better to distinguish the role played by status, we obviously must look where it is most important—that is, at the level of aristocratic lineages and of the relationship with Nambudiri. Some Nayar men told the anthropologist that they were proud of having Nambudiri blood in their veins. It is clear, first of all, that the relative status of lineages rests on the status of those who consent to act toward them as "wife-takers"—above all, in the *tāli* ceremony. It is also clear that the system results in giving the Nayar men nephews superior in status to their sons, as the latter are by definition members of lineages inferior to their own. There is thus a close interconnection between status, transmission in the maternal line, and the formula of marriage (especially *tāli*-marriage). Take, for example, succession to the throne in a royal lineage. Some would be inclined to attribute to the king a tendency to favor his own son over his nephew; but even if we suppose that the king could identify his eldest son, he would be of irremediably lower rank than the nephews. Here an objection can be raised: if the father's status is really so important, how is it that no effort is made to register paternity more clearly? Gough sees in the multiplication of *sambandham*(s) a means for the lineage to confuse the question of biological paternity; and, more generally, she sees in the distinction between the two sorts of marriages a way of denying to the de facto husband and biological father any juridically and socially meaningful role in relation to his wife and children (1955, 53). There is no doubt that here the lineage asserts itself as a corporate subject as against the unacknowledged individual subject.[18] As we have seen in the case of affinity, status attaches to the lineage and not to its members (which does not prevent distinctions being made as usual within the lineage according to age, etc). We saw the Nambudiri counterpart of this arrangement: with them, only the eldest brother goes through a (main) marriage.

We conclude that the more we go up in the Nayar hierarchy, the more strongly we perceive the functional linkage between, on the one hand, the quest for affines (*tāli*-husbands) of the highest possible status, and, on the other, the perpetuation of the "maternal" institutions of the Nayar.

The Nambudiri Viewpoint

It is not enough for the symbiosis to have been advantageous to the Nayar; it must also have been profitable for the Nambudiri. The system favors the senior Nambudiri over their juniors, who bear the whole burden of it. For Brahmans, among whom the father-son relationship is so very strong (since a deceased man finds his way among the dead only if his son carries out the prescribed ritual),[19] it is impossible to conceive a harsher rule than the one that deprives all junior men of the ability to perpetuate themselves. Must we admit that their most sacred interest is simply sacrificed (and to what end?). Or should we suppose that they conceive their peculiar situation as being part of their role as embodiments of value in the society, in the sense that they thus maintain their hold on Shudra people? It is somewhat surprising that our author, who is inclined to materialistic explanations, has not seen the probability that the Nambudiri may have obtained quite palpable benefits through their association with the Nayar. Yet that is what comparison suggests. We see that the Nambudiri Brahmans, by virtue of their own

18. This being so, we may ask whether it is justifiable—whether it does not introduce a factitious precision—to give an account of such a system, as did Gough (1959, 30), in terms of the diverse sorts of "rights" that would attach to the individual in each kinship role.

19. For Nambudiri see above ("The Indian Distinction . . .") and, from recent literature, Gough 1956 (Tamil Brahmans) and Derrett 1960.

religious preeminence, give prestige to the Nayar—prestige here being a reflection of religious merit. The dharma treatises eulogized, celebrated, and catalogued a device for transforming material goods (in themselves devoid of value) into merit: the *gift* to the Brahmans—actually an exchange of goods for merits. The transition from merit to prestige, and from the Brahman to any man of superior status, is seen in the North Indian formula of true hypergamy, where one "gives a girl" (in *kanyādān*) and goods to a man or family of superior status only for the sake of the prestige that reflects back on the giver.[20] Against such a background, it seems highly improbable that the Nambudiri would not have derived substantial profits from their association with the Nayar. Two features would tend to confirm such a surmise. It is known that in their own marriages the Nambudiri attach the greatest importance to the particularly sumptuous prestations accompanying the "gift of a girl."[21] What is more, we find the Nambudiri in Kerala in a situation quite peculiar for Brahmans. In general, Brahmans are spiritually superior but materially subordinated and needy. Therefore, pious kings settled them in special establishments (through the gift of land) and attached to the temples rich foundations for the maintenance of the priests. Elsewhere Brahmans have also been seen to exchange their traditional functions for that of rulers. In Kerala, the Brahmans, the Nambudiri, without ruling in the strict sense, are nevertheless closely entwined in the political organization. Not only do they live in comfort, but they occupy important positions in the pyramid of benefices which, from the king down to the Nayar commoners, ensures the livelihood of the warriors.[22] This is a somewhat anomalous situation; and just as our author underlines the correlation between "hypergamy" and the distribution of power, we may also suppose that the exceptional situation of the Nambudiri is related to the functions of affines and ritual fathers, and even of "genitors," which they are so good as to fulfill in favor of the military class. These functions themselves are in their turn exceptional and, combined with a

20. Although not yet described at length in a monograph, the fact is known from authors like Risley and Blunt; and Kingsley Davis (1941) understood it. (See also note 4, above.)
21. Thurston and Rangachari 1909, 5:158, 187: "Property alone is the real thing to be considered."
22. Gough 1955, 54. The Nambudiri are often village headmen (1955, 46; 1952, 24). Innes 1908 gave them as predominant in Walluvanad.

drastic enlargement of primogeniture—itself probably very profitable to the maintenance of the caste's material position—they entail among them a quite extraordinary separation (extending from status to juridical condition) between seniors and juniors.[23] On the whole, it is probable that their tying the *tāli* to the girls of Nayar chief lineages was very profitable to the Nambudiri, and that the sacrifice of their juniors on the religious level was compensated not only by sexual facilities but also by a secure corporate opulence which may have even facilitated the cultivation of the religious tradition.

From another angle, it must certainly be supposed that their relationships with the Nayar were perfectly compatible with the orthodoxy and sacerdotal pride of the Nambudiri. The point is easily verified with respect to the *sambandham*: for them, it is concubinage pure and simple; and the offspring born from it do not concern them, absorbed as they are in the inferior caste. But how did the Nambudiri tying the *tāli* to a Nayar girl regard his act, which for the Nayar was a ritual marriage? Being devoid of Vedic rites, the ceremony could not be a marriage for the Brahman. Moreover, in their own marriages, the *tāli* is tied *by the girl's father*, before the religious ritual that constitutes the marriage proper. Thus the Nambudiri could see himself, when he tied the *tāli*, as a priest accomplishing a rite appropriate to the status of the Nayar and for their benefit. Even real cohabitation, if it were to follow, would have been mere concubinage to him.

To conclude: the *tāli* rite probably corresponded to an exchange between Nambudiri and Nayar, the former giving prestige and the latter giving power (that is temporal goods). The two parties must have had, in principle, quite different views of the ceremony—so different that we may wonder how the two views have come to be combined or, so to speak, how there ever arose this comedy in which the Nambudiri allows the Nayar to mystify himself.

The Kshatriyas

One element in the situation can help us understand it. I shall underline the point, for Gough hardly brought it out. She first

23. This passage, inexact in the original, has been slightly expanded for clarification.

spoke of "royal lineages" among the Nayar; then, among the royal houses, she said that some claim to be "true" Kshatriyas, while others are more or less considered as such. In fact, the difference in status between Kshatriyas and Nayar is considerable. The Kshatriyas are a caste, or rather they are the second of the four *varna* (the classes into which the society is theoretically divided: Brahmans, Kshatriyas, Vaishyas, and Shudras), whereas the Nayar belong to the fourth *varna*—Shudra. The impurity of death lasts ten days for Brahmans, eleven days for Kshatriyas, fifteen days for the Nayar. Moreover, in Kerala the Kshatriyas are like the Nayar in that they transmit everything in the maternal line; universally, they are similar to the Brahmans in being "twice born" and entitled to the Vedic ritual for their family ceremonies. No doubt Gough was correct in noticing, with other authors (Innes 1908, 113–4), that a series of minute transitions leads from the best-authenticated Kshatriyas to people of intermediary or doubtful status and to Nayar pure and simple; and she may have thought that the Kshatriyas were in fact Nayar who had managed, at an earlier or later date—as a result of having exercised for a long time, without contestation, the royal function—to be acknowledged as Kshatriyas. All that is likely (and in no way contrary to principle). Yet, in the end, Kshatriyas and Nayar are distinct; and the Brahmans celebrate Vedic rites for the former and not for the latter.

Gough mentions that in the royal lineages acknowledged as Kshatriyas, the girls married Nambudiri men while the men married Nayar women.[24] That is to say that the Kshatriyas functioned as intermediaries, in the chain of intermarriage, between Nambudiri and Nayar. We can even, with the information provided by our author, slightly complicate the scheme by intercalating not one but two royal houses—one Kshatriya, the other non-Kshatriya—between the two extremes. The first intermarriage represented (fig. 20), between Nambudiri and Kshatriya of Beypore, is not documented but it conforms to the general rule. The Zamorin of Calicut, a *sāmantan*,[25] had conquered the Beypore

---

24. On this point, Thurston and Rangachari (1909, 5:156) mention—but without precise reference—an inscription of the Chalukya period, according to Subramania Aiyer.

25. The *sāmantan* are given as a Nayar subdivision intermediary in status between "royal lineages" and village headmen (Gough 1955, 46). Innes (1908, 114)

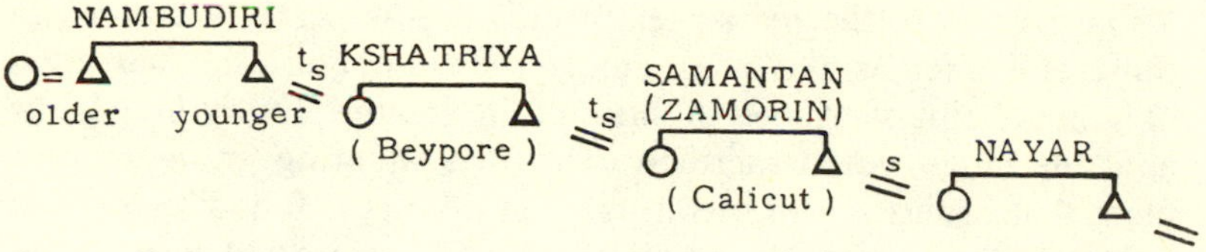

Fig. 20. Partly hypothetical chain of intermarriage. t = *tāli;* s = *sambandham.* Vertical spacing represents difference in status.

kingdom, but he continued (as is seen on the diagram) to recognize the superior status of that house.

This arrangement holds certain interest for us. In trying to understand the institutions of the Nayar, we were led to consider them at the level on which status is most important: that of royal lineages. Now we find that a part of those royal lineages were considered to be not Nayar (i.e. Shudras) but Kshatriyas. The latter's status being much nearer than the Nayar to that of the Nambudiri, it is much easier to imagine *sambandham*—and even more likely, *tāli*—relationships between them.[26] Moreover, those Kshatriyas, who are few and are grouped in distinct lineages, marry exclusively outside the caste (actually outside the *varna*), upward for women, downward for men. As a result, the status difference between a man's son and his nephew is quite drastic, his

---

classifies them between Kshatriyas and Nayar, and includes in that group the Zamorin of Calicut and the king of Walluvanad. (cf. Anantakrishna Iyer 1912, 146).

26. Yet a difficulty remains. We may suppose that, the Kshatriyas having the Vedic ritual, the *tāli* rite among them was part of a (Vedic) marriage between a Nambudiri man and a Kshatriya woman; Thurston and Rangachari (1909, 4:90; s.v. Kshatriya) give this impression. Such a marriage—of course, secondary for the Nambudiri—was perhaps not impossible. We have an example in Nepal (Fürer-Haimendorf 1960, 17), and, apart from the ritual, the Shastras' only condition seems to be that the children should be inferior in status to the father, which is the case. But then we are faced with only two alternative possibilities: either no *sambandham* followed (but Innes asserts that there is *sambandham* in all castes where transmission is from uncle to nephew [1908, 96]; and we shall see, further on, a reason to think that it is so), or the Vedic marriage had to be dissolved, which is difficult to suppose. There is a gap here in the evidence. Let us note, in passing, a peculiar formula of affinity, or marriage alliance, in North Kerala: the royal lineage of Kolattiri is said to have brought Koil Tamburan people from the South as *tāli*-tiers for its girls.

son being a Samantan or a Nayar and only his nephew being a Kshatriya. Here the marriages of men are as neatly sacrificed to those of women as we found, among the Nambudiri, the marriages of juniors being sacrificed to those of the seniors. Everything looks as if the kings would sacrifice their own offspring to an arrangement that brings a gain in status. And all this is found again, in a milder form, among Nayar aristocrats. We were led to consider Nayar marriages mainly from the point of view of the woman, who is the main subject on account of the mode of transmission; but what can be said of the men's marriages? Like the Nambudiri juniors, they have no main marriage; like them again, they hardly have sons properly called. The system subordinates the male viewpoint to that of the female in the matter; but, as compensation, it gives the men a satisfaction regarding their status.

We are thus led to suppose that the Kshatriyas have served, genetically, as intermediaries between Nambudiri and Nayar—that the configuration of marriages we are studying originated with them. In the Indian milieu, the extension of the pattern appears quite natural: the imitation of superiors by their inferiors, the Nayar's thirst for prestige, and perhaps the Nambudiri's greed would have brought about the spread of the pattern—first to the Nayar chieftains[27] and then to all "aristocrats," who could thus have prestigious affines and even high-status "fathers" (in a corporate and ritual sense) while perpetuating their lineages in the maternal line and holding in check the pretensions of *patria potestas*. From there the pattern would have spread even to the Nayar commoners, among whom it has no longer really a function of status but only of kinship.

Parallel between the Nayar Girl and the Basavi

Up to this point we have shown the compatibility, the probable interconnection of several features in the Nayar formula of two marriages; we have not as yet demonstrated its necessity. For example, why could not the Nambudiri, after tying the *tāli*, immediately enter into concubinage with the Nayar girl? Is it only because that would be incompatible with the definition of the girl's

27. Gough indicated one transition of this kind—a very valuable piece of evidence—when she wrote (1955, 47) that for a part of the girls of the Zamorin's lineage, the Nambudiri had replaced the Kshatriyas as *tāli*-husbands.

primary marriage, or because the matrilineage has an interest in multiplying the genitors?

Once more, comparison comes to our rescue. There is a striking parallelism between the *tāli* rite among the Nayar and tying the *tāli* in some other Dravidian-speaking groups. Tying the *tāli* is— generally, but not universally, in that milieu—a rite of the primary marriage, more or less stressed according to the group. In the case of the Devadasi ("god's servants," temple dancers and prostitutes), tying the *tāli* is [= was traditionally] part of the girl's ritual marriage to the god (represented by his image or by a sword.[28] Gough (1955, 52, n.4) refers to this well-known custom without pursuing the comparison. Among the Devadasi as among the Nayar, the ritual marriage takes place before puberty, and the girl may later on have intercourse with men relatively freely but not without restrictions (in Thurston and Rangachari 1909 s.v. Devadasi, 2:125ff.). While these Dasi constitute more or less a caste that is relatively degraded on account of their promiscuity, the similarity to the Nayar goes further and is somehow juridical for another category of women, the Basavi. As noted by Fawcett (1901, 231), the Basavi, if they are ritually married to a god as the Dasi are, do not lose their rank, nor do their children: "Their children are under no degradation." We read that, especially in the Bellary district, among certain castes

> a family which has no male issue *must* dedicate one of its daughters as a Basavi. The girl is taken to a temple, and married there to the god, a *tāli* and toe-rings being put on her, and thenceforward she becomes a public woman, except that *she does not consort with anyone of lower caste than herself.* . . . Contrary to all Hindu law, *she shares in the family property* as though she was a son. . . . If she has a son, he takes her father's name, but if only a daughter, this daughter becomes a Basavi. The children of Basavi *marry within their*

---

28. In general, an absent bridegroom can be represented by an object—e.g., a sword or a stick. A Brahman may avoid the inauspiciousness of a third marriage by marrying the *arka* plant *(Calatropis, or Asclepias, gigantea),* so that his real marriage will be the fourth (Thurston 1907, 41–44).

There is a striking parallel in Nepal: the Newar girl is first married to the fruit of the *bel* tree, so that her real marriages will then be secondary marriages (Fürer-Haimendorf 1956, 37); Kirkpatrick saw the similarity as early as 1811: "It is remarkable enough that the Newar women like those among the Nairs may, in fact, have so many husbands as they please, being at liberty to divorce them continually on the slightest pretences" (p. 187).

own caste, without restrictions of any kind [Thurston and Rangachari 1909, 2:129; from the 1901 Census Report; my emphasis].

We must understand that the Basavi do not constitute a caste; the term designates only women who have been dedicated by their parents. They do not cease to belong to "their own caste"—that is, as other texts confirm, to the caste in which they were born. The device is meant for procuring male offspring to the family of origin; and one judge recognized the parallelism with the *putrikā* or *putrikāputra,* the "appointed daughter" of Hindu law (ibid., 150).[29] In the absence of a son, the daughter thus "appointed" was treated as a son and was put in charge of procuring a son for her father. She was not dedicated to the god as was the Basavi, and did not prostitute herself (which, according to some sources, the Basavi did not do either; ibid., 135). Francis (ibid.) insisted on the fact that the Basavi's children were legitimate children, and that neither they, nor their mother were in any way treated as inferiors.

Clearly there is more here than what occupied us heretofore; it is now not only a matter of the purely ritual primary marriage as a preliminary condition of sexual life, nor of the greater freedom of secondary unions. Here, in groups where inheritance and succession are from father to son, a woman is made capable, in certain conditions, of assuming a male role, inheriting from her father and perpetuating the male line through her son. It is as if, in modern times, that could not take place through a primary marriage and as if, in order to bypass the male monopoly in the matter, the woman had first to go through a fictitious primary marriage in order to be able afterward to assume, through secondary marriages or unions, the juridical role normally reserved for men. Were she not first married to a god, in place of becoming a Basavi the woman could be only the means through which a man acquires children; however, by becoming a Basavi (that is, a special sort of married woman with whom men can have only subsidiary unions), she acquires the faculty of acquiring children for herself—actually, for her father, from whom she also inherits as if she were a son.

29. According to Kane (1946, 3:647ff.) and the Dharmashastras, there are two ways of considering the institution—or maybe two ways of interpreting the word *putrikāputra,* according to whether it is applied to the girl herself ("the son who is (in fact) a daughter, *putrikā*") or to her son ("son of the *putrikā*"). The Nambudiri are the only group among which the institution is acknowledged by modern law (cf. Thurston and Rangachari 1909, 5, 176; s.v. *sarvasvadānam*).

The obvious parallel with the Nayar brings up a crucial question. Everything among Nayar is *normally* transmitted in the mother's line. How is it that they apparently resort to the same stratagem that some castes employ when they want to *make an exception* to their transmission in the father's line? If, as I believe, we are dealing with the same fact in both cases, we obviously must answer that with the Nayar it is a matter of adaptation to the environment, a way of inserting their "maternal" institutions into a "paternal" sociological milieu. We have already learned that they were not independent in relation to their Nambudiri neighbors, and that they shared, in particular, a universal idea of hierarchy. But the dependency is now seen as more strict. It is as if the Nayar, recognizing in the primary marriage the "paternal" value it has for most castes, had recourse to the secondary marriage to escape it, as some of those other castes do. We note that this "paternal" value was not apparent in the ordinary case. It is only the exceptional arrangement of the Basavi and the Nayar that makes us see that transmission becomes maternal and, as far as we can see, can become maternal only in the secondary marriage or union: in other words, *the woman, being the secondary subject in the primary marriage, can become the main subject in the secondary marriage* (or union), and there only. Thus we understand the necessity for the distinction of marriages among the Central Nayar: there must be a primary marriage, and it must be made fictitious in all respects except ritual, so that in the secondary marriage the woman may keep her residence and the children can belong to the mother's lineage, inherit and succeed in the mother's line. The point is very clear in the context of the symbiosis with the Nambudiri. We note that the distinction between primary and secondary marriage, which is in the general case only an affair of status, is here at the same time an essential juridical matter. The same is true of the Nambudiri senior/junior distinction. It is obvious, a posteriori, that the similarity of the two situations demands this parallelism: we should have been able to deduce it logically.

The Basavi case is instructive on another point. The Basavi is first married not to a man but to a god or an object. Therefore, the presence of a man, of a real husband, in the Nayar *tāli* rite does not seem to be necessary for getting rid of the *patria potestas;* it seems rather to be only a matter of status and/or kinship (e.g. the case of the ritual husband and father being mourned). The trait is thus relevant for the lineage (the lineage being the subject of status and kinship), while the Basavi seeks only to perpetuate her father, or the individual line, and not the lineage as a whole. We thus come back to the complementarity between the characteristics that are transmitted without regard to the ritual and biological fathers and, on the other hand, the status and kinship conditions that must be met for this transmission to take place. Those conditions are especially prominent in the primary or principal marriage, and they finally encompass the distinction between the two kinds of marriages. Hierarchy (or affinity) and marriage distinction are thus closely tied together.

Conclusion

The Nayar are generally considered to be exceptional. I believe that their case illustrates the general impossibility of studying an Indian caste [or group] independently of its environment—as a self-sufficient society—and demonstrates the necessity of regarding it as a particular case of a common configuration. Indeed, what is exceptional here? There are of course, on the one hand, all those "maternal" features, the combination of which is so extreme that the Nayar are famous as an anthropological rarity. But this set of features—which anthropologists were wont to isolate and to compare to corresponding features of societies elsewhere in the world—is linked with other features that testify to the Nayar's integration in the society of castes. We can also ask ourselves what makes the Nayar exceptional in comparison with ordinary castes. What differentiates the Nayar here is a narrower dependency, an integration that is stricter than in the general case. At first sight, the Nayar seem to be an exception to the "law" of caste endogamy. However, this is only an appearance. In the first place, endogamy pertains mostly to the primary or principal marriage, which is here reduced to pure ritual. But, even more important, the real law is that a superior caste should not intermarry with an inferior caste;[30] and we have seen that for the Nambudiri there is no question of marriage in their relationship with the Nayar. In fact, the apparent exception of the Nayar is the mark of an extreme dependence on other castes. The analysis has shown that the two

30. Endogamy is only the general result of the operation of the hierarchy principle (Dumont 1980 §52 ff.).

sorts of aspects go together; and it is highly probable that, if the Nayar are extreme in their maternal (or, as they were first called, "matriarchal") features, it is due to the fact that they are not an isolated tribe but a caste that is all the more strictly linked to its neighbors because of its difference from them. There is a deep connection between the originality of the group and its integration in the caste system. But we should not see in that singularity a cause nor in the integration a consequence. Quite to the contrary, the fact that in the whole world the Nayar show up as having unusual traits warns us that they probably owe them to being both antithetic to and backed up by a solid "paternal" environment, and that adaptation to the Indian milieu has probably made possible an extreme development of those features—for instance, the Indian formula of the two types of marriages may have been an excellent device for holding in check the pretensions of the *patria potestas*.[31]

Appendix: A Tentative Generalization

In this article I have dealt only with the Nayar of Central Kerala, not with the other three groups studied by Gough in 1955. This singling out of one group, when all four—and others with them— seem to share the same institution, could be objected to. However, not only does the institution itself vary slightly from one group to another, but there is also a considerable variation in the context, so that the study of the institution in its context would require a separate analysis in each case. We shall be content with a few remarks.

Many questions arise as soon as one tries to widen the limited area on which comparison has thrown light. Can we say that the woman becomes the main subject of marriage *only* in secondary marriage? What does this rather stenographic expression "main subject" mean beyond the sole case in which everything is transmitted in the same line? To put it another way: if, starting from the extreme formula we studied, we imagine for a given group

31. There are general questions that remain to be discussed. Beyond those already mentioned, the use of the words "caste" or "subcaste" for designating certain Nayar groups that are not endogamous (either absolutely or predominantly), and the very nature of the vast set of groups called Nayar, represent problems I reserve for a paper making use of Nepali (Newar) data for comparison. (See Dumont 1964, 90 ff., especially the brief statement on p. 98.)

a gradual decrease in both its degree of dependence on others and its degree of "maternal" transmission, at what stage will the distinction between types of marriages become superfluous? It is the more difficult to answer such a question, as one comes to suspect that another factor is at play in the groups actually observed. I believe it is legitimate here, in certain conditions, to attribute the presence of a custom to inferiors imitating their superiors. For instance, if the *tāli* rite is found in a lower caste without what appeared in the analysis as its raison d'être in an upper caste, and if no other reason can be discovered, we shall admit that it is in this case due to imitation. To do so would obviously be dangerous if the generalization were made in a facile manner. Only what we know of the Indian milieu in general authorizes such a step. There is a phenomenon with which many features—even major features—of Indian civilization seem to be connected (*Contributions to Indian Sociology*, 1:19–21; 4:43ff.). In the Indian environment we must acknowledge, for any given feature, alongside its intrinsic function, an important "extrinsic function"—essentially, its prestige value. The latter may be enough to account for the presence of a given trait in certain circumstances. Authors familiar with the domain tacitly or expressly admit the point. Thus, in the matter at hand, Aiyappan (1944, 160–61) mentions an Indian theory of imitation; and Gough herself resorted to that type of explanation: in a study of the funerary rites of the Nayar (1959*b*, 257), she attributed to imitation the presence of features borrowed from the Brahmans.

The clearest case is that of the Central Tiyar–or, as we should rather say, the Iravar. Gough calls their *tāli* ceremony "a mock-marriage" (1955, 62). Aiyappan had already written (1944, 161–62) that for the people themselves (in the recent past, at any rate) it had no meaning other than that of an "initiatory rite, preliminary to attaining marriageable status"; and he had emphasized, as a proof of its having no real function, the ease with which reformers had suppressed it almost everywhere. Actually, among people who in the past practiced fraternal polyandry and who are *patrilineal* and patrilocal, the essential function of the *tāli* rite falls away. There was a preference for cross-cousin marriage, but the *tāli* does not seem to have played any role on that level either. The *tāli* was tied by a boy of the caste taken from an affinal (or unrelated) group. Yet the ceremony was relatively elaborate, with ritual divorce. Obviously we must remember that we are here in Central Kerala, where the rite was very important for the Nayar: synchronically, at least, the Iravar imitated a prestigious ceremony of their local superiors. Aiyappan furnishes the counterproof when he explains how the reformer of the caste, Sri Narayana Guru, put an end to the custom: "He stopped a few aristocratic families performing the rite, . . . and the rest of the people followed the example of the local leaders" (1944, 154). Here we have, rather than an "initiatory rite," a good example of extrinsic function: an imitation of marriage.

Now about North Kerala; and first, the Nayar (cf. Gough 1955, 54). In contrast to the Central Nayar, *sambandham* is here virilocal and monogamous, and often between cross cousins; and the *tāli* is tied by a Nambudiri. It is easy to see that most of the meanings we attributed to the distinction between marriage types are absent here. In particular, it seems that the quest for a high-status husband is confined to the *tāli;* the kinship rules, to *sambandham*. The association with the Nambudiri is less close, less linked to their place in the distribution of power; their role appears as a matter of etiquette. Yet the essential "function" we attributed to the distinction between marriage types is perhaps present. For here also the Nayar are matrilineal and in general "maternal"; residence returns to matrilocality for the children at puberty at the latest: a son then goes back to live, permanently, in the *tarvād* where his mother was born. We might think that he could not do so if he had been born from a primary marriage, but is it really so? To be able to answer positively, we should be sure that the "paternal" pressure of the environment in which the Nayar insert their maternal transmission is still present. We just saw that the link to the Nambudiri is much looser. Is it that the external pressure is replaced here by an internal "paternal" pressure, of which the virilocal and monogamous *sambandham* is testimony? We conclude, then, that in all likelihood the distinction between marriage types here keeps its essential function. But the same is not true of the Nambudiri tying the *tāli;* except for the prestige that he imparts to all Nayar lineages indiscriminately, he could be replaced by a god or an object: his presence seems a matter of imitation or merely formal tradition.

Interpretation of the case of the Tiyar of North Kerala (cf. Gough 1955, 56–59) is a more delicate matter. With them, *sambandham* is virilocal (as it is with their superior neighbors the Nayar), but their virilocal residence extends in time—in some cases, at least—up to three or four generations; if descent is matrilineal, residence seems on the whole indifferent. The distinction between marriage types has no kinship function, for cross-cousin marriage is preferred and the *tāli* rite is not used to dispose of it in favor of other marriages (Gough 1955, 59§2). It has no status function either. It is noteworthy that the *tāli* rite and the *sambandham* do not differ as to the person of the husband, who is not physically present in the *tāli* anyway. Aiyappan (1944, 59) says that in general the *tāli* was tied by the girl's mother's brother's wife—the mother of the preferred husband—but by the boy's maternal uncle's wife "if the girl is already betrothed."[32] Moreover, the girl is secluded for three days *before* the ceremony, as for a puberty ritual, which probably marks a contamination with that ritual (regionally very widespread but not mentioned by Aiyappan in his monograph on the Tiyar-Iravar).[33] On the whole, the ritual is relatively vague and confused, compared to that of the Central Iravar. The difference reflects and magnifies what we encountered among the Nayar. The confusion with the puberty ritual seems to indicate that the *tāli* rite is vaguely conceived of as a *rite de passage,* feigned puberty and the shadow of a marriage. All in all, the evidence indicates that the *tāli* rite, here as in the central region, has only an extrinsic function—a function of prestige.

1981 Comment

This note will not review the literature that has appeared on the subject since 1961, but will only discuss major criticisms and divergent views as they have been put forward in the main by two authors.

32. Original corrected.
33. It is positively known that there is a ceremony for the puberty of girls among Nayar (for instance "thirandukuli" in Cochin, according to Anantakrishna Iyer 1912, 29). The Ambalakkarar of Madura present the remarkable case of a ritual which the informants report as a mere simulation, imitating in its externals the circumcision of the boys (see Dumont 1957*b,* 245). The ceremony brings an income to the parents, through the prestations of relatives. Such does not seem to be the case with the Tiyar. Otherwise Thurston has at least two instances of an "auspicious ceremony" celebrated for girls of seven to nine years; the *thanda-kalyānam* among the Thanda Pulayar of Cochin, and the *vīlakkīdu-kalyānam* ("to set, or light, the lamp") among the Karkattu Vellalar of Tamil Nad (1907, 121; 1909, 7:380).

My Nayar article is relatively marginal in relation to the study reprinted above as chapter 2 in the sense that, having no field experience of the markedly different social organization of people of the West Coast, I simply tried in it to apply some general principles I had abstracted from my study in the eastern region. It is therefore rather paradoxical to find that it has met with greater comprehension and approval than the altogether more solidly based study.

In the first place, Kathleen Gough herself, so much discussed in the above as *the* Nayar specialist in those years, while, as we have seen in the comment on chapter 1, she otherwise disagreed with many of my views, and felt the need, regarding the Nayar themselves, for reservations on other points, nevertheless acknowledged in 1965 that my "suggestion of primary and secondary marriages . . . is probably the most appropriate way to view the system" and that it helped "very much to place Nayar unions in a more general Indian context" (Gough 1965, col. 11b).

Another author, Joan Mencher, who did fieldwork after Gough among both Nayar and Nambudiri, accepted the general interpretation I had given of the Nambudiri-Nayar symbiosis, which is in a sense the crux of the matter. True, she stated that it was not connected with the *tāli* rite as I had surmised from the literature, but only with the *sambandham* union, but she added that "correction of [Dumont's] statements about the Nambudiri does not change the force of the main argument about the Nayar" (Mencher and Goldberg, 1967, note 7). Indeed her description of the sociopolitical functions of the Nambudiri in relation to their drastic limitation of marriage to the eldest son (Mencher 1966, 186, 188) and their concubinage with (kingly or) Nayar women is quite consonant with my general point about the Nambudiri-Nayar relation having been essentially an exchange of prestige or status versus tangible goods and profitable functions.

Earlier, in a long article published in 1963, "On the Purity of Women in the Castes of Ceylon and Malabar," Nur Yalman accepted in part my argument but thought to draw more completely than I had done "all the logical conclusions" from "the fundamental structural factor (i.e. caste)" and offered in fact an alternative interpretation based on what amounts to a theory of castes ("a model for endogamy and hypergamy," pp. 39–43). For what concerns us here, Yalman started from the fact that "the preoccupation with caste purity" undoubtedly entails a preoccupation with "female purity" and "female sexuality" (1963, 39), that an "anxiety about preserving the purity" of women "arises directly from a regime of castes" (p. 45). This will be easily granted and is in immediate relation with the Brahmanical institution of prepuberty marriage, the classical prescription that *"all* orthodox Hindus *must* marry their daughters *before* puberty" (ibid.), which was, as Yalman states, generally observed in those circles. He adds that the *tāli* marriage is "a particular form of prepuberty marriage," which is literally true, and that "any explanation of one must cover the other"—which does not seem to be the case, as the *tāli* marriage is obviously something else or something more than the ordinary Hindu prepuberty marriage, which binds a woman to a husband exclusively and for life.

But the Brahmanical prepuberty marriage was only a part, and not the central part, of Yalman's argument. His consideration centered largely on a quite different ritual, which he described in detail for the Sinhalese, and which is widely found in South India, among people who do not have the Brahmanical infant marriage. This ritual accompanies the first menstruation of a girl, it is a puberty ritual, a *rite de passage* which has nothing to do with marriage except in sofar as it solemnizes, and almost advertises (p. 32), the maturity of the girl to be subsequently married. Now we all know that a menstruating woman is impure, and in that sense the puberty rite of girls has obviously to do with purity. Whatever the precise symbolism of the ritual (Yalman's fragmentary and "intuitive" interpretation has been aptly queried in Leach 1970), one thing is sure, it is that the rite cannot be considered as similar or homologous to a marriage as Yalman would have it (note 25, cf. Leach p. 826). The concern with purity here lies only in the fact that the temporary impurity of the girl has to be lived through (in seclusion) and to be properly liquidated or evacuated, which is done in this case with particular elaboration and solemnity.

It is not easy to see how Yalman justifies his conflating two rituals as different as the Brahmanical prepuberty marriage (which is simply a Hindu marriage performed when the girl is still a child, so that it does not conclude in her cohabitation with her husband) and the South Indian and Sinhalese girl's puberty ceremony (which can hardly be taken as an "initiation" either, as it is a purely individual affair). The reference to "purity" does not suffice to unite them, as it works very differently in both cases: there is in the latter case no dread of women's sexuality as potentially endangering the status of the group as in the former, on the contrary the sexuality of the new woman is frankly asserted. In actual fact what seems to happen in Yalman's study is that the bridge between the two heterogeneous rituals is provided precisely by the Nayar *tāli* rite in sofar as it can be seen as participating of both: on the one hand we have seen it taken as a prepuberty marriage, on the other hand advantage is taken of the fact that the girl is secluded, i.e. "is treated as if she had menstruated" (p. 45). But it is the more difficult to take the rite as a puberty ceremony, as the Nayar had the latter as a quite distinct institution.

Yalman himself sensed "the considerable difference between South Indian [=*tāli*] and Sinhalese rites" (p. 45) but at the same time he curiously reduced it to a question of "timing, emphasis and elaboration" to be related to the nature of the marriage tie (ibid.). In some cases, like the Sinhalese, "there is less reason to hold very elaborate *puberty or pre-puberty* rites" (my emphasis) (yet the Sinhalese have an elaborate puberty rite). In other cases, like the South Nayar, "an elaborate ceremony is called for" (p. 46). The upshot of this is that "a complete substitute marriage" (Nayar) differs from the Sinhalese puberty rite only through a superior degree of "elaboration" (ibid.). This is of course hard to accept, and we cannot here go into the elaborate theory through which Yalman tries to make of the "purity of women" a fundamental principle of the caste system itself. He certainly was right to insist on its importance in a general sense and on its two, for us, different aspects. (For a relevant comparison of the puberty ceremonies among different people in Sri Lanka, see Winslow 1980).

The Nayar are fortunate in that they attract the almost continuous and close attention of anthropologists. After Gough and Mencher, C. J. Fuller worked among them in the early seventies. He did fieldwork among the less typical southern Nayar and his book, as indicated by its title *The Nayars Today*, is concerned in the first place with the present state of things (Fuller 1976*a*). But Fuller is careful to set the present in historical perspective, and his book has a chapter on the Nayar's "traditional marriage system" which contains a seasoned *mise au point* of the questions debated here. Fuller also published an article "The Internal Structure of the Nayar Caste" (1975).

In his book, Fuller sums up with great care and discusses in detail, among others, some of the views put forward by me (see esp. 1976*a*, 105–14). He acknowledges in general the usefulness of restoring "the Nayars definitively to a place in Indian society" (p. 114), and restates very clearly my arguments about affinity and the like. Here, then, it seems, we get a chance of finding out how a new generation of researchers looks at those questions. Actually Fuller's consideration is restricted to the first part of my paper. He dismisses as "not very enlightening" what he calls a long development on "hypergamous" relations (p. 119) and silently skips the concluding pages as well. He himself candidly acknowledges that "many of the issues raised by Gough and Dumont have not been tackled" by him (p. 120) and that "many aspects of Nayar marriage . . . continue to baffle" him (ibid.). Of course a writer has a right to abstain from discussing certain issues, yet I cannot help wondering why he does so and what the sources of his uncertainties are.

What seems to be the case in relation to my theses is that Fuller retains in a measure, and with the modifications he finds fit, the similarities between the Nayar case and the "ordinary" Indian or South Indian case (see his conclusion p. 120) while he rejects what relates to the interdependence between the Nayar and their social environment.

Regarding the *tāli* rite and the *sambandham*, it is striking to find that Fuller simply does not mention what to me is the decisive point. Should it be summarily restated? In India the first marriage of a girl (the "primary marriage") results in the children's being attached to their father's group. The Nayar—owing to Brahmanical pressure or otherwise—admitted this principle and therefore had to perform such a marriage and to get rid of it in order to be able, through "secondary marriages," to attach the children to their mother's group without in the least contradicting the Indian or Hindu principles. More generally, the anthropologically problematic aspects of the Nayar makeup are seen as the condition for their "maternal" system to be integrated in the paternal Indian milieu. Why does this global conclusion escape discussion, while many minor points are considered? A highly selective treatment is preferred to facing the fundamental issues squarely. Along with the illumination of certain areas by Fuller's searching discussion, there are patches of darkness.

My argument bore largely upon the reciprocal adaptation of Nambudiri and Nayar, through the intermediary of Kshatriya (and Samantan Nayar). On this point we found that Mencher's description and understanding of Nambudiri institutions on the one hand and her direct statement regarding the Nayar on the other were positive. In contrast, Fuller's reserve is puzzling. It would seem, given his general orientation and his Cambridge pedigree, that he should be particularly interested in matters of material goods and political power. Certainly, and contrary to Mencher and Goldberg's concluding warning (1967, 103), Fuller tends like others to isolate the Nayar internal organization from their external relationships. For instance, he treats of "hypergamous" relations among them only after he has exhausted the nonhypergamous aspects, while the reverse seems preferable. But perhaps we can find in his text indications as to where more precisely the problem lies.

It is true, Mencher and Goldberg have introduced an important modification. I had surmised from the literature that the tying of the *tāli* by a Nambudiri Brahman to a (chiefly or) Nayar girl was a case of the well-known Hindu, caste-relevant type of exchange where the superior person gives status or prestige to the inferior, while the inferior gives tangible goods or power to the superior. Mencher and Goldberg have asserted that "Nambudiris never tied the *tāli* to a Nayar girl" in Central Kerala (1967, 93) but only to the (Kshatriya) Cochin princesses. But they have maintained the existence of an exchange of the kind I suggested between Nayar and Nambudiri on the occasion, not of *tāli*-tying, but of *sambandham*. They said that "the advantage to the Nayar family was usually one of social prestige, whereas the other advantages were more likely to be one-sided in the Nambudiri's favour" and graphically described the situation (1967, 1). Directly in support of my argument (1967, n. 7), they added: "It was quite common for the Nayar family to give temporal goods as well as sometimes even political power in exchange for the prestige brought to their *taravād* . . ." We shall see that Fuller totally neglects these statements. He fastens on the only case of *tāli*-tying by Nambudiris left standing by Mencher and Goldberg, that of the Cochin princesses. They quoted an informant saying,

[The] Nambudiri who performed the ceremony was considered something like an outcaste. He was paid by the royal family, sometimes two or three thousand rupees. Nowadays he is not considered as polluted, but traditionally that was so [1967, 93–94].

Lest the word "outcaste" in this statement is taken too seriously, it must be pointed out that neither was the man expelled from the caste nor does the relative degradation seem to have endured in any way: it is not mentioned when the differences of status among Nambudiri are considered, and seen to be quite minor (all Nambudiri dined together, etc.; cf. Mencher 1966, 188). The relative degradation of the *tāli*-tier is of course not unexpected, but it is clearly not more than a secondary aspect of the exchange in terms of the groups concerned.

Fuller has chosen to look at the transaction in a different way, as "a kind of status exchange," "the Nambudiri tier losing status as the Cochin royal family gained it, the loss being compensated by payments" (p. 118). The notion is strange on several counts, but I must be brief. It looks as if some powerful unstated premise had led Fuller to refuse to see that two different kinds of things are here exchanged, as is implicit in the Brahmanical theory of the gift, and in keeping with what I called the thorough distinction of status and power in the caste system. The surmise that the refusal of this distinction may be covertly at work here is confirmed by a contemporary text where, studying the Syrian Christians, Fuller states that this distinction is not present in the ideology of the people but only in their theology (Fuller 1976, 66–67). But what when the "theology" becomes hard fact?

In order to be complete on the point, I add some remarks which will take the form of a triangular discussion with Fuller and with Mencher-Goldberg. As noted earlier, Fuller was careful to set out my arguments about matters of affinity. In the end he came to consider the question of affinity in *sambandham* unions and concluded that affinity was practically absent there, or more precisely that "the most important characteristics of affinity" were not found (p. 115). A new and interesting insight, in keeping with what we know of secondary unions in general. Now, unlike him perhaps, I should prefer not to think of Nayar institutions as having quite different characteristics in the "isogamous" and in the "hypergamous" case. What was quoted above from Mencher and Goldberg goes to show that sambandham was consequential in the "hypergamous" case. Conversely, if we admit Fuller's conclusion, and if we think that affinity is important in the system, then we must search for its presence on the *tāli*-tying level, and suppose that the *tāli* ceremony will be, in the extreme case when we cannot speak of affinity proper, much more charged with exchange values than the *sambandham*. If this is so, then a considerable pressure must have been exerted on the Nambudiri, if not by Nayar proper, at least by others than the Cochin raja, for one of them consenting to tie the *tāli* to girls of prestigious and rich families in matrilineal groups. Will the Nambudiri have been able in all circumstances to withstand that pressure? Given the general makeup, and given the very good reasons one can find for present-day Nambudiri to have forgotten all about rather debasing events the estimated consequences of which have not been registered in their internal ranking, I would incline, unlike Fuller, to challenge the categorical denegation of Mencher and Goldberg. For it to be solidly established, it should at any rate be documented in much more detail than has been done hitherto.

Fuller is careful to dissociate himself even from views he partially accepts. In his 1975 article he quotes a development taken from a comparison of the Nayar with the Newar of Nepal where I had stated that neither Nayar nor Newar were actually castes but rather conglomerates or populations whose "subdivisions" were essentially status groups "which may be absolutely (or practically) endogamous at the one end, and exogamous at the other" (Dumont, 1964, 98), that is to say that *all* subdivisions are status groups, of which *some* may be called castes and others cannot. Which is very much what Fuller in the end admits (as Mencher did explicitly for the Nambudiri; Mencher 1966, 188 n. 1). At the same time he presents my text as an "over-radical reinterpretation" according to which "neither the Nayar as a whole, nor any subdivision within that whole, form a unit which can meaningfully be called a caste" (1975, 290–91). What is "over-radical" here is actually Fuller's reading of my text. Yet the latter is quoted at length. Only Fuller left out the Newar (and the comparative viewpoint), which led him to introduce seven cuts (six marked and one unnoticed near the end) and to obscure the text, as the plural covering Nayar and Newar: "these conglomerates" seemed now to bear on Nayar groups. These are admittedly details, but as I do not want my suggestion to remain buried in Fuller's unilateral and careless quotation, I may perhaps be permitted briefly to reiterate it. The concern was to draw attention to the fact that those two populations situated in remote, backwater areas in relation to Hindu India present similar patterns which differ from the ordinary caste pattern and which can be interpreted as resulting from their relative isolation, and a less massive and continuous interaction with the evolving Hindu culture than in the ordinary case, or, as I then wrote perhaps all too briefly, "patterns resulting from the early, limited and regionally encapsulated impact of Hinduism on local populations" (ibid., p. 98). I mentioned two hypotheses, which do not exclude absolutely each other, first that "a name endowed with prestige (Nayar: 'ruler') may have been "borrowed by lower levels of society and become a blanket term for most of the native population." This might be the case for the lowest castes, as drummers, oilmongers, Untouchables, that Fuller still lists as Nayar "subdivisions" without telling us whether they really are part of the Nayar caste as he understands it. The other hypothesis was that Nayar as well as Newar are "an old population which has adapted itself to Hindu influence by inner (caste-like) stratification and close combination with Hindu castes."

Finally, Fuller's stand seems to me to embody under a new form an attitude that was familiar in an earlier period, or in other words to reassert an earlier position while making the necessary allowances for changed circumstances. It so happens that what it is convenient here to call alliance theory, i.e. essentially the importance of marriage and affinity in South Indian society, and in some measure even the structuralist view of caste cannot any more be simply brushed aside, as was done as an instance for the former in its budding state by Radcliffe-Brown. Just as some years back Robin Fox was seen integrating it clandestinely, as it were, in his textbook on kinship (see above, chap. 2, n. 13), so C. J. Fuller has carefully extracted from those views a few elements which in his opinion can now hardly be done without, and rejected the rest, his stated hope being to integrate those elements in a theory which will as far as possible preserve the former assumptions. He wrote in the conclusion of chapter 5 of his book:

> To produce a genuinely satisfactory analysis, we need, I think, some sort of fusion between Gough's perspective, which derives predominantly from functionalism and descent-theory, and Dumont's, which stems mainly from structuralism and alliance-theory [1976a, 120].

I hope it is permissible to see the tendency in a slightly different way by looking at the author as located within a certain tradition, and thus distinguishing between the continuity of that tradition and the occasional borrowings from outside. If Fuller's conclusions remain incomplete, as he admits, it is apparently because the attempted synthesis is still in the making, and if I am not mistaken we shall hear more about it, and be given more complete and perfect constructions in the future.

4

Stocktaking 1981:
Affinity as a Value

What is intended here is a limited stocktaking, a review of the professional reception of the preceding studies, extending to alternative views or related original contributions but falling short of a general survey of the study of South Indian kinship in the intervening period. For instance, uncle-niece marriage falls outside our purview, and therefore Kodanda Rao's contribution, important though it is, will not be considered for its own sake. The discussion will center on the major paper (chapter 2) without excluding the others. Special points relating to sections 1 and 3 have been dealt with separately.

What has become of marriage alliance in subsequent literature dealing with South India? There has been some degree of agreement, more perhaps about minor theses than about the major one, and the new evidence that has come to light seems by and large confirmatory, but I shall deal mainly with disagreements, which are more vital. Given the bulk of the relevant literature and the inordinate length demanded by the precise consideration of a given text, the discussion has to be selective, to concentrate on central issues, and as far as possible to disregard chronology and subordinate authors to themes. When needed, I shall not try to demonstrate but only offer indications for those who would care to pursue the matter in detail.

"Hierarchy and Marriage Alliance in South Indian Kinship" was completed, as initially indicated, in 1953. Looking back a quarter-century one finds that the development has been anything but straightforward. Only rarely is it possible to point to a question asked twenty years ago having received an answer since, as was done by Kodanda Rao (Rao 1973; cf. Dumont 1961)[1]. At first sight, the literature in general gives an impression of discontinuity and divergences more than of cumulation or convergence, so that a wider question looms in the background: what is the measure of consensus, and of diverse tendencies in competition?

It is all very much a matter of interpretation, the interpretation of sets of data on a regional basis, or a "regional theory." The obvious presupposition then is that the theory is not dead, or absolutely superseded, but still deserves consideration. Actually there are found in the more recent literature both a rejection of the legitimacy of the regional basis and a claim to supersession. The latter part of this discussion will try to show that the tendency is misguided and the conclusions unacceptable.

A still more basic presupposition that is also challenged in the tendency just referred to is that there is a domain or system of kinship. It is well known that David Schneider has subtly argued and vehemently contended that there was not such a thing, that kinship was a nonsubject (Schneider 1968). He has been directly and indirectly influential in the area that concerns us. But, if only one thinks of it, one finds that other tendencies have a similar effect. Thus, when Tambiah singles out affinal prestations in order to account for them in materialist terms, with the stated intention to replace the abstractions of kinship by more tangible factors such as property (Tambiah 1973), or when a stranger to the Indian field like Scheffler dogmatically asserts that it is wrong to look at the kinship vocabulary as a whole and see it in relation to kinship as a whole and advocates instead an opaque algebra of "extensions"

---

1. I do not mean that the pattern revealed by Kodanda Rao will be found with all the groups practicing this type of marriage, as we know from other reports that this is not the case. What makes it important is that it answers systematically, in a typically Indian way, the problems that this sort of marriage posed for the anthropologist, and thus in the first place confirms that those problems exist for the people themselves. See also the contribution of Beck 1972.

(Scheffler 1977), are they not also contributing to the destruction of kinship as a concrete domain? Of the latter point I find a confirmation in the fact that Carter, while combining a general recognition of affinity with an attempt at componential analysis, does away not only with the no doubt imperfect expression of "cross-cousin marriage" but also at the same time with the most clear-cut feature of South Indian kinship that the expression conveyed hitherto (see below).

Yet there was agreement among those concerned during the period considered, until the last developments, about the existence of the domain. Moreover, there *is* agreement at least on one point, namely the importance of affinity in South India. But such a phrase refers only to a very vague perception, and as soon as we try to make it more articulate we encounter divergences. Actually any untutored observer of the region would be struck by that aspect of its social life, and an anthropological consensus restricted to it is a poor thing indeed.

Let us try and be more precise. Suppose we say that the importance of affinity there is linked in some manner with the kinship vocabulary. The statement would presumably be endorsed by every one with field experience. A footnote of Carter's, rebuking a person he was otherwise trying to emulate, can be taken as expressing in technical language the general sentiment in the matter. He wrote: "I think Scheffler himself errs in assuming that kin terms must always have consanguineal kin-types as their foci. I already have shown how this view fails to fit the facts in the Marathi case and how, in this regard at least, Dumont's argument has validity" (Carter 1974, 52, n. 14). That is to say, there is a fundamental content of affinity in some of the kinship categories. Further than this point the agreement does not seem to go, and that is why I felt impelled to add in the above a sort of elucidating justification to the analysis of the vocabulary.

If we suppose that there is agreement on the existence of the domain, the first and foremost question that comes up is about its definition, and in particular about the nature of the connection between features that are found to exist in association: whether their connection is merely accidental or necessary, empirical or logical, extrinsic or intrinsic to the domain as a system.

This point was raised early about descent. Yalman, having observed among Kandyan Sinhalese a similar system devoid of descent groups, argued that the descent groups present in my

South Indian material were not "intrinsically associated" with
marriage alliance (Yalman 1967, 357). Actually Yalman (ibid., p.
355) and others wrote that I had posited a complementarity
between descent and alliance, and here I must introduce an
elaborate commentary in order to dispel all misunderstanding.
Descent—I mean exclusively unilineal descent—appears here in
the abstract as a particular form of consanguinity. That is how,
discussing preliminarily Emeneau's views on unilineality, I could
hint at a (factual) complementarity of descent and marriage alliance. Yet it should be clear that, at the most general *representa-
tional* level, the complementarity is between consanguinity and
affinity, or alliance, and that descent as such has no place at all. It
is only when descent groups exist that we can speak of a complementarity, the more so if we find descent groups linked by
marriage alliance. I never asserted the presence of descent groups
as necessary on the empirical level either (see the discussion in
Kaplan 1973, 556–58). I could therefore agree with Yalman that
"the feature of descent is not a primary variable at all" (ibid., p.
355), were it not that different levels of consideration must be
distinguished.

Let me take the occasion to generalize from descent groups to
groups pure and simple. It is widely admitted that a relationship
like marriage alliance, being not purely individual but essentially
collective, must bear on groups or supposes the existence of
groups united by that relationship. Indeed, in a review of Lévi-
Strauss's *Elementary Structures* Harold Scheffler quoted a passage
where I seem to say the same thing. It is taken from an article on
"Marriage Alliance" in *International Encyclopedia of the Social
Sciences*, vol. 10, col. 21b (Dumont 1968). Scheffler's quotation
(Scheffler 1970, 252) is correct, my text is not. As printed, it reads
"[Lévi-Strauss] was concerned only with the forms and implications of intergroup marriage," and Scheffler, quite appositely for
his purpose, underlined the word "intergroup." Now my manuscript actually read: "was concerned only with the forms and
implications of intermarriage, not with the juridical aspect of
marriage." The change was introduced by the editor of the article.
Certainly I accepted it, and I admit my guilt for so doing,[2] yet I

2. I can plead extenuating circumstances, namely that, after I had refused even to
   consider a too heavily edited version of the article (in which the passage in
   question was entirely omitted), and when I received a much more acceptable

want to put it on record that the mention of groups was not originally intended.

The question is whether and how we can think of a collective relationship otherwise than between stable or permanent groups. In fact it is all a matter of where the value lies. In modern common sense, and with anthropologists in Cambridge and elsewhere, value attaches to group(s), by preference corporate group(s), while the relationships between those groups, being less valued, can be left to fluctuate, change, or vanish. But if value attaches to the relationship, it will be thought as permanent, and the groups (of the different levels), being less important, will not be thought as necessarily enduring parallel to the relationship. Instead of relations appearing as a complement to groups, groups will appear as a complement to relations, and relations will be the necessary condition for anything of the nature of groups to appear and maintain themselves. At least this is the sort of disposition that we should train ourselves to expect.

But to return to extrinsic and intrinsic. It was once contended that affinity itself, or rather the elaborate South Indian construction of it, was extrinsic to the arrangement of categories. The argument, logically decisive, was that vocabularies of Dravidian type were found elsewhere (outside India) without any association with marriage rules. If such was the case, then it should be admitted that I had committed the monographic fallacy, to which the functionalist is prone, of confusing an empirical juxtaposition with a necessary combination. I am referring to a paper by Scheffler (1971). Fortunately, his evidence was shaky, partly by his own admission (1971, cf. p. 236 and n. 16), partly because he had conflated the Dravidian with the Iroquois type, which, if similar, is by no means identical. After all, the massive Indian evidence is stronger than such a flimsy construction, as Carter had the good sense to recognize, saying that Scheffler "perhaps fails to grasp the full implications of his own methods. It seems quite possible that

---

version, I thought that I had to make some concessions. I distinctly remember thinking at the time that, if the editor, who had been trained in anthropology, could not understand my phrase, it was, after all, useless to maintain it. Certainly, as the event proved, I was wrong. Yet the incident also says something about the evils of editing, in the United States and elsewhere. I may perhaps add that the notion of "exchange between groups" was seriously relativized in the sequence of the article (see esp. col. 22*b*).

'Dravidian-Iroquois' systems have been grouped together merely
on the basis of surface structure similarities'' (Carter 1974, n. 14).[3]

In general, this question of intrinsic/extrinsic is obviously linked
with that of the definition-cum-consistency of the domain: where
does kinship begin and end, and is it a system in the real sense or in
the purely nominal or analytical sense of a more or less convenient
anthropological abstraction? But just as there is a question about
extrinsic features being unwittingly taken as intrinsic to the system, there is a converse question about the possible imposition of
an alien framework onto the evidence, such as David seems to
impute to me when he presents on a par my view and that of
Radcliffe-Brown and others arguing, ethnocentrically according to
David, that the mother's brother *must* be a consanguine (David
1973, *init.*). Yet the statement of David's informant that follows
immediately—if shorn of David's own interpretation—shows that I
have not interpreted but only transcribed. There is another kind of
imposition when solid evidence is brushed aside because it does
not fit a preconceived scheme. I am thinking of Rodney Needham,
armed with his exacting requirements for the recognition of
"prescriptive patrilateral cross-cousin marriage," who declared,
when faced with the (I dare say) compelling example of the
Nangudi Vellala chieftains (genealogy above fig. 8), that the case
was extremely complicated and required additional information
(Needham 1958: 214–15). If such a case does not fit the theoreti-
cian's criteria, one might conclude that those criteria badly need
revision. Again I cannot help sensing a similar imposition or misfit
in the case of componential analysis, when the cumbersome
hypothesis of "extension" is forced upon a nomenclature like the
Dravidian, whose simplicity cries for a more direct understanding.

The next most important and most frequently recurring disagreement surely lies in the admission or denial of different levels in the
analysis and, I surmise, in the system itself. Many objections and
discussions stem from a divergence on that point. This was seen
early in Radcliffe-Brown's criticism (above, chap. 1, Correspondence). As already noticed (chap. 1, Comment), Kathleen Gough

---

3. Cf. the remarks on Kariera below, chap. 5. Actually Lounsbury had already
   stated in 1964 that "Dravidian and Iroquois are systems premised on very
   different principles of reckoning and deriving from social structures totally
   unlike" (Lounsbury 1964:1079 n. 4).

repeatedly protested my putting the father's sister on the affinal side of the vocabulary in the name of descent and descent groups. Clearly such a stand implies that the level of descent is the only one to be considered, and that all other aspects have to fit that level, and will therefore be either modified or ignored if they don't. When Yalman claimed that I had never stated "the direct interconnections between the kinship terms as categories, the cross-cousin marriage rule, the question of alliance and the gift-giving, and so on" (Yalman 1967, 357), I suppose that his emphasis was on the word "direct" (for surely I have otherwise stated some of the relations he required). If so, then the real reproach is for not having set everything on one and the same level, and for thus having shown only "indirect" relations. No wonder then that conversely Yalman's own theory has been taken by Tambiah as failing to distinguish between an ideological level and an empirical level (Tambiah 1965).

Yalman's monolithic frame of mind is clearly responsible for his incomprehension of my contribution. As his Sinhalese system ignored descent, he postulated that descent could not be "intrinsic" to a system of the same sort, that it could only be associated with it by accident, but, by a characteristic survival of what looks like descent worship, the presence of descent was made to dominate my own argument. For instance it was the fact of "operating with the concept of 'exogamous' lineages' " that had prevented me from stating "the direct interconnections in the system" (1967, 357). According to Yalman, even the distinction between consanguineous and affinal relatives was tinged with descent. He stated that I had "expressed the matter still in lineal terms as an opposition between "kin" and "affines" (p. 359), and again that such a distinction arose "only in unilineal contexts" (p. 358). As lineality is clearly out of the question, what I understand here is simply that Yalman was not at all concerned with the dichotomy of the vocabulary as a whole, beyond the distinction of marriageable/unmarriageable "cousins." In effect he was content with hinting at "rules governing the interconnections between the categories" (p. 357). He stated that the categories of the vocabulary determine (directly?) everything (p. 357), that "the entire structure is terminological" (p. 358) and saw no need for the "clumsy" (p. 219) or "complex distinction" (p. 358) of terminological kin and affines, that is, here again no need for distinguishing levels.

Yalman nevertheless borrowed the expression of "marriage alliance" (it is the title given to the eighth chapter of his book); he occasionally agreed on the repetition or perpetuation of intermarriage (e.g. p. 219); but he could not accept the idea that affinity is transmitted from generation to generation. To speak of the transmission of affinity is to reify it (p. 358); only "rights and obligations" can be transmitted, perhaps under the "guise" of affinity (ibid.). Affinity remains a mere incident of kinship: "the system is one of kinship which entails affinity" (p. 219). In the last analysis, Yalman refused to upgrade affinity as I had proposed in order to do justice to the system. What did he offer instead?

Two things. On the one hand, marriage alliance is intrinsic to a cognatic system with small kindreds or "micro-castes"; on the other, it springs from the reciprocal rights and obligations of brother and sister. Comparatively, the first point is anything but obvious, for kindreds are not generally accompanied by a vocabulary of Dravidian type. Nor is a logical connection between the kindred as an amorphous bilateral group and the pronounced dichotomy of the vocabulary immediately apparent. Actually the link Yalman had in mind is functional, or so it seems to me. The idea is that, in the absence of clear-cut exogamy, there is a need for distinguishing marriageable from unmarriageable relatives, and the vocabulary answers that need. In other words, there is something of an equivalence of function between exogamy and a Dravidian vocabulary. Thus "this problem of differentiating and at the same time reconciling consanguineous ties and ties of marriage appears in all endogamous castes where concepts of lineage exogamy are not strongly developed" (p. 171). This is specious, for in most "endogamous castes" exogamy is "strongly developed." (For a criticism of Yalman's construction of the "kindred," see Tambiah 1965). Yet, in fairness to Yalman's argument, some new evidence must be mentioned. He had insisted on the existence of (let us say) micro-castes in some South Indian castes, and the point has since been confirmed (Barnett 1976, 139 ff.). Moreover, it could be argued that exogamy, whether by itself or in association with other features, can weaken the application of the terminological scheme in its systematic aspect. An example was given here itself with the KK. Maravar (chap. 2, "How the terminology is applied"), but more recently Brenda Beck has given evidence that a patrilineal dominant group (also prone to uncle-niece marriage) could disregard more than others the principle of closure (that affines' affines

= consanguines)[4] and I find that the same applies to Barnett's TK.
Vellalar as against David's Jaffna Tamils (Barnett 1976, 150 n. 16;
David 1973).

We have seen that Yalman wanted to substitute for what I called
affinity "rights and obligations." They are those "of brothers and
sisters" (p. 358). We return here to the conception of cross-cousin
marriage in terms of the reciprocal "claims" of brother and sister
on each other and on their progeniture. Two observations should
suffice. First, Yalman hardly makes clear how one can speak of the
"restatement" or "reiteration" (p. 153–54, 358) of claims from
(unmarriageable) siblings to (marriageable) cross cousins.[5] Second
there is a wide gap between the (terminological) "categories"
stressed in the above and the immediate genealogical relationships
involved here (ibid., p. 152; cf. Kaplan 1973, n. 2), with the result
that Yalman's theory falls into two parts that are juxtaposed rather
than combined. Yet Yalman's insistence on the brother-sister link
may be faithful to the "feel" of the culture. It may well be the case
that cross-cousin marriage is more categorical among South Indi-
ans, more "genealogical" among Sinhalese.[6]

While in the sixties the major theoretical obstacle to the recognition of marriage alliance in South India was, quite naturally, the
predominance of the concept and the theory of descent, by and
large Cantabrigian, whether in its positive form as with Gough or in
its peculiar negative form with Yalman, the seventies brought to
prominence another approach, the "symbolic analysis" or "cultural analysis" of Chicagoan parentage. As I read it, the evolution

4. See Beck 1972: 221–26. Actually Beck concluded more generally that "parallel
   terms are given great importance when descent is weak or absent" (p. 226), a
   finding that would fit Yalman's argument as understood here. (Beck's table p.
   223 should not include ZD; Carter has noticed that Beck failed to distinguish the
   sex of speaker in relation to such relatives, cf. Carter 1974, 42, 54).
5. Beck describes a ceremony through which a brother, before his marriage, is
   thought to promise to his sister his future daughter in marriage for her own son
   (1972, 238 ff.).
6. More precisely, there is likely to be a link between the stress on the brother-
   sister relationship and the "cognatic" or "undifferentiated" aspect of the
   Sinhalese system at large. Recent work on some Oceanian vocabularies based
   largely on the primacy of the distinction between same-sex sibling and other-
   sex sibling goes to show this, and it is hoped to publish some results in the near
   future. Then the Sinhalese specificities on which Yalman has insisted would
   appear to be "extrinsic" to the terminology of Dravidian type.

has been from downright rejection of marriage alliance in the first stage to an attempt, which may be taken as still in progress, at superseding or bypassing it. In the latter approach, the importance of affinity in South India is not altogether denied or neglected, on the contrary the original findings, widely confirmed in the meantime, are acknowledged, but the conclusions are modified. There are wide differences between the three authors to be considered but they have in common the claim to unify the whole field of study better than I did by focusing on what one of them has called "overarching cultural concepts." This unification operates in two dimensions, singly or in combination; between kinship and caste and between North and South India. Somewhat paradoxically the central vocable is "substance" and the central operative concept is segmentarity. Actually it's all very simple. If man is made of a substance, then that substance should be found on the level of caste as well as on the level of kinship: the boundary between the two domains is gratuitous. And if the difference between North and South centered on the different relation between kinship and caste, then it has evaporated.

Now the idea of substance (as a paramount conception) seems so incongruous in relation to South India, where all the effort of the present writer had been to get rid of such conceptions in order to give a faithful portrayal of the society and culture, that it is natural to ask where the notion comes from. It comes from David Schneider, and the claim is that the datum confirms it. To the datum we shall return. Let us first look at the origin. At first sight, the notion of substance perfectly fits West European or American (US) kinship (as it fills modern ideology in general), to the extent that a rapid inspection of the vocabulary of kinship in current French led immediately to introduce the idea, and the word (Dumont 1962, 35, line 5 from bottom). The same is true of the American case, there is therefore nothing surprising in David Schneider's stressing substance in his study of American kinship. (That he actually contrasts "substance" and "code" is immaterial here; cf. Schneider 1968.)

What takes some wonder is how the notion has migrated, without more ado, to the quite different Indian, and especially South Indian climate. That would perhaps be inexplicable without another influence, that of McKim Marriott and his modified transactionalism (Marriott 1976). Both influences are present, in varying proportions, with our authors dealing with South India:

here is "the Chicagoan parentage." Once in India, substance undergoes strange avatars. With two of our authors it becomes "segmentary." What is meant is that it takes different meanings on different levels of experience or of social organization. Yet it is hard to imagine how a substance, a self-sufficient entity by definition, or, with a change of emphasis, a material entity can change its nature according to situations. Let us be serious. To speak of "segmentary substance" is simply to paper over the chasm between structure ("segmentarity") and its contrary ("substance"). We may of course be told that this is how the informants think, but then we should be on our guard.

In this trend of thought, the theoretical focus moves from the traditional framework of kinship and caste to cultural analysis in terms of how the people studied conceive man, and especially man's generation or conception, the "construction of the person." It is not quite caricatural to say that the motto is "Tell me how you conceive the conception of man, and I shall tell you how your society is organized." The general result of the inquiry is that man is a substance, or is made up in the main of a substance, most often blood. For such a conception to apply to the essentially relational world of South Indian societies as we all know it, it has of course to undergo drastic transformations. "Natural substance" becomes "segmentary" with David (David 1973, 522, and chart p. 525), while with Barnett (1976) blood becomes "blood purity," the latter in turn being made up of body and spirit. It is difficult to deal with such fairytale accounts, unless one isolates more circumscribed and "substantial" issues. It should be clear that when these authors deal with the present writer's findings and conclusions—which they do pretty often—they do not actually continue his effort but they are busy transcending it and reformulating the data in a quite different paradigmatic framework. For my part, while I am of course ready to learn of the people's "cultural categories," I would reiterate a point made earlier about the kinship vocabulary: I hold that kinship terms, being the terms in which the people actually think their kinship relationships, are more important than the terms in which (they tell us that) they think they are thinking.[7]

The divergence of views can be seen from the start in Kenneth

7. On this point I may be taken as contradicting myself. I hold in general that the primary determination of a subsystem lies in its relation to the system of which it is a part. It might be applied to the case at hand by saying that the

David's treatment of the broad kinship categories of the Tamils of Jaffna, which are very close to those of the groups I studied. He claims to avoid the arbitrary choice of analytic categories (of Dumont and others) by following the native mode of thinking. He introduces three indigenous categories "which exhaustively classify all kin terms." (David 1973, 521). The first two are those I translated as consanguines and affines. The third one I noted as "affines' affines" or "consanguines by convention" (cf. 1957b, IID2d, p. 185–86). (To mark the difference with earlier writers, let us note in passing that here the MB is unambiguously recognized as an affine in terms of the vocabulary). So far, there would only be a question—or a difference—as to the status of David's third category, which in my own account is only a subdivision of the first. But then David becomes quite arbitrary: he presumes to translate all three categories in terms of one and the same "bodily substance". Affines (*sambandikkārar,* literally "those of the [inter-] marriage, or link") thus become "uniters of bodily substance" (1973, 522). This obscure expression transforms a relation—affinity—into an attribute or factor of "substance" ("uniters of . . ."). And so David goes on, but I must be brief.

The TK. Vellalar of Steve Barnett are altogether less similar to the castes studied in the above; his account is also more subtle than that of Kenneth David. Barnett's essay (1976) is part of a collective effort to unify South and North India while doing away with the distinction between kinship and caste (Fruzzetti, Östör, and Barnett 1976; see my general criticism, 1980, xxxiv–xxxv). I shall be content here with reviewing the core of his account of "relational identity" or "the cultural construction of the person." It is made up of several elements.

The best piece is an impeccable indigenous theory of cross-cousin marriage. Two elements are combined in a child: its body comes from its father, or in the father's line, and corresponds to the exogamous clan, while its life or breath (Barnett says "spirit")

---

general ideas and values of the culture command the kinship distinctions found on one particular level of that culture.

But the very way in which the cultural or symbolical analyst derives his "overarching categories" suffices to show that they are not part of the fundamental ideas and values at work in the *society-and-culture,* while it is clear from the institutions and behavior as well as from the kinship vocabulary itself that affinity is.

comes from its mother, or in the maternal line (cf. David 1973, 523; similar theories are known outside India: bones and flesh etc.). Barnett's interpretation is questionable: what the theory means in the first place is that *cross cousins are the nearest relatives* that are different in both elements and therefore marriageable, not the relatives "with whom you share the *least*" (p. 148) but relatives with whom you share *as little* in terms of the two elements as with any unrelated person within the endogamous group. Barnett tries in vain in a long footnote (n. 12) to apply the theory to adoption and to ZD's marriage. Clearly it does not apply; it is only a theory of cross-cousin marriage. Therefore Barnett's disparaging of the anthropologist's diagrams (p. 149) is out of place, for the theory says essentially the same thing as they do. Culturally, the informants' analogy with Shiva-Shakti is less apposite than the dictionary's reference to grammar: consonant-vowel (in the syllable) (cf. David, loc. cit.). The claim of a hierarchical relation between the two (p. 147) does not seem substantiated.

A second element is the "transubstantiation" of (the "body" element in) the woman at marriage. The idea expresses the fact that she then ceases to be a member of her father's clan to become one with her husband and his group. The idea is widespread and probably of Brahmanical parentage; it contradicts lower caste usage and the fact that the married woman does not change her usage of kinship terms for that of her husband: his brothers remain her "cross cousins." This representation has a very restricted bearing: it does not bear at all on the generation of children, as these receive only "breath," and not "body," from their mother; and it does not bear on status, because the conception refers to the clans and the clans are all equal. The only link with the previous item lies in the consistent place of the "body" element. Moreover, given the exogamy of the clan, the idea that marriage makes the woman belong to it makes the clan reproduce itself as a kind of substance. The idea is thus as opposed in spirit to the neat complementarity of the cross-cousin marriage theory of "body" and "breath" as Brahmanical ratiocination is to South Indian structural practice and thinking.

For the same reason I am very suspicious regarding Barnett's "blood purity," which looks a little too much like a "natural substance" (p. 143). Actually one finds that his people speak of pure and impure very much in the usual terms (ibid.). What is new here is this: "KVs say caste purity is located in their blood" (ibid.), and apparently the fact justifies Barnett in speaking all along, not of purity, but of "blood purity." I am sorry, but I suspect that substance, or "blood," is here a Western importation. We should not forget that India was long under the British, and under British education. It is especially true of people who live in the city of Madras and its surroundings and who have not been impervious otherwise to Western ideas (cf. the "self-respect" movement). Indeed it seems strange that as excellent a fieldworker as Barnett has sensed no incongruity on this point. Yet he is not alone, and we must make do with "blood," if not with "blood purity." One thing is sure, it is that "blood" has absolutely nothing to do with the dichotomy of "body" and "breath," although the contrary is asserted with assurance (p. 147).

Actually "body" and "breath" are one thing, "change of body" or "transubstantiation" is another, and blood, semen, breast milk, and what not are still another. Hard as Barnett tried to amalgamate them, they do not combine. They are only connected through the anthropologist's claim to combine kinship and caste, to unite better than his forerunners, or to articulate more precisely "equivalence" and "hierarchy." We find that, in fact, clan ("gotram") and change of body as well as body-and-breath have nothing to do with caste but are purely a matter of kinship, while purity has nothing to do with kinship, were it not for the metaphor of blood. Kinship and caste remain here very much in the same relation that I had portrayed, relatively independent from each other as "equivalence" within "hierarchy." The point is morphologically clear, as TK. Vellalar have ranked microcastes (*vageirā*) within which only kinship operates.

Although I must be brief, and although I should not like to overcriticize an author who stands closer to my endeavor than others, I must add two general points that go some way toward explaining what I take to be Barnett's failure. One is his imperfect application of a structural—or "structuralist"—approach. In one place, recording that X designates both an entity and its relations, he separates these two aspects as two different meanings of X (it is about the "family," p. 141). But a theoretical statement in the introductory part of the paper is more spectacular. Barnett writes:

> Conception and behaviour are thus linked by KV ideas about blood purity, a natural substance enjoining code for conduct. The term "enjoining" is meant to convey the significance of *relation* in analyzing caste society; we must begin with rela-

tions, not with antecedent autonomous units, to remain true to Indian modes of conceptualization [p. 134].

What is strange here is that the author has done the contrary of what he preaches, he has "begun with antecedent autonomous units." To start from "the cultural construction of the person" presupposes precisely such a reference. And if in the end the reference proves negative, it has yielded in the meantime, not unexpectedly, a self-sufficient entity, namely a "natural substance." What the statement actually means, if taken in the context of the whole endeavor, is that we may conceive everything in terms of substances provided we do not substantify the individual actor. The antisubstantial, structural approach is thus actually encompassed within its contrary.

The second point is about the lack of a sound comparative ethnography of the region. It applies to other authors as well and in general. Barnett has found microcastes while others have not. Yet he posits them as universal in Tamil Nadu (p. 162). While not referring on this point to Dumont's evidence, which is negative, he is content about prestations on the contrary to state that they are "basically similar" to Dumont's account (p. 141). Yet we want to know what varies with what. We lack in the first place a less exclusively problem-oriented ethnographic description of the group. With the slow accumulation of monographs, the ethnographic basis should become surer and surer—and the description be simplified. Instead we most often have only the choice between X's and Y's views centering on a particular group and generalizing too much from it alone. Is there any hope of reestablishing the conditions of a sound collective advance? South India with the richness of its material and its indefinite variations on common themes is an outstanding laboratory for anthropology. Will it come to be used reasonably?

A. T. Carter's study "A comparative analysis of systems of kinship and marriage in South Asia" (Carter 1974) is no doubt very different from the preceding ones. It could almost have been considered in our first section—for it deals first of all with kinship vocabularies—were it not for its length, technicality, and above all its ambitiousness, which require a separate treatment. It is an elaborate piece of scholarship, precisely argued most of the time, which fairly discusses previous contributions. What the author is doing in that work, at first sight at any rate, is to combine componential analysis—which thus made its appearance in the Indian field—with some elements taken from previous Indian studies in order to offer a new and more satisfactory theory, especially in the sense of better unifying North and South India.

What has been gained in the end? Looking at the conclusion as summed up in a chart (table 12), one is not struck by its intrinsic novelty. Everything that the chart shows, with increased (but perhaps questionable) precision, was there before, as the author justly and repeatedly indicates (see col. 30a). Yet something has been effected. To put it in a nutshell, what distinguishes South India from North India is cross-cousin marriage. Carter has done away with cross-cousin marriage as a "surface" feature, so that the unity of India is now perfect. In other words, once kinship is reduced to what is immediately relevant to caste, North and South present mere variants in the configuration of intermarriage. There is thus a suggestive parallel between Carter's endeavor and the joint enterprise of Fruzzetti, Östör, and Barnett (1976) in the sense that both tend to unification in both senses. Only Carter's title is inaccurate, for important aspects of South Indian "kinship and marriage" go overboard for the sake of this double unification.

How was Carter led to take such a course? He was dissatisfied with previous accounts. Regarding North-South comparison, I am blamed for my "remarkably inconsistent" reasoning (col. 45b; I thought I had forestalled this objection, see 1966, 103; but the point lies beyond the present concern). Regarding South India (and Lanka) which is discussed at length (p. 39–44), previous authors in general are said to have been content with the incomplete consideration of "surface structure" (sic), including cross-cousin marriage (col. 41b). As far as I am concerned, it is clear that there are many misunderstandings bearing on the vocabulary analysis. In particular the author as others before him did not see the crucial role played by the radical distinction of sexes. My comment (see chapter 1 above) should make those questions clearer. On one point I must protest. Quite similar general categories are taken as belonging to kinship in Marathi (in Carter's account), and as extraneous to it in Tamil (in my own account) (compare 41b with 43a–b). Carter does not want to speak of "consanguines" and "affines," therefore he is at pains dismissing the similarity (ibid.). But what does he actually do? In the componential analysis of his Marathi kinship vocabulary, he introduces a rule whose effect is "to divide the kintypes of Ego's own generation and of the first

ascending and descending generations into two intermarrying classes" (p. 37), that is, he transcribes in his manner, and so far as it
goes, the alliance distinction while avoiding two things: (1) locating
the Ego somewhere, and (2) attributing either a consanguineal or
an affinal quality to a given (type of) relative. It may be, at best, a
refinement of the original thesis. That is not enough, for after re-
jecting my argument that the alliance distinction necessarily cancels
itself in the extreme generations (for a clarification of the argument
see above chap. 1, n. 8), Carter has to accommodate the fact by
introducing a second rule with "the effect of neutralising the distinction in the second . . . generations" (p. 37). Yet he claims to
"account fully and *economically*" for the data (my italics).

Apart from all dissatisfaction with previous accounts, Carter's
approach is grounded on the conviction he shares with Scheffler,
that all kinship terms have a primary meaning and are "extended"
to secondary meanings, and the originality of the approach lies in
the fact that he admits, against Scheffler, that affinal meaning is
sometimes primary. The problem is then to reconcile componential
analysis with the recognition of the importance of affinity. This is
achieved, to a large extent, through segmentarity. It is axiomatic
for Carter that all Indian systems of kinship and caste are "segmentary," and this seems to imply for him that affines must also be
at the same time and in some way consanguines. (This is not
stated, at least in this form, but it seems to be implicit.) This
assumption of segmentarity, or of continuity between caste and
kinship, is common to all "cultural analysts"; it poses a fundamental question, and I shall return to it later.

Carter's own construction proceeds in three stages. He first
studies the system he knows at first hand from Maharashtra,
including a componential analysis of the vocabulary; at the second
stage he generalizes his findings to South Indian or Dravidian
systems; at the third stage he offers a componential analysis of a
North Indian vocabulary. The conclusion is, in the main, that the
South is isogamous, with systems made up of two intermarrying
classes, while the North if hypergamous, with systems of three
intermarrying classes. My remarks will bear on the first two stages
only. The first reason for dissatisfaction lies in the ambiguous
relation that prevails throughout between the "Marathi non-
Brahmin" system and those from Dravidian languages. By and
large, they are identified, or rather a thoroughgoing similarity
between them is asserted. At the same time a difference between

them is admitted, now implicitly, now explicitly. At the start, the author brushes aside the received idea of Maharashtra as a zone of transition between North and South, and maintains that the non-Brahmins of Western Maharashtra have a system with "thoroughly 'Dravidian' credentials" (30*a*). In particular, cross-cousin marriage occurs and is looked upon with approval. Yet later we learn that it is a "surface" feature. More precisely, advantage is taken of the relative weakness of cross-cousin marriage in Maharashtra for downgrading it, a downgrading that is in a second step extended to Dravidian systems. Not only does the logic of the argument appear questionable but I shall try to show, further on, that Carter's very procedure in the analysis of the Maharastrian vocabulary itself belies his attribution of a "surface" status to cross-cousin marriage.[8]

In passing, one must protest against the high-handed rejection of the current view, which for once is reasonable, about the place of Maharashtrian culture between North and South. It is characteristic of the insensitivity and arbitrariness of the mode of analysis Carter has chosen that it misses, in the kinship nomenclature itself, unmistakable marks of the mixture of Northern and Southern features or rather structural principles. Both Hindi and Tamil offer a systematic, if radically different, classification of relatives in the parents' generation. If the principles outlined above in chapter 1 are followed,[9] it will be seen that the North (Hindi) distinguishes four couples of spouses, that is, it groups husband and wife uniformly under one term, while Tamil segregates the two sexes and has two terms for each sex. What Carter's Marathi vocabulary shows is an irregular mixture of the two principles, culminating in a disposition unheard of in the context, where father's brother and sister are classed together. This local probe shows, without any appeal to linguistics, a mixture of North and South bordering on

8. What is a "surface" feature for Carter, and what not? He writes sometimes as if the "equivalence rules" chosen by the componentialist for his analysis were the only non-"surface" features. It is true that some of Carter's equivalence rules (e.g. the first rule above) actually inject sociological principles (the principle of alliance) into the technical analysis.
9. The main principle is not to mix up radical distinction and mere affixal distinction (cf. above p. 25 and what was said of the meaningful difference in the treatment of the sexes, ibid.) Here I had to leave out the detailed demonstration. The Dravidian form is found above (chap. 1); the Hindi form can be found in e.g. Dumont 1975*b*.

disorganization. It may be admitted that, starting from such a system, Carter will have no difficulty in showing that North and South are at one: the enterprise is tautological. If we leave out the relation to Northern India and keep in mind only, in relation to Carter's immediate argument, that with the South, then the least we must say is that we have to do with a distinctly weakened form of Dravidian systems. That the ideology of cross-cousin marriage is relatively weak among these Maharashtrian people we shall be prepared to believe. And yet, even here to do away with it takes some boldness, as we shall see.

But perhaps we should first ask what exactly is meant by "cross-cousin marriage." In a sense, Carter is completing or perhaps extrapolating a historical change in the meaning of the expression. For our forerunners, it was a label designating a particular form of marriage between close relatives. Then, on closer inspection, it turned out that there was a transition from the immediate *genealogical* cross cousin to more remote relatives falling in the same *category*. Once the category itself had been structurally defined in the vocabulary, the traditional expression "cross-cousin marriage" corresponded to forms of intermarriage between categories—or between groups—*as well as* to marriage between identifiable close relatives. No hard and fast line was drawn between "marriage alliance" in general and "cross-cousin marriage" in any of its acceptations, the latter remaining rather, in sofar as it was maintained in its vague sense, an equivalent of the former expression. What Carter is doing is to separate the two and to maintain the existence of "intermarrying classes" while denying that marriage with the immediate genealogical cross cousin plays any significant role. This denial is unlikely to correspond to the facts, for he admits even for Maharashtra that the native idea is that marriage is between people standing reciprocally in a certain category, whose members closest to Ego are genealogical "cross cousins." It is of course true that to translate the *category* as "cross cousin" is misleading. Roughly speaking, I proposed to translate it as "affines," and in a sense Carter is now following this suggestion, but by a sort of overbidding he goes on to repudiate not only the old label but, together with it, a part of the content and, as it were, the genealogical anchorage of intermarriage.[10]

10. The evidence in Carter's table 6, (1974, 42) is irrelevant, unconvincing, or marginal.

But let us see how he proceeds. We have seen that he transcribes the postulated existence of two intermarrying classes into equivalence rules, allowing him to deduce some secondary meanings of kinship words from their assumed primary meaning. Let us now look at his treatment of the category for "cross cousin" (*mehuna, fem. -i*). Componential analysis requires that one (or two) primary meanings of the word be isolated, to which all other meanings will be referred back by application of the "equivalence rules." But here the author is in a quandary: he has announced his intention neither to reduce affinity to consanguinity nor to do the reverse. He is therefore compelled to treat on a par the two kinds of "meaning" of "cross cousin," and to posit no less than *four* primary meanings of *mehuna:* MBS, FZS, WB, ZH. It is not for me to say whether this step is in conformity with componential orthodoxy, but rather to stress that Carter has been led to it by his recognition of affinity as somehow fundamental. He has had to stretch the "primary" meaning of *mehuna* in order to reconcile Marathi affinity with componentialism.

Carter's decision has the virtue of laying bare the logic of his whole endeavor. First, it is in keeping with his presuppositions: that affinity and consanguinity are irreducible to each other on the one hand, but also, on the other hand, that, in accordance with the "segmentary" view of kinship (and caste), affines are at the same time consanguines in a sense. In the primary meanings of *mehuna*, both elements are equated but remain distinct: MBS = FZS = WB = ZH. Now we must reflect a little about what the componentialist is doing when he attributes a primary meaning to a kinship word or "term". He makes a postulate such that, once that postulate is granted, all other meanings of the same word will be deducible from that one through "equivalence rules." In other words, everything in the vocabulary will be explained by the operation of the equivalence rules, *except the postulated primary meanings*. They escape all verification, explanation or "prediction," with the result that the complete vocabulary, the vocabulary as a whole, will never be grasped. In the present case, in particular, Carter will never have anything to say about why MBS and FZS are equivalent, or about why, as the further equivalences indicate, "every marriage is reputed to take place between cross-cousins." He has done away with the problem by locating it in his presuppositions. What is the use then of the complicated kind of algebra he resorts to, and of his "two intermarrying classes" which are unable to account for the crucial fact? Moreover, there is an unredeemable contradiction when the same author who has, so to speak, pushed cross-cousin marriage under the carpet builds his whole pan-Indian construction on the exclusion of cross-cousin marriage as a mere "surface" feature.

As we have seen above, Carter's construction is based to a large extent on the assumption that "in North India as in South India, concepts of kinship are segmentary" (col. 45a). The issue is central to this new school of thought in general, and I shall end this stocktaking by a discussion of it regarding South India. Granted that caste is "segmentary," the idea is that there is no discontinuity between caste and kinship, or again that the principles at work are the same whether external relations (caste) or internal relations (kinship) are considered. I shall argue that, regarding South (or Dravidian-speaking) India, this is wrong, that there *is* a discontinuity there, and that the arguments to the contrary are unfounded and the segmentary view specious. Carter has a long discussion that leads to the statement that "the issue of lineality versus cognatic kin groups may be resolved by a proper recognition of the segmentary nature of the phenomenon" (col. 44b). For lack of space, I take this discussion as inconclusive and the "segmentary concepts" of kinship and marriage that would be "intimately related to the problems posed by caste society" (ibid.) as nonexistent.

The only formal presentation of segmentarity for Dravidian-speaking people is to my knowledge that of Kenneth David for the Tamils of Jaffna (David 1973). It is absolutely unconvincing. David makes reference to the "Jaffna segmentary theory of natural substance," but his informant on kinship says nothing of the sort. We may well apply to this case Carter's formula of an "overarching cultural category" (in this case "natural substance") not being immediately related to actual kinship categories. Whatever can be said of that presumed concept of "natural substance," the informant's kinship categories are very clear, and they do not in the least warrant the "segmentary" chart that the author makes of them in his fig. 1 (p. 525). Briefly, the "segmentary" division, i.e. encompassing disposition, at the bottom of the diagram, where "non-sharers," i.e. affines, divide into themselves and others, contradicts both the informant's statement (p. 521) and the terminology (alluded to near the end of p. 522). (On the "others," *sagalār,* cf. Dumont 1957*b*, 185–86). What David actually did here was to elevate a secondary aspect (cf. this volume, fig. 18 and text) to the primary level of classification.

Steve Barnett has attempted in a different way to build a continuity between caste and kinship. I have shown above that he relied in actual fact on an amalgam of heterogeneous features or representations—some of which are stressed also by David and Carter—which, on close examination, are seen to relate either to caste or to kinship but by no means to unite both.

I shall not consider Carter's segmentary chart for Maharashtra (table 1:31), as it falls outside South India proper. Here, as in our authors in general, North India seems to have somehow contaminated South India, a fact that is rather strange as regards the scholars, in sofar as the South Indian pattern is the more clear-cut of the two and, one would think, the easier to understand. Just as it takes some pretension to "evaporate" cross-cousin marriage from South Indian kinship, it takes some insensitivity to remain blind to the tremendous difference *in form* between the kinship makeup in the two regions as seen in their vocabularies or to imagine, for instance, that it may result from a mere difference in the number of "intermarrying classes."

Let me then focus for a while on *form,* in the hope of setting into relief the ineradicable specificity of South Indian kinship representations. North India presents us, in the vocabulary itself, with a clear case of what is here called "segmentarity": the word *bhāī* "brother" effectively bridges kinship and caste by taking increasingly wide meanings when we ascend from the immediate relationships to wider and wider circles. It thus repeatedly encompasses on the higher level what was its contrary on the lower level. It is a case of what our authors call "segmentarity," or of that "inclusion" of one category in another which, together with the "overlap" between categories, has been rightly taken as an obstacle or a difficulty in the structural (simple) mapping of categories, an obstacle that actually made me stumble in my first attempt at analysis (Dumont 1962; cf. Dumont 1975*b*). I prefer to speak of the phenomenon as the "encompassing of the contrary" or *hierarchical opposition* (Dumont 1980, 239–45). In the Southern vocabulary we find nothing of the sort, the (main) categories show no overlap or inclusion; they stand in neat distinctive opposition, an opposition in which the two poles or terms have the same status and which we may call, to distinguish it from the former, *equistatutory* *opposition*. This goes to show, to my mind, that the hierarchical principle of caste, which is quite in keeping with the *bhāī* disposition,[11] on the contrary does not enter the basic framework of South Indian categories.

Here we may return to Conklin's distinction between a "paradigm" (a scheme based on what we just defined as equistatutory oppositions) and a "hierarchy" characterized by successive levels of "inclusion" (cf. above, chap. 1). South Indian kinship presents us with a contrast of that sort: something like an island of equality in an ocean of caste.

Such a conclusion will arouse protests, and the formula is a little too sweeping. I must show more precisely the articulation of the two domains. The presence of caste hierarchy has been emphasized in this very book on several occasions, and in one place the original version went too far (see chap. 2, note 3) in stressing it against the opinion according to which Indian kinship is a perfect stranger to caste. But if we look closely at those occurrences of hierarchy, we shall find that they do not bear on the *basic level,* I mean the level of definition of the basic categories, of kinship. They bear, so to speak, on levels above or below that one, with one exception, to be dealt with presently. *Above* that level, we have the segmentation of the caste, to which is devoted the first part of chapter 2, clearly separated from the kinship inquiry proper. Here the articulation between the two domains is delicate; it is found in the relation between the formal or theoretical unit of endogamy in terms of caste and the circle of actual intermarriage, which may be much smaller and remain purely empirical, unformalized (cf. chap. 2, note 7).

Otherwise, hierarchy is present essentially in the senior/junior distinction, which is put to multifarious uses, bearing now on same-sex siblings (chap. 2, notes 9 and 10), now on types of marriages and/or kinds of sons (chap. 2, sec. 1, "Senior and Junior"; chap. 4, "The Indian distinction . . ."). Each of these status distinctions is located, encapsulated as it were, within one of the pigeonholes or niches provided by the grid of categories, that is, so to speak, *below* the level of that grid. With one exception, though: on one point, the age distinction—inseparable, I argued,

---

11. I am not implying that the hierarchical opposition is always linked with "social stratification." It is in itself an independent conceptual device, of probably very widespread occurrence.

from the status distinction—contributes to the grid by splitting Ego's generation into two. But such a split, together with the succession of generations, is fairly widespread in kinship vocabularies at large, and (caste) hierarchical status should be taken here as only reinforcing a nonspecific device; it is only for the sake of completeness that I admit an "exception" on this point.

Apart from that rather common "vertical" succession of generations and age groups, the grid of categories is determined by a specific conjunction of the consanguines/affines opposition with the absolute distinction of *(equal)* sexes. In other words, the alliance relationship provides the backbone of the classification of relatives. Here is the island of equality, even though the ocean of hierarchy invades it here and there, with the effect of adding status distinctions within the framework.

Thus we may say that, within kinship proper, i.e. within the domain defined through the system of kinship categories, hierarchy plays its role within a framework it does not determine, and is thus conceptually subordinate to kinship.

Let me make a similar point about one detail: to reject the notion of the "change of body" of the woman in marriage as extraneous to the system and therefore as useless for its understanding is not to deny its presence in certain groups as a piece of brahmanical sophistication, that is, more or less as an importation from the North. We should note both that the feature is present and that the contradiction it bears to the system as a whole is apparently not felt by the informants.

Before closing this account, I should like to avoid all confusion about its generality, the geographical and social range of its relevance. True, the localization of the inquiry itself (chap. 2) is not in doubt, but the discussion made one speak elliptically of a "South Indian system" in a way which might be misleading. First, the West Coast is quite apart, even if we could apply some of our general principles to the Nayar question (chap. 3). East of the Ghats now, the main obstacle to straight generalization is the wide prevalence of uncle-niece marriage. The individual systems admitting uncle-niece marriage are very troublesome. On the one hand they do not represent another kind of model as compared with those which admit only cross-cousin marriage, but rather variants of the same. On the other hand those variants strike at the roots of some of the principles of our model, and do it, not in a homogeneous way, but in various and more or less idiosyncratic ways. This is a rough estimate, but it has to be borne in mind whenever we talk of a "South Indian system."

I don't want to discuss once more (cf. Dumont 1961) this difficult question, but only to take advantage of Mr. Kodanda Rao's article on uncle-niece marriage among some fishermen of Andhra Pradesh (Rao 1973) with regard to our problem of the relation between caste and kinship, or hierarchy and equality, in South India. Accepting Rao's presentation of the case, there is intermarriage between two lines belonging to patrilineages of unequal status. The crux of the matter is that the superior line and the inferior line agree on differing, namely on taking two contrary views of the same chain of intermarriage: while the superiors marry a cross cousin (MBD), the inferiors marry a niece (ZD), all along. Now the author claims that the categories of kinship remain unchanged. This does not seem to be the case in his somewhat incomplete account, but even if it were so, the fact that the two lines look at their intermarriage in quite different ways suffices to show that status difference is asserted here at the cost of the normal reciprocal play of the system of categories. In other words, hierarchy is paramount and imposes a drastic modification of the kinship system. I thought the fact was worth singling out.

Yet this spectacular example lies outside our present field of study. Regarding the latter, I submit that we must recognize a discrepancy between two subsystems—that of caste, where hierarchy and hence "segmentarity" prevail, and that of kinship, where hierarchy is not absent but is contained within a fundamentally equistatutory system of oppositions.

Or is the present writer mistaken, contrary to all appearances? Let us leave the question open. Regarding the vocabulary, or the categories, the debate with the "segmentarity" thesis is easy to settle by answering a single question: when consanguines and affines are merged, are they merged in consanguinity, or in a superior category? It is true that, due to the literature considered, we have dealt mainly with the anatomy of the kinship system, not with its physiology. The account of ceremonies and presentations presented above in chapter 2 has not been much supplemented, and has been little queried in subsequent literature. Again let us leave those questions open for studies and scholars to come.

Yet one cannot help wondering why the three authors last considered have not recognized the discrepancy or discontinuity between caste and kinship. They seem to have been misled by an uncritical urge toward unity and simplicity and by flimsy, so-called "overarching" conceptions. Ethnographic faithfulness has here been supplanted by the need for closure of "symbolic analysis." Simplicity of principle has been bought at the price of disregarding the unmistakable clues that a detailed ethnographic description would impose to attention.

This is the natural result of our having been exposed for too long to a hollow doctrine that amounts to treating the data as subordinate to the individual researcher's interest or to the professional fad of the day. Quite to the contrary, I would plainly maintain that the data do *prefer* one frame of reference to another and that the job of the anthropologist consists in finding out which and in subordinating oneself to that tendency of the data.

In this case, we must recognize the full status of affinity in the system, a status equal to that of consanguinity, and not let it be erased—as by the downgrading of cross-cousin marriage, or drowned in consanguinity as it is with us—by its "segmentary" inclusion on a level superior to that of its distinction. Hence the title of this little book: what the crystalline form of the South Indian vocabulary enshrines is, with the transmission of affinity from parents to children, the assertion of affinity as a value equal to that of consanguinity, the assertion, that is, of identity and relation as indissolubly solidary. This solidarity, itself a (second order) relation, is thus substituted for what we call substance. No trivial lesson, I should think.[12]

Postscript

I feel the need for bringing out more clearly a general conclusion of the study in chapter 2. It is about symmetrical and asymmetrical aspects, obligation and preference, regional pattern and makeup of

---

12. I regret that the monumental and long-awaited book by Professor Thomas R. Trautmann, *Dravidian Kinship* (Cambride University Press) reached me too late (September 1982) for the relevant discussions that it contains to be taken into account here, even in a special postscript. A review by C. J. Fuller has just been published (*Times Literary Supplement*, 24 September 1982). I must also be content with referring the reader to a recent study bearing on one of the groups considered in chapter 2: Anthony Good, "Prescription, Preference and Practice: Marriage Patterns among the Kondaiyankottai Maravar of South India, *Man* 16/1 (March 1981): 108–29.

the individual group, and has remained scattered in different places—pp. 79 (fig. 13), 86 (n. 16), 92 (n. 18), 102.

The terminology is symmetrical, it does not distinguish between patrilateral and matrilateral cross cousins. Yet the fact does not correlate as might have been expected with double cross-cousin marriage or sister-exchange, which is disliked. Rather, the terminology provides a common, regional conceptual framework, making affinity the equal of consanguinity. Corresponding to it we find in each group a symmetrical background in the statistical outcome of intermarriage as well as in the form of exchange in ceremonial prestations and counterprestations.

Against this symmetrical background, each of the groups studied presents a particular pattern made up of descent on the one hand, affinity preference or hierarchy on the other. Paternal elements being generally present (locality, authority), there is a neat complementarity on that level: for example, corresponding to patrilineal descent there is a matrilateral marriage preference together with the preeminence of the mother's brother as ceremonial affine—the foremost affine being always the one who should in principle give his daughter in marriage to the (male) subject.

From a regional-comparative point of view, there is a hierarchy: the common terminological framework is actually *mandatory*, and within it is developed in each case the particular *preference* (as it were) of the particular group.

Australia

5

The Kariera Kinship Vocabulary: An Analysis

The primary purpose of this paper is to draw attention to an often-neglected though noteworthy difference between the Kariera vocabulary and that of Dravidian type.[1] I take this occasion to offer a rigorous and detailed analysis of the Kariera system; however, for lack of a wider comparison, the conclusions remain incomplete and hypothetical. Therefore I shall be brief and shall reduce to a bare minimum the preliminaries and commentaries, discussions and references.

Here, as elsewhere, the intention is to treat the vocabulary as a subsystem of the kinship system. The aim is to bring forth as much as possible the structure or texture of the vocabulary taken separately, before looking at it in relation to the other distinguish-

This paper was first published in French in J. Pouillon and P. Maranda (eds.), *Echanges et Communications, Mélanges offerts à Claude Lévi-Strauss* (Paris-La Haye: Mouton, 1970), p. 272–86.

1. The two systems are often taken as one and the same. Neglecting my brief indication of the difference, Radcliffe-Brown (1953) not only criticized a Dravidian analysis from an Australian point of view, but strongly insisted on what he called "the 'Australian-Dravidian' type of terminology" (see above, chapter 1, note 9 and Correspondence).

able subsystems (in this case, the section system). It is not what is usually done; there is often a mere bringing together of isolated local features of the vocabulary and institutional features that seem to correspond to them (unilineal descent, for example). In the Kariera case, some authors have been pleased to note that there exist precise relations between some of the kinship terms and the sections that make up Kariera society and in which, once an Ego has been located, it is possible to distribute his or her different relatives.[2] Similarly, the recurrence of the same terms in the extreme generations was interpreted as an index of the "cycles" or "couples" that descent—whether matrilineal or patrilineal, documented or surmised—had to go through in such a section system. But all this was seen not as the congruence of two consistent subdomains (i.e. of a terminological consistency with an institutional consistency) but rather as the points at which the insubstantial web of the vocabulary was anchored in the hard facts of institutions. Otherwise, how could one at the same time have entertained the idea that the Dravidian vocabulary, which is unconstrained by sections, could be of the same type as the Kariera?

In a broad sense, it is true that the Kariera, like the Dravidians, distinguish two categories of relatives: "parallel" and "cross."[3] But while in the Dravidian case this distinction accounts for the form of the system as a whole—at least in my interpretation, and against the background of a linear succession of generations and relative age groups[4]—it is not so in the Kariera case. Let us try then, with the utmost circumspection, to construct the Kariera vocabulary as a system. Everywhere, except in the grandchil-

---

2. In a paper entitled "A Simplified Model of Kariera Kinship," Romney and Epling (1958) used the vocabulary in a four-column table in order to show, for a male Ego located in a given section, the distribution of his different kinds of relatives into the "moieties" at birth and into local groups corresponding to the "moieties" after marriage.

3. The point was clearly acknowledged by Radcliffe-Brown from his 1913 article onward. The 1913 text contains more detail relevant to our interest than does the 1930 study: two genealogical charts—one for a male Ego, the other *for a female Ego*— and a description of the self-reciprocal usages.

4. The distinction opposes persons related through consanguinity and persons related through permanent affinity or "marriage alliance." As such, the distinction cancels itself in the grandparents' generation. [The analysis that follows rests on the same principles as the foregoing one, chapter 1 above].

dren's generation, the terms for male relatives are radically different from those for female relatives. We may therefore try to
construct the two halves of the vocabulary separately, and then
bring them together.

Let us begin with the male relatives. There are two terms for
each generation, or age class. The question is how we should
arrange them into a chart, how generations can be superposed on
each other according to a single principle. We designate the
generations, beginning with that of Ego (Gen. 0), −1, −2 upward,
+1, +2 downward. We suppose that the categories are well-
enough known, in general, for each to be identified by our simply
indicating a close relative who falls into it. Let us posit Ego, his
brothers (older and younger), and his father F (see fig. 21). The
cross cousin (C.C.) and the mother's brother fall into place. Also,
FF must be above F, and MBF above MB. Similarly the places of S
and ZS, SS and DS are determined. The recurrence of the terminal
term (MAELI, TAMI) in the same column is satisfactory. It should
not be concluded that we have put the agnates on the left and the
nonagnates on the right, for FF is only one of the denotations of
MAELI, while many others (MMH, etc.) do not represent agnates.
What is true is that all agnates fall into the same column, and that
the two columns are opposed like the two "moieties" of the
society. Moreover, this arrangement is not the only one possible
for this fragment of the vocabulary taken in isolation; we could
have chosen to put MB instead of F above Ego, and to continue on
following that principle. Such an arrangement would also ensure
the recurrence of MAELI and TAMI in the same column; it would
not, however, correspond to Kariera social organization.

The construction of the chart for female relatives must be done
mutatis mutandis as for males. This time, taking a female Ego as
point of departure, we place in the first column (the terms
corresponding to) her sisters (elder and younger), M and MM
(above), D and DD (below); facing them will come C.C., FZ, FM,
BD, SD. This way of proceeding is justified for it supposes only
that the vocabulary treats the father-son and mother-daughter
filiation relationships in the same way, which is obviously the case;
also, we thus avoid any mixing of the sexes—anything resembling
"crossing"—in the filiation chains.

Here again there is another possibility: following the pattern of
the one indicated above for men, it would consist in placing FZ
immediately above the female Ego, and so on. Considering all

−2	MAELI (FF)	TAMI (MF)
−1	MAMA (F)	KAGA (MB)
0	KAJA (eB) Ego MARGARA (yB)	KUMBALI (C.C.)
+1	MAIÑGA (S)	KULING (ZS)
+2	MAELI (SS)	TAMI (DS)

Fig. 21. Male relatives of a male Ego

those relatives as attached to their group (section) of birth (and not of marriage), one will have the satisfaction of seeing that our columns correspond to the social "moieties." We thus find that the one arrangement that brings about this result for one sex excludes it for the other sex, which shows that *the dichotomy of the vocabulary does not purely and simply express the division of the society into "moieties."* It could have been foreseen, as we know that women change their residence on marriage and subsequently have the same "sons," etc., as their husbands.

Hitherto we considered only an Ego of one sex or the other. We should now include an Ego of the other sex (female for the first figure, male for the second). At the same time, we shall fuse the two charts into one by bringing together the first columns (i.e., in the first approximation, "parallel" relatives) and the second columns (presumably "cross" relatives). Some complications occur for the central generations, though only for cross relatives. In detail: a female Ego says ÑUBA (not KUMBALI) for her male cross cousin, TOA (not KULING) for the male cross relative of the son's generation; conversely, a male Ego says TOA (not YURO) for his cross aunt, ÑUBA (and not BUNGALI) for his female cross cousin. The case of NGARAIA is regular: the term corresponds to the cross niece, that is, ZD for a man and BD for a woman. The case is exemplary as it contradicts two interpretations of the vocabulary that have been proposed. First, we see that a brother and sister designate as NGARAIA persons located in two different "moieties," which shows that the category is not contained in one section or "moiety" of the society. Second, if as a result of the fascination I mentioned elsewhere[5] one were tempted to substitute in the analysis the opposition "agnates/nonagnates" for "parallel/cross," one would be compelled in the present case to suppose that the same term falls on one side or the other according to the sex of the speaker. To do this would be to go back to the times before Morgan; yet it has been done.[6] The first advance in these matters had consisted in seeing that the meaning of such terms was actually independent of the sex of Ego, that it was a relative instead of an absolute meaning. Is that lesson, which seemed well established, now being forgotten?

Let us return to the cross relatives in the middle of the chart and look at the arrangement in a more straightforward manner. What brings up the complications is the existence of two reciprocal terms between cross relatives of opposite sex: ÑUBA designates, self-reciprocally, a cross cousin of opposite sex, and also the potential (or real) spouse. TOA self-reciprocally designates the cross aunt of a man and the cross nephew of a woman and, in contrast to ÑUBA, corresponds to a strongly stressed prohibition, which

---

5. See below, Chap. 6, "The Spell of Underlying Descent."
6. Epling 1961. The article contains a table of the terms, free of any interpretation (p. 153b). Burling (1962) saw the difficulty, and proposed to remedy it—while holding to the agnatic hypothesis—by adding one more dimension of (local) distinction. The case is exemplary, for it shows that in these authors' approach (that is, in "componential analysis" as they practice it), the recognition of a mistake can be easily replaced by the introduction of a supplementary complication. My method is quite different: I propose to utilize the particular or local feature for an understanding of the system as a whole. This might be the occasion to inquire into the almost automatic use of an apparently quite arbitrary distinction—agnates/nonagnates—in the study of vocabularies. I found that Lounsbury (1956, 168), accepting for his own use the "eight fundamental categories of difference" of Kroeber, had seen fit to complete the seventh ("consanguines/affines") by introducing *within the consanguines* the agnates/nonagnates distinction. The adjunction itself—which was presented as self-explanatory—is very interesting; even more so is the fact that the new distinction has, in effect, swallowed up the former one: under the cover of a pseudo-structural approach, descent has banished affinity, substance has replaced relation.

-2	KANDARI (MM)	KABALI (FM)
-1	NGANGA (M)	YURO (FZ)
0	TURDU (eZ) Ego MARI (yZ)	BUNGALI (C.C.)
+1	KUNDAL (D)	NGARAIA (BD)
+2	KANDARI (DD)	KABALI (SD)

Fig. 22. Female relatives of a female Ego.

Radcliffe-Brown presented as rather like a generalized form of the mother-in-law taboo; the case is very clear, for to lift the taboo the term is ceremonially replaced by another *(yumani)* (Radcliffe-Brown 1913, 156). There is apparently no similar prohibition between cross uncle and niece. (In an exception to the method we generally follow, we have here gone beyond the vocabulary and singled out the two cases of self-reciprocity, and seen them in relation to the regulation of sex and marriage.) Once the two self-reciprocal terms are posited, they entail the necessity of four different terms to designate similar relationships between persons of the same sex. We note that whereas in the case of NGARAIA there is absolute connotation of the sex of the object designated, ÑUBA is entirely relative, indicating only cross relationship, different sex, same generation. As for TOA, it is absolute only as to the relation between relative generation and absolute sex. We recall that there is nothing of the sort in Dravidian: there, every-thing happens as for KAGA and NGARAIA here.

We now reach the crucial point: the generations of grandparents and grandchildren. The terms for the former (see top of fig. 23) are the same for speakers of both sexes. Regarding the latter (bottom of fig. 23), there are complications. First, each term for Gen. +2 designates persons of either sex, with no differenciation—a unique exception in the whole system; thus MAELI designates SD as well as SS. The recurrence of the term from Gen. −2 to Gen. +2 simply expresses its self-reciprocity. That the sexes are not differenciated in Gen. +2 is entailed by that self-reciprocity *if we posit at the start the term* in Gen. −2, for if his grandchildren call a certain grandfather, and him alone, MAELI, and if the appellation is self-reciprocal, then this same grandfather (and he alone) must call both his grandson and granddaughter MAELI. In other words, self-reciprocity transfers, in one of the two uses of the word, the sex distinction from the object to the subject. Similarly the corresponding grandmother in our chart KANDARI (MM) will call not only her DD, but also her DS, KANDARI. Here a remark is called for: to set together MAELI and KANDARI in Gen. +2, as it results from figs. 21 and 22, is to define the category *relatively;* KANDARI represents for a female Ego the equivalent of what MAELI is for a male Ego—that is, DS instead of SS. If we had chosen the *absolute* aspect, MAELI would have been accompanied by KABALI (SD, female speaking). Our procedure is consistent. It leads to extend to those generations the "parallel/cross" distinction usually reserved to the middle generations. To formulate this extension *in the present case,* we shall say that a relationship of reduplicated filiation is parallel if the two upper generations in it are of the same sex (maternal grandmother and, conversely, children of the daughter of a woman), and that it is "cross" if they are of opposite sex.

We shall come back to these questions. We must first pay attention to the very fact of reciprocity between grandparents and grandchildren, irrespective of its particular aspects. In the Dravidian system, the two kinds of relatives who are distinguished in the middle region of the vocabulary are merged at the two ends, so that there is only *one kind* of grandparents and *one kind* of grandchildren—there being, beyond Gens. −2 and +2 (ideally or really) a *linear sequence* of generations, each with a distinct term. In Kariera, on the contrary, nowhere do the two kinds of relatives merge; instead, each of the two closes up, as it were, upon itself. This is best seen from a diagram showing (or at least suggesting) the coincidence of grandparents and grandchildren terms, as compared to the corresponding Dravidian diagram (see fig. 24).

On the right-hand side we see a continuous flow which divides into two branches in the middle region; on the left-hand side, two circles face each other, each closing in upon itself. True, there is between those two circles (or rather, between corresponding

	"Parallel"		"Cross"	
Gen.	m	w	w	m
−2	MAELI	KANDARI	KABALI	TAMI
−1	MAMA	NGANGA	(m) TOA (w) YURO	KAGA
0	KAJA .... MARGARA	TURDU .... MARI	(m) ÑUBA (w) BUNGALI	(m) KUMBALI (w) ÑUBA
+1	MAIÑGA	KUNDAL	NGARAIA (m) (ZD) (w) BD	(m) KULING (ZS) (w) TOA (BS)
+2	(m) MAELI	(w) KANDARI	(w) KABALI	(m) TAMI

Fig. 23. The vocabulary as a whole. — m = man. w = woman. (m) = man speaking. (w) = woman speaking.

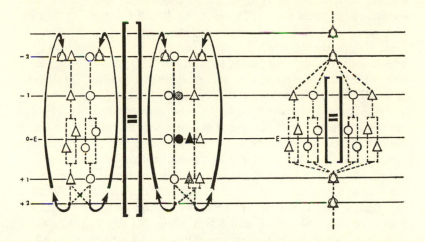

Fig. 24. Kariera vocabulary (on the left) and Dravidian vocabulary (on the right). (Hatched symbols = Toa; black symbols = Nuba; cf. note 11).

elements of the one and the other) a relation of affinity or intermarriage similar to that which on the right separates and unites the two median branches; but on the left that relation prevails throughout the chart, not only on local levels but on the global level, between the two circles themselves. The whole set of relatives (that is to say, virtually the whole society as seen by a given subject) is divided into two different species. There is obviously some relation between this dichotomy and that of the society into "moieties"—not in the sense that each of the two circles representing the vocabulary would correspond exactly to one of the "moieties" (for we have seen that such was not the case in our women's chart, but only for men seen from a male point of view) but in the sense that on the one hand the society, on the other the vocabulary operate a dichotomy of the whole social body, and that the link between the two halves is the same in both cases—that is, intermarriage.

We propose to now study the relation between the vocabulary (sub-)system and the section (sub-)system. As mentioned above, our predecessors often considered the relation between termino-logical categories and social groups. We shall use a technique they often employed: projecting the vocabulary scheme, category by category, unto the section scheme. Beginning with the circular aspect of the vocabulary, let us consider, for simplicity's sake, only men. We know that Kariera society is made up of two kinds of local groups (here called, for brevity, exogamous "moieties") in which men remain from father to son, but with successive generations alternating between two sections. Let us call the "moieties" A and B, the sections A1 and A2, B1 and B2: if the father is A1, the son is A2, the grandson A1, etc. In other words, Ego, his FF, and his SS are members of the same section, say A1; and his F and S belong to the alternate section A2. We can depict the circular vocabulary as in fig. 25—we could represent similarly, on a plane parallel to that of the first circle, another circle corresponding to the second column of our chart (MF-DS, MB, C.C., ZS). We note two things: the vocabulary makes a distinction within the sections: Ego is opposed to his FF and SS in A1 as F is to S in A2. Yet it does not, for all that, ignore the unity of A1 and that of A2 as opposed to each other within A (and as opposed to the corresponding section of B). There is reciprocity between Ego and his FF-SS; Ego himself is FF-SS of his FF-SS (and the same is true between F and S from their viewpoint). All in all, Ego and FF-SS are primarily identical in relation to those outside; they are differentiated only secondarily, as Ego distinguishes his F from his S. In the final

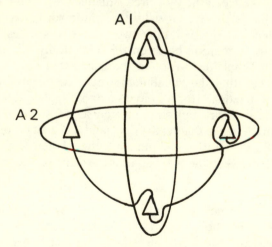

Fig. 25.

analysis, the circularity is coterminous with the oscillation between A1 and A2, *plus* an internal and relative distinction within
each of the two sections.

Using *a* and *b* to refer to the subdivisions of each section to
which the vocabulary points, we can attempt to distribute the
categories of the vocabulary into those subdivisions. The matter is
immediate for male relatives, delicate for female relatives. A
general question comes up: namely, whether women should be
placed in the section of their birth or that of their marriage.
Experience shows that the decision taken on this point is likely to
reflect the theory of the researcher. One might contend that there
is no reason for locating women once and for all, as their normal
destiny is bilocal.[7] The question is, rather, whether there is or is
not in the indigenous mind (as we can reconstruct it) a link between
the vocabulary—including its feminine aspect, without which it
would be much impoverished—and the section system. We shall
see that there are reasons to answer in the affirmative, though
without denying that in some cases the link to be established
between a category and a (subdivision of a) section is a matter of
predominant rather than exclusive representation. Moreover, we
shall find that the question is not without relevance to the most
general problems that the vocabulary suggests.

We can distinguish moieties, sections, and subdivisions in a
symmetrical fashion as in fig. 26, where the generations succeed
one another by regular rotation in the direction indicated on each
side by an arrow. If Ego is placed in A1b, the grandfathers will be
respectively in A1a and B1a (in the lower part of the sector); the
other male relatives (in capitals) of a male Ego easily fall into place,
down to the grandson (MAELI in the upper part of A1a). The
places of some female relatives (in lowercase letters) seem to result
from that of the males. Thus "sisters" come naturally with
"brothers" in A1b, the "daughter" in A2b and the "grandmother"
kandari with MAELI in A1a. The last point is important, for we
saw that the two terms were homologous in the vocabulary; by

---

7. Thus Romney and Epling (1958) locate women both directly in the "moiety"
where they reside after marriage and indirectly in the section of their birth (thus
in all generations). Contrary to appearance, their chart has nothing to do
with the problem of the relation between the vocabulary as a whole and the
system of sections—a problem which, it must be said in all fairness, the authors
did not set themselves.

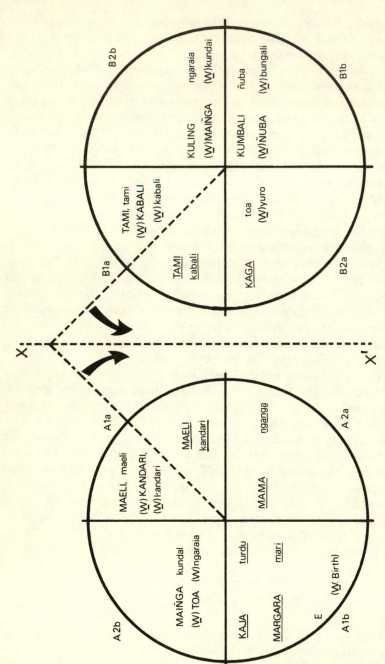

Fig. 26. System of the vocabulary and section system. (W) = woman speaking.

inscribing them in the same section, we admit that *kandari* is seen in her place of birth (and not of marriage)—and actually the self-reciprocity of the term does not allow otherwise. The same applies to the corresponding categories in moiety B. In contrast, I place the "mother" *nganga* on the A side, and the "cross aunt" *toa* on the B side; in both cases this is in the place of marriage, not of birth. In so doing I may provoke controversy, but it seems that to do otherwise would be gratuitously to complicate the relations between vocabulary and social morphology. The mother-children relationship is terminologically homologous to the father-children relationship; there is therefore every reason to suppose that the mother is seen, together with her homologues, as situated (pre-dominantly, at least) in the same subdivision as the father—which also corresponds to the experience of the children as such. On the contrary, the strongly stressed prohibition applying to *toa,* pater-nal aunt (etc.) and mother-in-law, seems to indicate that she is viewed in a cross-position—that is, in B. The emphasis could even be explained, better than by the relative age of the parties, by the fact that, among the women attached to the alternate moiety, *toa* is the only one that is there by marriage, the only one of consanguine-ous origin—all the others having been born under the category of affinity, whether or not they belong to the subdivision in which one normally takes one's wife. Lastly, we see that the terms for males and females used by a male Ego fall into the subdivisions as pairs of siblings except for the generation of the parents, where they are couples of spouses.

Let us now take a female Ego who would be the sister of the previous Ego, born in the same place (A1b). A number of terms are the same as previously; they are underlined in fig. 26. The specific arrangement of grandchildren is known. Some terms are special to the woman [(*w*) is for "female speaking"] *yuro* (instead of *toa*), *bungali* (instead of *ñuba*). Some terms are identical but designate a different person for *(w):* ÑUBA for male cross cousin, TOA for brother's son (in A2b), *ngaraia* for brother's daughter (A2). Lastly, the woman, once married (in B1b), sees her children MAINGA and *kundal* in B2b. To stress the point: a brother and a sister born in the same place see their children and their cross niece in two different moieties. No effort of the imagination can alter that fact.

On the whole, what do we see? The difference between the sexes, their different destiny, and the conditions under which they combine complicate the terminology in the middle generations; this point had already emerged in the foregoing. What appears so forcefully now by contrast is the reunion that takes place in the last generation (A1a and B1a), a reunion aptly mediated precisely by the sex difference. There the terminological loop, so to speak, closes up—a little like the Dravidian schema, but on two different poles. That is the point of rest, the point at which the torsion marked in the place of *nganga* and *toa* and in the cross-arrangement of the children of a man and of a woman disappears. This is bought, it is true, at the price of an irregularity: the sex of grandchildren is not differentiated. But this fact has been seen to result from reciprocity. It is therefore the reciprocity between alternate generations of the same section that marks the consummation of the torsion between the vocabulary and the sections.

Finally, this reciprocity is seen to correspond both to the closure of each "moiety" and to the alternation of sections, as the grandson comes back to the section of his grandfather. Now, what is the relation of this reciprocity between the extremes with the double median reciprocity, apparently of a very different character? Should we rest content with admitting that they are only juxtaposed, without any internal relation, the slightest homology, or any functional similarity? For the time being, we can at least propose an observation. If the former reciprocity is related to the alternation of generations, the latter is related to the intermarriage between sections, or between corresponding generations in the two "moieties." As has been shown elsewhere,[8] these two elements (alternation and intermarriage) are precisely the two basic principles of the section system. We may then say that, taken together, the two reciprocities found in the kinship vocabulary put on it, as it were, the imprint of the global social system. To put it another way: they represent the intersection of the *local* plane of the kinship relationships of a particular Ego with the plane of the *global* organization; they are the tangible proof that here the regulation of marriage is collective before being individual. At least such are the hypotheses that may be formulated in this particular case, in the absence of any general notions or theory of reciprocity in kinship vocabularies.

There remains an important problem. We have employed throughout, provisionally, the expression "parallel/cross." This expression takes a somewhat different meaning according to

8. See below, chap. 6 and fig. 27.

whether we consider it only in the comparison between Dravidian and Kariera or from a more general viewpoint. In the Dravidian case, I had proposed to replace this anthropological, analytical, and obscure expression by the distinction *consanguines/affines*. Once thus defined, the distinction disappears in the grandparents' generation, for nothing prevents us from crossing the filiations: mother's father and father's father may be taken *ad libitum* either as consanguines or as affines. In the Kariera case, on the contrary, the distinction extends to Gen. -2 and $+2$. Therefore the distinction is not exactly *the same* in the two cases. One can explain the difference by saying that it is the holistic formula, the division of the society into two "moieties" and the operation on that level (or that of the sections) of the intermarriage relationship that demands that the distinction be carried on for the grandparents. But this supposes that such a possibility is inherent in the distinction, that the "crossing" of sexes can play the same role in repeated filiation as between siblings in relation to their children.[9] Genetically we probably ought to reverse the sequence and say that the parallel/cross distinction can disappear between grandparents when, as in the Dravidian case, intermarriage is no more present on the global, but only on the local, level. Of course all that presupposes that our descriptions are accurate, and in particular that the picture of the extreme generations in Dravidian is actually as we presented it.

In conformity with the logic of those systems, distinguishing two kinds of grandparents entails distinguishing the two sexes among them; but in the Kariera case the holistic formula entails the self-reciprocity of those terms, which in turn entails obliteration of the sex distinction in the grandchildren's generation. The formula is avowedly still complicated, but I can propose no simpler one that would account for this remarkable configuration.

From a general point of view, the foregoing hypothesis would seem to require for its confirmation that the distinction between grandparents—wherever it appears in that type of system—should be combined (whether synchronically or not) with a social dichotomy, a global dualism. This may be too strong a demand. Moreover it was recently stressed that the "parallel/cross" distinction can designate very different things (Buchler 1967, 23). No wonder, since it expresses only an external view, a view devoid of

---

9. Bernot 1965. The purpose of the author is slightly different from my own; he formulates the parallel very clearly, and refers to Rivers (Buin and Pentecost).

meaning—an "analytical" view, as it is called. Until the question is cleared up, it is apposite to qualify the expression and speak of this distinction as found among Kariera, for example, or among Iroquois, etc.

To conclude, it should be clear in what measure our analysis is incomplete, and more hypothetical than definitive. What I hope to have shown is simply the difference between Kariera and Dravidian vocabularies—that it is not insignificant, and that it corresponds to the presence or absence of a close link between the vocabulary, on the one hand, and, on the other, a global form of the society which is found in the Australian section systems but not in South India. It has already been emphasized (Lévi-Strauss 1949) that, in systems with positive marriage rules, the determination of the spouse can be effected either through a system of classes or by tracing individual relationships. Similarly, it is likely that we should make a fundamental distinction between cases in which a global formula is present in the minds of the people and cases in which it is absent. When only individual or *local* determinations are in evidence, the attempt to unearth a *global* formula[10] whose existence on the empirical level would presumably be entailed by those determinations appears once more as highly problematic in the light of the present comparison.[11]

Postscript

The above may be compared with the contemporaneous but very different analysis of Goodenough (1970).

Harold Scheffler has added to his review discussed above two pages (1977, 876–77) dealing nominally with the present paper. Unfortunately I find it very difficult to make sense of his criticism *in relation to this text*. Not only does Scheffler deal with other authors for half of the space, but he has actually mixed up this analysis of Kariera vocabulary with the article on Australian

10. For a somewhat similar orientation, see Service 1960. For some of its remarks (p. 425–26), this article should have figured in the bibliography of my next chapter.

11. My fig. 24 is imperfect in that I have not always managed to make the different usages of the same Kariera term coincide. The representation is tolerable for Ñuba (in black) but insufficient for Toa (hatched), where the generation difference should be shown as suppressed.

section systems (which follows hereafter), and the only two references he makes bear on the latter. Moreover, the critic capitalizes on two expressions of which one, "local patrilineages" was nowhere used by me, while the second, "moieties," which, in fact, I enclosed in quotation marks throughout, was glossed in one place as follows: "two kinds of local groups (which we have called to simplify matters exogamous 'moieties')." Regarding the "structure of the system of kin classification," presumably Kariera, which alone interests us here, I am said to have reduced it, contrary to my purported intention, to "the structure of the section system." How can Scheffler make me say that "The male terms . . . designate relative positions in the 'moiety' system," or pretend that in my model, "the proper application of kinship terms is dependent on relative section affiliation"? I leave it to the reader to decide what relation these statements bear to the real text they are intended to criticize. Actually, the real text is simply ignored, including the footnote (6) bearing on componential analysis.

6

Descent or Intermarriage? A Relational View of Australian Section Systems

The intent of this paper is to propose a view of some classical Australian or Australoid section systems which is at variance with the prevailing or, at least, the predominant view of the matter. But an apology and some explanation might well be required of one who is not a specialist on Australia, if he presumes not only to meddle with this area but to restrict his consideration to a few groups and their subsystem of sections (or "subsections") or marriage classes alone, i.e. to only one aspect of the kinship system. The present sketch might begin with the same words as W. E. Lawrence's noted contribution of 1937: it "seeks to clarify certain matters which seem unnecessarily abstruse in much of the literature" (Lawrence 1937, 321). Even Lawrence's title might have been borrowed, for it will be seen that a major emphasis will be on "alternating generations."

This paper was first published in *Southwestern Journal of Anthropology* 22/3 (Autumn 1966): 231–50. Reprinted by permission of the *Journal of Anthropological Research*. The argument is presented in summary in section 1 of "Marriage Alliance," an article prepared in 1963 for the *International Encyclopedia of the Social Sciences* (Dumont 1968).

Looking at Australia from a Dravidian angle, I began by doubt-
ing the often assumed structural identity between Dravidian and
Kariera kinship vocabularies. I was then struck by a situation so
strange as to warrant criticism and a passing intrusion into a
foreign field. What looks very strange in retrospect to the present
author is the fascination exerted on most anthropologists' minds by
the idea of "descent." If its exclusive use, its privileged status, is
objectively unwarranted, there is room for a critical study of the
explanatory value of the concept, or rather of its relation to the
anthropologists' mental makeup and subjective—if collective—
needs. I shall be content in the following with a discursive
highlighting of some aspects of this question. The proposals that
follow are tentative, of course, and are offered for critical apprais-
al. They are formulated as affirmative statements only for the sake
of simplicity. As to the narrow restriction of the subject matter, the
author is conscious of the risks involved. Although the inquiry may
well not have been wide enough, it has gone beyond the present
topic. A study of Kariera terminology will be published subsequently.

The Spell of Underlying Descent

There is widespread agreement on the nature of Australian, and
especially Kariera and Aranda, section (or "subsection") systems.
Most often, they are considered to be based on "double descent";
in this view, their four or eight known and named sections or
classes are explained by the combination and cross-cutting of two
sets of moieties, patrilineal and matrilineal. Actually the moieties
are either nonexistent or unnamed. Matrilineal moieties do not
exist among the Kariera and Aranda, nor do patrilineal moieties
among the Aranda, and we shall see in what sense patrilineal
moieties can be said to exist among the Kariera, who do not
distinguish them by name. To explain groups and arrangements
(positive marriage rules) that consciously exist by groups which do
not exist, or of which the people are not conscious, may seem a
dubious procedure unless one recognizes the advantages involved
in terms of general anthropological theory. The procedure was
questioned recently by Goody (1961), although from a point of
view completely different from the present one, and R. B. Lane,
on the same occasion, recalled Elkin's position (Lane 1961, 16;

Elkin 1953).[1] But double descent has been the dominant approach to the problem since Radcliffe-Brown drew attention to the horde as a universal patrilocal exogamous group. Insofar as there were, among Kariera, only two kinds of observed but unnamed local groups, the tribe could be considered to be divided into two unnamed patrilineal moieties, or as having what I shall call "holistic patrilineal descent." Radcliffe-Brown had only to combine this feature with the earlier recognition of a supposedly "underlying" matrilineal dichotomy in order for Australian systems to be accepted as based on double descent.

When one reads successively the authors who either claimed or acclaimed the discovery of underlying matrilineal moieties as a complementary principle of holistic descent, the repetitive emphasis displayed begins to look somewhat uncanny. And if one is inclined to admit that anthropologists may sometimes agree for the wrong reason—I mean for a reason which springs from their own mentality and their *initial* assumptions, and not from their conversion by the evidence—one grows suspicious of a "discovery" which has called forth such overemphatic agreement among people who otherwise disagree widely among themselves.

Let me provide a few examples. Brenda S. Seligman expressed ingenuously the tendency to reduce matrimonial classes to descent groups:

> Although it may appear that the type of marriage is the dominant factor in the formation of the social group, the point I want to bring forward is that it is the *recognized* form of descent that really shapes both the groupings and the marriages [Seligman 1928, 534].

Radcliffe-Brown was not content with stating that underlying matri-moieties had to be supplied where they were not present for the sake of a uniform theory of section systems; he insisted that they actually existed everywhere:

> This [Kariera] system . . . involves a division of society into two matrilineal moieties and also a cross division into two patrilineal moieties. . . . It is important to note that the moieties exist in every section system whether they are named or not [Radcliffe-Brown 1930, 39, 439].

1. There is no mention of matrilineality in a recent study of Kariera by Romney and Epling (1958). Instead, the distinction of generations is taken as one of the principles on which the system rests.

Yet, notwithstanding his insistence on confusing the real and the actual, essence and existence, Radcliffe-Brown never introduced the interpolated moieties in his symbolization of the systems. Lawrence did so, after others (cf. fig. 1b and 2b). Where Radcliffe-Brown was still struggling against his own resistance, Lawrence is all of a piece:

> Tribes throughout the class area are divided, not only into the petty local patriclans, but also independently into two matrilineal divisions . . . It is this combination which causes alternating generations to be classed together [Lawrence 1937, 323].

> Four divisions, called "sections" if they bear names, are formed because the patrilineal moieties and the matrilineal moieties bisect each other [ibid. p. 324].

Lawrence did still more for the apotheosis of descent. Radcliffe-Brown had maintained that the section arrangement was secondary in relation to the arrangement of relationships, including marriage rules, as centered on an individual subject; in other terms, the global or *holistic* aspect (the section system) was merely a formalization of the *ego-centered* aspect (kinship as referred to one Ego). Thus, according to Radcliffe-Brown's theory of Australian kinship, the significance of the interpolation of matrilineal moieties or holistic matri-descent remained limited. Lawrence (1937, 336ff.) criticized this point and reversed the relation: the section or holistic system was primary, individual relationships secondary. This modification may have been correct, but its effect was to increase seriously the function of the interpolated holistic matri-descent in the kinship system at large. Double descent was not only the basis of a secondary holistic image of the tribe; it had become the crux of the whole of kinship. In particular, the significance of marriage rules had almost vanished, and "horde-sister exchange" was the only feature of affinity that Lawrence deemed necessary to stress (1937, 331ff.).

Lawrence's general achievement made Murdock enthusiastic to the point of forgetting Radcliffe-Brown's contribution:

> From the time of Galton their [the sections'] bilinear character had been dimly recognized. Knowledge of the subject was greatly advanced by Deacon. It remained for Lawrence . . . to clear up the entire matter in what is certainly one of the most original and significant contributions in the entire literature on social organization. . . . Lawrence is right whereas Radcliffe-

Brown has been consistently wrong. . . . Such [kinship] systems result from the interaction of patrilineal and matrilineal kin groups in the presence of moieties and rigorous exogamy. Radcliffe-Brown . . . ascribes them to the influence of kinship terminology (1949, 51–52).

It should be clear that the disagreement with Radcliffe-Brown bears only on the relation between the subsystem of sections and the kinship system at large, or between the holistic and the ego-centered aspect.

If proof is wanted that an unconscious urge or a powerful spell has acted upon one scholar after another for the triumph of one aspect of kinship over others and over the whole, it will be found in the very author who has done so much in the opposite direction. In his *Les structures élémentaires,* Lévi-Strauss devoted the better part of a chapter to putting the reader on his guard against the explanation of cross-cousin marriage in terms of double descent (1949, 138) and, in general, against the reduction of marriage rules to hypothetical descent groups:

Dans la plupart des cas . . . c'est le sociologue qui, pour rendre compte d'une loi compliquée de répartition des conjoints possibles et des conjoints prohibés, invente une hypothétique division du groupe en classes unilatérales [rather "unilinéaires"] [1949, 140–141; quoted in Goody, 1961, 9, fn.].

The laws of logic are invoked against such a procedure, and a reference to Seligman's complicated constructs is appended. What is more striking is that Lévi-Strauss (1949, 202ff.) did not apply his theory to the Kariera and Aranda directly, but accepted and elaborated Radcliffe-Brown's and Lawrence's treatment to the extent that he finally took the existence of names for the moieties for granted, thus reifying Lawrence's symbols of hypothetical groups ("A and B represent the names of moieties." Lévi-Strauss 1949, 209). On this particular point, Lévi-Strauss yielded to the song of the siren. The circumstance urges us to stuff our ears until we understand the nature of the spell.

Some writers are careful to distinguish between overt and latent features. Thus J. P. B. Josselin de Jong's recognition of latent elements is far-reaching, perhaps because he does not intend to set any store by them:

Any system of a stable number of unilineal groups intermarrying according to fixed rules is latently bilineal. When there are e.g., *n* patrilineal clans with positive rules of marriage there are also *n* latent matrilineal groups intersecting the former.

This has already been clearly demonstrated in 1935 by Van Wouden [1952, 55].

Other authors, such as Layard and Lane, maintain the distinction but deem the latent features indispensable to anthropological theory. Layard (1942, 104) distinguishes between "overt" social organization and matrilineal descent, "which is less obvious on the surface but nevertheless forms the foundation of the whole social system." He adds:

Bilateral cross-cousin marriage, when repeated in every generation, automatically gives rise to a system of matrilineal moieties . . . and, equally automatically, to a simultaneously operating system of patrilineal moieties resulting from the same set of causes [1942, 105].

Similarly, R. B. Lane remarked:

With small, relatively stable residential groups based on a unilocal principle, or with localized lineages, certain types of marriage regulations automatically create dual divisions of the society of oppposite linearity to that given recognition through residence and/or descent [1961, 16; cf. R. B. Lane and B. S. Lane 1962, 52].

The latent features thus appear as entailments of the overt features. As Lane puts it: "the [implicit] moieties are structural epiphenomena" (1961, 16). Why should such epiphenomena be considered essential to the theory? Lane justifies it by repeating that

in Australia, systems with "unnamed" or "implicit" moieties operate in precisely the same way as systems wherein these categories receive explicit recognition [1961, 16].

Whatever the precise meaning to be attached to the expression "systems . . . operate in the same way," implicit in this argument is an important premise, namely that moieties, even when implicit, are endowed with greater explanatory power, or comparative value, than features which happen to be explicit everywhere in the area. More precisely, let us distinguish what is actually given from what has been construed by the anthropologist. In both the Kariera and the Aranda cases, there are: (a) a number of named sections (or "subsections"); (b) rules of intermarriage between these sections; (c) rules that determine to which section the children of each kind of intermarriage belong. (Here the sex of the parents is distinguished; the children of an A man and a B woman and those of a B man and an A woman are classed differently.) This last feature leads the anthropologist to construe rules (c) as rules of filiation (or "descent") between father and children and between mother and children. We note here the first twist taking us from a system stated in terms of its elements [the sections, (a)], the relations between the elements [(b), intermarriage], and the recruitment into the elements [(c)], into a system based on the unilineal transmission of qualities from an individual to his children. But be this as it may, it is essential to note that rules (b) and rules (c) so construed are not independent. *Given the rule of patrilineal filiation and the rules of intermarriage, the rule of matrilineal filiation is entailed.* More generally, any two of these elements imply the third, and a choice is thus open to the anthropologist. Thus Seligman (1928, 534) proposed to reduce the "type of marriage" to "forms of descent," however complicated the latter may sometimes be. This may be legitimate, but is it economical?

Radcliffe-Brown's attitude is not so simple. He insisted that the horde or local group was composed of people related in the father's line, i.e. it was based on patrilocal residence. In the Kariera case, he noted the existence of a number of such local groups, all of which fall into two kinds only, being made up of two of the four sections into which the tribe is divided. Thus, not two local groups—the point is sometimes forgotten—but *two ideal kinds of local groups* confront each other: those composed of sections Karimera and Burung, and those made up of sections Palyeri and Banaka. They think of each other as "our side" and "the other side," and there is no reason to believe that actual local groups cannot be individually distinguished in the language by names of locality, totemic centers, etc. But the two kinds of local groups are generally taken as "unnamed." It is true that they have no *simple* names, but in the above did we not unwittingly give them names made up of two components? Is, then, a pair of names no designation for the anthropologist? Does not this designation tell us that each of them is a whole made up of two opposite and complementary parts, and not, as apparently we should prefer, a unit designated by a simple name?

Let us complete the description of the Kariera arrangement. (1) The two named sections of each observed patrilocal group represent alternating generations; if the father is Karimera, the son is Burung, the son's son Karimera, etc. We may call A and B the two "unnamed" kinds of observed local groups, A1 and A2 the alternating generation sections of A (e.g., Karimera and Burung).

(2) The marriage rule enjoins exclusive and reciprocal intermarriage between A1, A2, and the corresponding sections of the alternative kind of local group B1 and B2 (Palyeri and Banaka). This holistic system of intermarriage between two sets of two locally alternating sections can be ideally represented very simply. The diagram, fig. 27*c*, where reciprocal intermarriage is represented by the sign [=], closely follows Radcliffe-Brown's description of the patrilocal horde with its sections and their matrimonial relations. Why, then, did that scholar feel the need to recognize implicit matrilineal moieties? Let us leave aside the historical situation. First, Radcliffe-Brown was concerned with discovering general patterns of kinship in Australia, which is quite understandable. He saw such a pattern in terms of matrilineal moieties because other tribes of the class area have them, and because those systems work in the same way. Secondly, double descent was used to explain the division of each local group into two alternating generation sections, also a widespread Australian phenomenon (cf. the quotation from Lawrence above, Lawrence 1937, 323).

This is a crucial point. The logic of the explanation is that a particular Australian arrangement—alternating generations—is shown to derive from a universal or at any rate a general phenomenon, i.e. descent. Radcliffe-Brown did not invent this procedure, but he was highly conscious of the transition: "By descent I understand membership of a closed group (social segment) determined at birth by the fact that a parent belongs to that group" (1929, 200; quoted by Goody 1961, 9a). By this definition Australian sections are not descent groups. Indeed this is the point that bewilders the student of descent when he makes his first acquaintance with Australia. And it is the point that was felt to necessitate reducing the section system to what in all rigor it is not. This is very clear in Radcliffe-Brown (1929, 200; quoted by Goody 1961, 9a): "The sections are not descent groups in the ordinary sense, but the system does really include two sets of direct descent groups, often anonymous."

It is only natural that people writing at the end of the previous century, like Galton and Matthews, should have thought in this way. But it is possible now to view the question in another light. We conceive of a unilineal group as a *line,* a continuous flow of generations maintaining a substantial unity; in short, a kind of collective, and thus permanent, *individual.* Indeed, the theory of descent groups—Evans-Pritchard notwithstanding—stresses this aspect more and more, insisting on the "corporate" character of the lineage, and for this reason, going to the extreme of confusing descent with inheritance (Goody 1961, 10b and n. 15).

What confronts us in Australia is a phenomenon of a quite different kind. Here, the son's son falls into the section of his father's father, as opposed to the section of which his father and his father's son's son are members. Instead of a line, there is an alternation of two kinds of generations. Instead of a collective unity or individuality, there is a whole based on the opposition between its two complementary parts, i.e. a structure. Do we "explain" anything when we reduce a structure to a substance? At any rate, we do not understand it. The contrast between what is there and what the descent theorist sees is complete. On the one hand, it is clear that the Kariera section system is built on two complementary oppositions operating crosswise: (1) between two kinds of local groups, ideally affines to each other; (2) between two kinds of generations which bisect each local group and which, as particularized in each kind of local group, are linked one to one by intermarriage. On the other hand, the descent theorist sees a set of four semi-independent essences, which do not appear as such or display their ordinary character because they cut across each other, and which intermarry as they do only because they cannot do otherwise.

There are several arguments in favor of discarding this type of individualist logic. (1) Alternating generations, not only in themselves but as the subject of intermarriage, represent a widespread Australian phenomenon of the kind that Radcliffe-Brown and others were searching for. (2) This would hold even if alternating generations were a purely regional phenomenon, but this is not quite true; witness the ubiquity of features which bring together, in terminology as well as in behavior, grandparents and grandchildren. It would be difficult nowadays to account for the worldwide distribution of such features by hypothetical survivals of dual descent, of patrilateral cross-cousin marriage, or the like. More probably, these characteristics are aspects of a universal tendency to group together alternating generations, a tendency which would have found its perfect development in Australia. We may even risk the evolutionary surmise that alternating generations are more primitive than a continuous flow of generations. In general, it is probable that we should be well advised to reverse our inherited view and to suppose that *structure or complementarity is necessar-*

ily and historically prior to substance and individuality, and in that sense complexity is prior to, and more explanatory than, simplicity.[2] If we do not realize this more readily, it is because we remain bound to our own modes of thought and because we more often look at parts than at wholes.

Two kinds of logic are at grips. In the following I shall try to develop a few consequences of one. There are certainly some who would prefer the other, if only because the view I am advocating will thwart an easy generalization by insisting on immediately irreducible concrete or regional features, such as alternating generations. Either I am fundamentally mistaken somewhere, or descent is here a misnomer. Some other difficulties it has introduced will be reviewed below. But to insist on a feature I have alluded to, how will descent theorists account for the lack of linear genealogical time and the presence of circular genealogical time in Kariera? Study of the terminology will confirm this feature, whose recognition the descent theory has hitherto prevented. More generally, how will they account for the fact that the Kariera have names for certain things, and not for others? Lawrence (1937, 327) attributes his own formulation to the Kariera: "If savages could invent this, any civilized reader is capable of taking pencil and paper and comprehending it." The difference between the two kinds of thought is thus blurred: it appears rather that the "civilized reader" has not yet comprehended what the "savage" invented.

Symbolization: From Artificial Complication to Simplicity

Kariera

In his study of 1930 Radcliffe-Brown symbolized the Kariera section system as represented in fig. 27*a*: A, B, C, D are the sections, marriage is between A and B, C and D, the arrows mark

---

2. From this point of view, the transition proposed by Lawrence from systems with "petty local patri-clans" and matrilineal moieties to four-class systems is unlikely. He attributes it to an "innovating extension of patrilineal descent" from the above patri-clans to the whole tribe, i.e. to patrilineal moieties (1937, 323–24). This would mean that, like the anthropologist, the Australians would have cared for the parts before the whole. Since the Australians have precisely developed holistic views of their kinship systems—that is, the section systems—this would be an unreasonable surmise. See note 5 below.

matrilineal filiation or "cycles," ACA and BDB (Radcliffe-Brown 1930, 38). In this disposition, the patrilocally paired sections or "couples" are AD and BC; diagonal arrows linked them in the similar diagram of 1913, but these "patrilineal" arrows disappeared, as did the graphic representation of "patrilineal descent" in all diagrams, in 1930. This change underlines the paradox of Radcliffe-Brown's attitude as a whole. On the one hand he insisted on the basic group being the patrilocal horde; on the other, when diagraming the section system, he chose to stress increasingly the hypothetical matrilineal aspect.

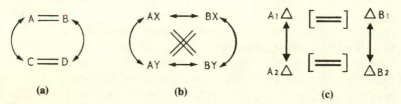

Fig. 27. Representation of the Kariera section system: **(a)** Radcliffe-Brown 1930; **(b)** Lawrence 1937; **(c)** Dumont proposal.

Lawrence refined Radcliffe-Brown's diagram in two ways (1937, 326, fig. 3). (1) He more clearly accommodated the patrilocally paired sections by bringing them on one horizontal line and linking them with arrows. As a result he represented intermarriage in the diagonals (fig. 27b). (2) He designated the hypothetical matrilineal moieties by A and B, and the "patrilineal moieties" by X and Y. Thus the sections A, D, C, B of Radcliffe-Brown were designated AX, BX, AY, BY. We see that the vertical dimension of the figure no longer corresponds to generation difference. A difference in generation is to be found between AX and BX as well as AX and AY, but not between AX and BY. It is not easy to state precisely what the letters represent in actual fact. A and B are the matrilineal moieties as they exist in other groups and are supposed to underlie this system. X and Y mark a fact of slightly different status, namely that there are only *two kinds* of local groups, but the symbols X and Y will be taken easily as representing actual local groups. This occurs in the work of Lawrence (1937, 331) when he reads AX=BY as entailing "horde-sister exchange." Actually this symbol is only consistent with such an exchange, for there are *n* local groups containing sections designated by BY, or by AX, and it is not a contradiction of the diagram for a man to marry in one Y local group and for his sister to marry in another Y local group.

I propose a different symbolization. A and B are the two kinds of local groups. They are divided into two generation sections: A1 and A2, B1 and B2. (If A1 is Karimera, A2 will stand for Burung, B1 for Palyeri, B2 for Banaka.) We may then represent reciprocal intermarriage between the sections, as symbolized by the sign [=] as it will be throughout hereafter, and their patrilocal pairing ("couples") as in fig. 27c. Women are not represented, but it is easy to reconstruct a maternal line by combining marriage and paternal filiation; the "matrilineal cycles" are diagonal: A1-B2 and B1-A2. This is a representation, close to the Kariera idea (intermarriage between sections) and practice (patrilocal residence), of the tribe as a whole. We should bear in mind that a symbol such as A1 does not represent the local group of a section, but rather the whole section as dispersed into a number of local groups.

Aranda

The Aranda possess four kinds of local groups instead of two, but each local group is divided into two generation sections as among the Kariera. The tribe is therefore made up of eight sections (or "subsections") instead of four. Radcliffe-Brown (1930, 39), who was eager to stress the fact that each Kariera section is here, so to speak, split into two, termed the Aranda divisions "subsections." In his diagram of the system (cf. fig. 28a) he used the symbols A1, A2, etc., for "subsections" and indicated matrilineal filiation by arrows. The patrilocal "couples" were given as follows: A1D2, A2D1, B1C1, B2C2. The irregular form of these "couples" is enough to condemn the formulation. The ordinary meaning of the vertical dimension in such figures is jeopardized, and the only intimation that the system is a holistic or closed one lies in the circular form of the "matrilineal cycles."

As he did for Kariera, Lawrence modified this diagram by bringing each patrilocal couple of sections on one horizontal line; marriage is shown obliquely (1937, 326, fig. 7). He then called the supposed matrilineal moieties A and B, while designating the four kinds of local groups P, Q, R, S. Each of the latter, in his view, was bisected into two generation sections by the operation of matrilineal descent; thus P was divided into two sections, AP and BP (fig. 28b). Compared to 28a, the matrilineal bias is maintained and the "cycle" is clearer, but the supposed logical link with the Kariera

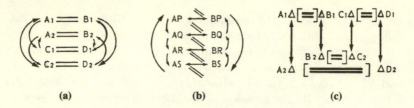

Fig. 28. Representation of the Aranda section system: (a) Radcliffe-Brown; (b) Lawrence; (c) Dumont proposal.

system is omitted; graphically, the chain of intermarriage is broken at both ends.

Let us call A, B, C, D the four kinds of Aranda local groups, and distinguish by 1 and 2 the opposed generations. The eight Aranda sections will be A1, A2; B1, B2; etc. Now, it may easily be verified (e.g. from Lawrence's diagram) that the difference with Kariera as regards intermarriage consists in the fact that the two generation sections of one local group *marry not in the same, but in two different kinds of local group.* If we assume that A1 intermarries with B1 and C1 with D1, it follows that A2 intermarries not with B2, but with D2 [it could be C2] and C2 with B2 [if not with D2]. This disposition is diagrammatically represented by fig. 28c. It is true that "matrilineal cycles," though easy to construct (A1, B2, C1, D2, A1 and A2, D1, C2, B1, A2), do not take a regular shape in this figure.

From fig. 28c, the Aranda section system is seen as linking by symmetrical intermarriage four kinds of patrilocal groups, as Kariera does for two only. The Aranda system thus accomplishes what has been declared impossible by some anthropologists, and it does it—a feat also declared impossible by some—by enjoining different intermarriages to alternate generations. We thus take a unified view of both systems by regarding them as holistic systems of intermariage between generation sections paired in patrilocal groups.

What is the equivalent picture offered by the double descent theory? This theory considers the whole system exclusively in terms of hypothetical moieties, and consequently it views inter-marriage not as an effective link between sections, but only as the negative corollary of descent; not as a positive rule, but as the residue of negative rules. According to this theory, in our fig. 28c A plus C on the one hand, B plus D on the other, form the equivalent of the Kariera "patrilineal moieties." Marriage between them is therefore impossible. But what is new in Aranda is that A2 does not marry in B2 but exclusively in D2. How is this to be explained? Radcliffe-Brown would refer us back to individual marriage rules: in this system Ego may not marry his MBD but only his MMBDD; as a member of A2 he may not marry in B2 but only in D2. Lawrence, on the contrary, holds that the section system is primary, and he is therefore reduced to state that: "a man is forbidden to marry, not only into the two patri-cycles constituting his own patrilineal moiety [i.e., A and C], *but also into one of the patri-cycles* [i.e., B] *of the opposite moiety*" (1937, 328, my italics). In my view, this statement in apparently innocuous anthropological jargon condemns the whole theory, for it does not in the least follow from the descent theory that such should be the marriage rule. Actually the statement is self-contradictory, for what is a "moiety" which does not exhaust the (patrilineal) ban on intermarriage? It is possible that Murdock perceived this, for he offers a different formula:

> [In the "eight-class system"] each section is subdivided into two *subsections*. This results from the imposition of an exogamous taboo upon one's mother's patrilineal kinsmen, which is extended throughout the society to form a third moiety dichotomy. This third exogamous dichotomy divides the members of each section into two groups, those belonging to one of the third pair of moieties and those belonging to the other [1949, 54].

I feel this is a monument to be left untouched for the glory of the double—or triple—descent theory. The weakness of the position is demonstrated by the necessity of relying upon a fresh set of "moieties," whether definable or not, to account for the passage from four to eight sections. Actually the patrilineal moiety hypothesis breaks down in the Aranda case, as is clearly seen from Lawrence's statement. The Aranda possess four kinds of local groups, where Kariera have only two; that is all. Murdock's statement demonstrates the extremities to which one may be driven when refusing to look at intermarriage as a positive phenomenon. Finally, it appears that descent, even under its holistic form (moieties), cannot account for these systems as wholes. The descent theorist can only represent matrilineal descent "cycling" through the generations, but this substantial and diachronic holism is a poor substitute for the synchronic and structural holism of the people themselves, who see the whole as made up of elements paired in local groups and *all linked together* by a *regular* chain of intermarriage.

It is true that the present theory does not account for the number of groups, but given the number of groups, it does account for the particular marriage rule as the only one that can link symmetrically all the groups into one whole. As to the passage from Kariera to Aranda, we can also diagram it simply. If the principle is set that A1 and A2 should marry in different patrilocal groups, then A2 can marry only in a different subdivision of B; i.e. the B kind of patrilocal group must split into two, and the same holds reciprocally for A. Let us call the subdivisions Aα and Aβ, Bα and Bβ. Then if Aα1 marries in Bα1, Aα2 will marry in Bβ2, etc. (fig. 29a). The

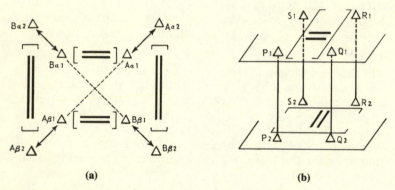

(a)   (b)

Fig. 29. Aranda section system: **(a)** transition from Kariera to Aranda; **(b)** alternation of intermarriage in alternate generations.

alternation of intermarriage in alternate generations is perhaps more graphically apparent in Fig. 29b, where the two horizontal planes correspond to the generations and the four local groups are labeled P1-2, Q1-2, R1-2, S1-2 (if P corresponds to Aα, R stands for Aβ, etc.).

Ambrym

Our mode of representation is immediately applicable to the Ambrym (Balap) scheme as represented in the sand by Deacon's informant (1927, diagram 4). The informant depicts three patrilocal groups, each divided into two generation sections in the Australian fashion. Compared to the Aranda (fig. 29*b*) we have in each generation a triangle instead of a parallelogram. It is impossible to relate the three groups by intermarriage in the same generation, for at least one intermarriage between different generations is necessary (e.g., A1 = B1, A2 = C2, and B2 = C1). By reasons of the odd number of groups, a regular formula entails a difference of generation *in each intermarriage, say:* A1 = B2, B1 = C2, C1 = A2 (fig. 30*c*). This is what Deacon's informant drew in the sand. Of course the difference of generation is not between individuals, but between the generation sections of the three groups.

It is tempting to diagram such holistic systems as the three we have studied in the form of a circle.[3] In fig. 30 the systems are reduced to their essentials, with *a* representing Kariera, *b* Aranda (North), and *c* Ambrym (Balap). The three systems appear graphically as variations on the same theme, linking by a regular chain of intermarriage the alternate sections of two, four, and three patrilocal groups. For those who may be interested, the supposed or implied "matrilineal cycles" are easy to draw: they will be two

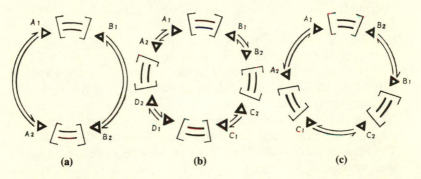

(a)	**(b)**	**(c)**

Fig. 30. Comparative structure of three section systems: **(a)** with two patrilocal units—Kariera; **(b)** with four patrilocal units—Aranda; **(c)** with three patrilocal units—Ambrym.

3. This form of diagram is not new. It was used by Deacon, Layard, Lawrence, and Lane. Yet the differences are obvious. For instance Lawrence in his fig. 10 (1937, 343) aims at a circular presentation of the "matrilineal cycles" among the Aranda. Intermarriage is indeed shown, but it appears in consequence as oblique. Furthermore, Lawrence superimposes on this holistic picture a distribution of the relatives of an Ego located in one of the sections, i.e. an ego-centered point of view.

diameters in the Kariera figure, two inscribed squares running in opposite directions for the Aranda, and two equilateral triangles for Ambrym.

The Murngin Section System

The Murngin kinship system has proved a very controversial ground for the exercise of anthropological theory. This is therefore the most tentative part of the present study. Yet, while limiting myself once more to the section system, it so happens that an hypothesis of Lévi-Strauss allows for linking this case clearly to the preceding ones. As described by Webb (1933) and others, the Murngin possess eight sections ("subsections") grouped into two patrilineal moieties. I accept the view of the eight Murngin sections as having derived from a binary division of the four sections of a system of Kariera type, and I shall symbolize them accordingly; thus Kariera A1 will be replaced here by two sections, A1a and A1b. The individual marriage rule is that a man marries his matrilateral cross cousin. In terms of sections there are said to be two kinds of marriage (Elkin 1933), one "regular," say between A1a and B1a, the other "alternate," between A1a and B1b, with the child of an A1a man belonging to A2a (by hypothesis) in the first case, and to A2b in the second.

This is where Lévi-Strauss's brilliant hypothesis comes in: he found a simple way of conciliating the individual marriage rule with the complicated rule of marriage and filiation in terms of sections. It consists in supposing that "regular" and "alternate" marriages must alternate (in a male line) with the generations (1949, 223–24). The hypothesis fits in well with the present approach, as we have seen alternate generations making in one way or another alternate marriages. Of course, matrilateral cross-cousin marriage entails that a brother and a sister should make different, here alternate marriages (one "regular," the other "alternate"). As opposed to the previous cases, we are dealing with a case of asymmetrical intermarriage; a given group takes its wives from one group and gives wives to another. Accordingly in the diagrams the signs by which we represent marriage will bear arrows, and a Murngin section will be seen as receiving wives from one section of the opposite moiety and giving wives to another.

The following questions immediately arise: (1) How far does a Murngin system automatically result from a Kariera system if it is prescribed that intermarriage be asymmetrical instead of symmetrical? (2) There are two forms of asymmetrical intermarriage, corresponding respectively to matrilateral and patrilateral cross-cousin marriage; given their general properties, the patrilateral form would be more likely than the matrilateral to issue directly from a symmetrical arrangement once asymmetry is prescribed. How is it that this is not the case here? (3) If Lévi-Strauss is right, it remains to be explained why the rule he discovered is not actually formulated by the Murngin, and why the two types of marriage can be described (by the anthropologist but no doubt somewhat in keeping with the Murngin view) as "regular" and "alternate."

The answer to the first question is simple. The Kariera sections must split into two once asymmetrical instead of symmetrical marriage is prescribed, since if a man of A1a takes his wife from B1a, then he must give his sister to a group which, while belonging to the same generation in the opposite moiety, i.e. belonging to B1, must be different from B1a, and must therefore be B1b. With respect to patrilineal filiation, if the eight sections are to remain distinct and not be reduced to four, the section in which a man marries must be relevant to the classification of his children. It can be so only if the alternate marriage brings the issue into the alternate section of the same generation; that is, if the child of a "regular" marriage of a man of A1a is in A2a, the child of an "alternate" marriage of the same man must be A2b, as there is no other possibility.

Everything will become clearer with the help of a diagram (fig. 31). The two moieties are A and B, the two alternate generations 1 and 2. Let horizontal lines correspond to "regular" intermarriage, which will allow us to posit A1a and A1b (corresponding for instance to Ngarit and Bulain) and, facing them, B1a and B1b (Balang and Buralang). We shall designate by A2a the section corresponding to the children of the "regular" marriage of a man of A1a (and similarly for the rest), and represent this "regular" paternal filiation *starting from generation 1* by vertical lines. Thus in the diagram A2a and A2b will represent respectively Bangardi and Kaijark, B2a and B2b Karmarung and Warmut. The words in italics are essential, for we shall see that the relation between marriage and filiation is reversed in generation 2; there, "alternate" marriage brings about vertical, or "regular" filiation.

Henceforth, in accordance with the diagram, we shall call horizontal marriage "straight" instead of "regular," and apply the

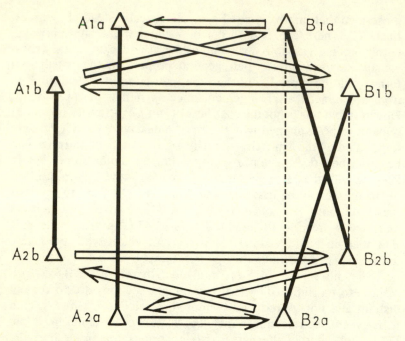

Fig. 31. Asymmetrical intermarriage in an eight-section system (one-half of the hypothetical Murngin system).

same word to vertical filiation. The alternate type of marriage will be termed "oblique" instead of "alternate," and similarly the nonvertical filiation. The existence of alternate marriages makes it impossible to represent the system as a whole on a simple diagram. If we start with A1a and consider only the case of the men of A1a who have made a straight marriage (horizontal arrow from B1a to A1a), we observe that this entails that their sisters should be given in marriage to B1b and so on. A whole chain of intermarriage in generation 1 is thus determined. The filiation of the children born of those marriages will be as on fig. 31: straight in moiety A, oblique in moiety B. The marriages in generation 2 are determined from our hypothesis, alternating in each case with the marriage of the father in generation 1. As the man in A1a has made a straight marriage, his son in A2a will make an oblique marriage. The direction of all arrows is reversed in generation 2. What is remarkable is that the filiation thus determined brings the children of generation 2 into the same section from which we started in

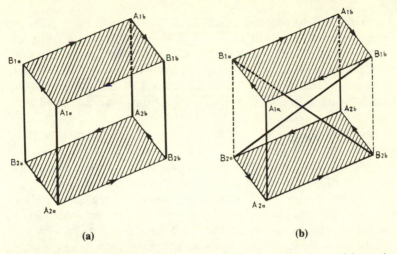

Fig. 32. Asymmetrical marriage alternating with generations in an eight-section system: **(a)** patrilateral cross-cousin marriage; **(b)** matrilateral cross-cousin marriage.

generation 1: the son's son is in the same section as his father's father. This result increases the likelihood of the initial assumption that marriage should alternate with the generations.

Examination of the second question requires that we ponder the asymmetry of our diagram: filiation is straight in A, oblique in B. It would be the reverse if we started from the opposite case of the men of A1a making oblique marriages. Indeed we should juxtapose the two pictures in order to represent the system as a whole. This asymmetry in the diagram obviously relates to the difficulty of producing a continuous and oriented pattern (matrilateral cross-cousin marriage) when starting from a symmetrical system of moieties. It can be demonstrated that a symmetrical diagram would correspond to patrilateral cross-cousin marriage. Let us represent the sections as we did for the Aranda (fig. 32a), and introduce in generation 1 a chain of asymmetrical intermarriage (the arrows). To introduce alternate intermarriage in generation 2, the only possibility is to reverse the arrows. But this is the classical diagram corresponding to patrilateral cross-cousin marriage; in terms of the nearest relatives, a man in A2a receives a wife from the line in which his father's sister was married, i.e., a FZD (and the same will be true of his son in A1a). If we wish to modify this in order to produce matrilateral cross-cousin marriage, the only solution at

our disposal is to proceed as in Fig. 32*b*. Let us bring in B2a, not
the children of B1a, but those of B1b, and the man in A2a will
marry a girl from the group from which his father has received his
wife, that is, a MBD. The *lines of filiation must cross* in one moiety
if they are straight in the other in order that the prescription of
alternate marriages in alternate generations may not produce a
patrilateral formula.

One of the three questions we asked at the outset remains. If the
system works ideally as we have described it, the rule that
marriage should alternate with generations in a male line explains
the rules of patrilineal filiation, and in particular the apparently
strange reversal in the relation between straight and oblique
marriage and straight and oblique filiation from one generation to
the other. How is it then that the Murngin themselves do not
simply state that marriage should alternate with generations? I
shall not provide a straightforward answer to this question, but
only observe that the paradox is related to a built-in discrepancy
between the manner in which a *particular situation* is seen in the
system as a whole, and as a relation between male lines.

In the first place, that such a system compels one to consider
particular situations is clear from the preceding analysis. In order
to devise the diagram (fig. 31), we had to start with one of the two
possibilities for the marriage of a man of A1a. Had we insisted on
representing the two possibilities at the same time, we should have
superimposed on fig. 31 a figure symmetrical to it. The result
would have been a diagram with double arrows and with both
straight and oblique types of filiation combined in both moieties.
However, this would have represented only the sum total of what
happens in the system and would have blurred its distinctive
asymmetry.

Now, to examine a particular situation, let us look at that of B2b
in fig. 31. A discrepancy arises, according to the way we look at it.
In terms of straight and oblique marriage, B2 alternates with B1, as
it receives in the straight line, and gives in the oblique line.
Absolutely, that is, the marriages of B2b can be said to alternate
with the marriages of B1a and B1b. But *this is not true in terms of
actual patrilineal filiation,* for the man in B2b gives to A2a just as
his father B1a gave to A1a, and he takes from A2b just as his father
did from A1b—and of course this continuity is essential in matrilateral cross-cousin marriage. What is *absolutely* an alternate marriage is thus at the same time an identical marriage in terms of the

particular patrilineal *filiation*. This discrepancy also relates to the fact that oblique marriage in generation 2 produces the same kind of filiation as straight marriage in generation 1 (in the case of fig. 31, straight filiation in A and oblique filiation in B). Taking all this together, we come to understand that the Murngin do not see marriages as purely and simply alternating in alternate generations. The "regular" form is regular in terms of the section makeup, but practiced alone it would reduce the whole to a Kariera system; the "alternate" form is entailed for an eight-section system by the existence of the asymmetrical prescription, but it appears in patrifiliation not as alternating with but as parallel to the "regular" form.[4]

Conclusion

Intermarriage between sections can be looked at either as a positive link which, together with the paternal pairing, unites all sections into a whole, or as the negative residue of real or hypothetical unilineal transmission of membership in holistic exogamous groups. We saw that the latter view failed in the case of the Aranda. It is still more clearly impotent in the case of the Murngin and the transition from the Kariera to the Murngin, which can be understood only by opposing two types of intermarriage, symmetrical and asymmetrical.

I have stressed intermarriage between sections in preference to hypothetical holistic matrilineal descent. This has led me to stress the generation section or "marriage class" as the real agent in those holistic systems; in other words, I have emphasized the alternation of generations as a basic feature, not to be reduced to others. The sections (including the so-called "subsections") are the agents of group intermarriage, and it is in terms of such

---

4. [1981 note.] In relation to the distinction between *local* or individual rule of marriage and *global* model of intermarriage (see previous chapter *in fine*) we noted above the discrepancy between the two aspects in the Murngin case. A similar discrepancy is present in Ambrym regarding the generations. We have thus two cases where the introduction of a new, particular or supplementary feature (an odd number of local groups in Ambrym, the matrilateral rule with the Murngin) brings about discord between global model and local view. The global (symmetrical) model cannot any more transcribe adequately the local situation.

intermarriage alone that the four systems can be considered as wholes and as logically related to each other. The device of reduplicated holistic descent offers only an *Ersatz* analysis in terms of self-sufficient substances, in contrast to the conception of a whole in terms of complementary relations, a conception in which the anthropologist is simply emulating the Australian or Australoid aborigines.[5]

Postscript

I should like to emphasize the limits of this study, as indicated at the beginning. Its intention was critical, and I have attempted to reconstruct only up to a point. Thus I have kept from the literature the term "section," but not that of "subsection." On one point, we have even strayed from the indigenous representation for the sake of immediate practicality: we have expressed as subdivisions (A1, A2) the named categories (Karimera, Burung); to follow the Kariera closely, we should posit: Karimera = A, Burung, = B, A + B for the ideal local group, and symbolize, if need be, the local dimension *on a distinct level*.

More importantly, the study is based only on the literature, sometimes secondhand. Yet, beyond the tendencies of the literature, there are the factual data. For instance, in an unpublished critique, Lorenz G. Löffler has, among other things, used the irregular marriages as showing that the filiation to the mother is fundamental for the classification of the offspring, cf. his published article (Löffler 1966). The full dimension and complexity of the problem will best be seen from a monograph of Mervyn J. Meggitt on the Walbiri of Central Australia (Meggitt 1965), for on the one hand one will find there many arguments to be opposed to the present thesis, but on the other hand one might also ask how far the description itself is independent of the presuppositions that are here criticized.

5. It will be objected that the Australians are also aware of moieties in other groups. But we are not concerned with developing a construct of an Australian tribe which would epitomize everything that is found within the "class-area." In the context the absence of simple names for Kariera patri-moieties should be explained. It would seem that Australians nowhere recognize a *double* set of moieties; it is as if one explicit dichotomy excluded the other. A possible reason for this is obvious, since intermarrying units are sufficiently defined in one line. Among Kariera, everything looks as if the four named sections excluded the possibility of named moieties, i.e. functionally replaced them.

Works Cited

Aiyappan, A. 1932. "Polyandry." *Man,* art. 337.

———. 1937. *Social and Physical Anthropology of the Nayadis of Malabar.* Bulletin of the Madras Government Museum, n.s., General Section, 2/4. Madras.

———. 1944. *Iravas and Culture Change.* Bulletin of the Madras Government Museum, n.s., General Section, 5/1. Madras.

Anantakrishna Iyer, L. K. 1912. *The Cochin Tribes and Castes,* 2. Madras.

Baden-Powell, B. H. 1896. *The Indian Village Community.* London.

Barnes, R. H. 1975. "Editor's Introduction." In J. Kohler, *On the Prehistory of Marriage,* translated from the German by R. H. Barnes and Ruth Barnes, pp. 3–70. Chicago.

Barnett, Steve. 1976. "Coconuts and Gold: Relational Identity in a South Indian Caste." *Contributions to Indian Sociology* n.s. 10/1 (January–June 1976):133–56.

Beck, Brenda E. F. 1972. *Peasant Society in Koṅku: A Study of Right and Left Subcastes in South India.* Vancouver.

Bernot, Lucien. 1965. "Lévirat et Sororat." *L'Homme* 5/3–4:101–12.

Blunt, E. A. M. 1931. *The Caste System of Northern India, with*

Special Reference to the United Provinces of Agra and Oudh. London.

Bouglé, C. 1908. *Essais sur le régime des castes.* Travaux de l'Année Sociologique. Paris.

Briffault, Robert. 1927. *The Mothers.* 3 vols. Vol 1. London.

Buchler, Ira R. 1967. "Analyse formelle des terminologies de parenté iroquoises." *L'Homme* 7/1: 5–31.

Bühler, G. 1886. *The Laws of Manu, Translated with Extracts from Seven Commentaries.* The Sacred Books of the East 25. Oxford.

Burling, Robbins. 1962. "A Structural Restatement of Njamal Terminology." *Man* 62, art. 201:122–24.

Carter, A. T. 1974. "A Comparative Analysis of Systems of Kinship and Marriage in South Asia." *Proceedings of the Royal Anthropological Institute for 1973,* pp. 29–54.

Conklin, Harold C. 1969. "Lexicographic Treatment of Folk Taxonomies." In St. A. Tyler (ed.), *Cognitive Anthropology,* pp. 41–59. New York.

Contributions to Indian Sociology. 1957–59. Vols. 1–3. L. Dumont and D. Pocock, eds. Paris, The Hague.

Crooke, William. 1896. *Popular Religion and Folklore of Northern India.* Delhi.

———. 1906. Art. "Dravidians (North India)." In *Encyclopedia of Religion and Ethics,* vol. 5.

Current Anthropology. 1966. CA* Book review of Louis Dumont, *Une sous-caste* and *Hierarchy and Marriage Alliance. Current Anthropology* 7/3: 327–46.

David, Kenneth. 1973. "Until Marriage Do Us Part: A Cultural Account of Jaffna Tamil Categories for Kinsman." *Man* n.s. 8/4 (December 1973):521–35.

Davis, Kingsley. 1941. "Intermarriage in Caste Society." *American Anthropologist* 43:376–95.

Deacon, A. Bernard. 1927. "The Regulation of Marriage in Ambrym." *Journal of the Royal Anthropological Institute* 57:325–42.

Derrett, J. Duncan M. 1960. "Law and the Predicament of the Hindu Joint Family." *Economic Weekly* (Bombay), pp. 305–11.

Dumont, Louis 1950. "Kinship and Alliance among the Pramalai Kallar." *Eastern Anthropologist* 4.

———. 1953a. "The Dravidian Kinship Terminology as an Expression of Marriage." *Man* 53, art. 54.

————. 1953*b*. "Dravidian Kinship Terminology" (Reply to A. R. Radcliffe-Brown). *Man* 53, art. 224.

————. 1957*a*. *Hierarchy and Marriage Alliance in South Indian Kinship*. Occasional Papers of the Royal Anthropological Institute, 12. London.

————. 1957*b*. *Une sous-caste de l'Inde du Sud*. Paris, The Hague.

————. 1960. "Le mariage secondaire dans l'Inde du Nord." *6e congrès international des sciences anthropologiques et ethnologiques* 2:53–55.

————. 1961. "Marriage in India: the Present State of the Question. 1. Marriage Alliance in S.E. India and Ceylon." *Contributions to Indian Sociology* 5:75–95.

————. 1962. "Le vocabulaire de parenté dans l'Inde du Nord." *L'Homme* 2/2:5–48.

————. 1964. "Marriage in India: The Present State of the Question. Postscript to Part One; 2. Marriage and status, Nayar and Newar." *Contributions to Indian Sociology* 7:77–98.

————. 1966. "Marriage in India: The Present State of the Question. 3. North India in relation to South India." *Contributions to Indian Sociology* 9:90–114.

————. 1968. "Marriage Alliance." *International Encyclopedia of the Social Sciences* 10:19–23.

————. 1971. *Introduction à deux théories d'anthropologie sociale: Groupes de filiation et Alliance de Mariage*. Paris, The Hague.

————. 1975*a*. *Dravidien et Kariera: L'alliance de mariage dans l'Inde du Sud et en Australie*. Ecole des Hautes Etudes en Sciences Sociales. Textes de Sciences sociales, 14. Paris, The Hague.

————. 1975*b*. "Terminology and Prestations revisited." *Contributions to Indian Sociology* n.s. 9/2:197–215.

————. 1980. *Homo Hierarchicus: An Essay on the Caste System*. (First English edition 1970; original French edition 1967.)

Elkin, A. P. 1933. "Marriage and Descent in East Arnhem Land." *Oceania* 3:412–15.

————. 1953. "Murngin Kinship Re-examined and Remarks on Some Generalizations." *American Anthropologist* 55:412–19.

Emeneau, M. B. 1937. "Toda Marriage Regulations and Taboos." *American Anthropologist* 39:103–12.

————. 1941. "Language and Social Forms: A study of Toda Kinship Terms and Dual Descent." In Leslie Spier, A. Irving

Hallowell, and Stanley S. Newman (eds.), *Language, Culture and Personality: Essays in Memory of Edward Sapir,* pp. 158–79. Menasha, Wis.

Epling, P. J. 1961. "A Note on Njamal Kin-Term Usage." *Man* 61, art. 184.

Fawcett, F. 1901. *Nayars of Malabar.* Bulletin of the Madras Government Museum, 3/3:179–322.

———. 1903. "The Kondayamkottai Maravars: A Dravidian Tribe of Tinnevelly, Southern India." *Journal of the Royal Anthropological Institute* 33:57–65.

Fox, Robin 1967. *Kinship and Marriage: An anthropological Perspective.* Penguin Books.

Francis, W. 1914. *Madura,* 1. Madras District Gazetteers. Madras.

Fruzzetti, Lina, Ákos Östör, and Steve Barnett. 1976. "The Cultural Construction of the Person in Bengal and Tamil Nadu." *Contributions to Indian Sociology* n.s. 10/1:157–82.

Fuller, C. J. 1975. "The Internal Structure of the Nayar Caste." *Journal of Anthropological Research* 31/4:283–312.

———. 1976a. *The Nayars Today.* Cambridge.

———. 1976b. "Kerala Christians and the Caste System." *Man* n.s. 11:53–70.

Fürer-Haimendorf, Christoph von. 1956. "Elements of Newar Social Structure." *Journal of the Royal Anthropological Institute* 86, part 2:15–38.

———. 1960. "Caste in the Multi-Ethnic Society of Nepal." *Contributions to Indian Sociology* 4:12–32.

Goodenough, Ward H. 1965. "Yankee Kinship Terminology: A Problem in Componential Analysis." *American Anthropologist,* 67/5, part 2: 259–87.

———. 1970. "Analysis of the Kariera Kinship Terminology." In *Description and Comparison in Cultural Anthropology,* pp. 131–42. Chicago.

Goody, Jack 1959. "The Mother's Brother and the Sister's Son in West Africa." *Journal of the Royal Anthropological Institute* 89/1:61–88.

———. 1961. "The Classification of Double Descent Systems." *Current Anthropology* 2:3–12.

Gough, E. Kathleen. 1952. "Changing Kinship Usages in the Setting of Political and Economic Change among the Nayars of Malabar." *Journal of the Royal Anthropological Institute* 82, part 1:71–87.

———. 1955. "Female Initiation Rites on the Malabar Coast."
Journal of the Royal Anthropological Institute 85:45–80.

———. 1956. "Brahman Kinship in a Tamil Village." *American Anthropologist* 58/5:826–53.

——— 1959*a*. "The Nayars and the Definition of Marriage."
Journal of the Royal Anthropological Institute 89, part 1: 23–34.

———. 1959*b*. "Cults of the Dead among the Nayars." In M. Singer (ed.), *Traditional India, Structure and Change,* pp. 240–72. Philadelphia.

———. 1959*c*. Review of "Une Sous-caste de l'Inde du Sud."
Man, art. 323.

———. 1965. "A Note on Nayar Marriage." *Man,* art. 2.

———. 1979. "Dravidian Kinship and Modes of Production."
Contributions to Indian Sociology n.s. 13/2, 1979: 265–91.

Granet, Marcel 1929. *La civilisation chinoise: La vie publique et la vie privée.* Paris. (English translation, *Chinese Civilization* by Kathleen E. Innes & Mabel R. Bradsford. London, 1930.)

Held, G. J. 1935. *The Mahābhārata: An Ethnological Study.* London, Amsterdam.

Hocart, A. M. 1937. "Kinship Systems." *Anthropos* 32:545–51. Reprinted in the *Life-Giving Myth* (London, 1952), p. 173.

———. 1938. *Les Castes.* Annales Musée Guimet, 54. Paris.

———. 1952. *The Northern States of Fiji.* Occasional Papers of the Royal Anthropological Institute, 11. London.

Hutton, J. H. 1946. *Caste in India: Its Nature, Function, and Origins.* Cambridge.

Innes, L. A. 1908. *Malabar.* Madras District Gazetteers. New ed. Madras, 1951.

Jagor, Fedor. 1914. *Aus Fedor Jagors Nachlass.* Vol. 1. *Südindische Volksstämme.* Berlin.

Jolly, Julius. 1896. *Recht und Sitte (einschliesslich der einheimischen Literatur).* Grundriss der Indo-Arischen Philologie und Altertumskunde, 2/8. Strasbourg.

Josselin de Jong, J. P. B. 1952. *Lévi-Strauss's Theory of Kinship and Marriage.* Leiden.

Kane, P. V. 1946. *History of Dharmaśāstra,* 3. Poona.

Kaplan, Joanna Overing. 1973. "Endogamy and the Marriage Alliance: A Note on Continuity in Kindred-based Groups." *Man* 8/4:555–70.

Kay, Paul. 1967. "On the Multiplicity of Cross/Parallel Distinctions." *American Anthropologist* 69:83–85.

Kirchhoff, P. 1932. "Verwandtschaftsbezeichnungen und Verwandtenheirat." *Zeitschrift für Ethnologie* 64:41–72.

Kirkpatrick, W. 1811. *An Account of the Kingdom of Nepal.* London.

Kulandaiveluccami, V. S., and A. V. Acirvada Udaiyarttevar. 1938. *maRavar çarittiram.* (Maravar History, in Tamil.) Srivaikuntham.

Lane, R. B. 1961. "Comment on Goody 1961." *Current Anthropology* 2:15–17.

Lane, R. B., and B. S. Lane. 1962. "Implicit Double Descent in Southeast Australia and the Northeastern New Hebrides." *Ethnology* 1:46–52.

Lawrence, William Ewart. 1937. "Alternating Generations in Australia." In *Studies in the Science of Society,* ed. G. P. Murdock, pp. 319–54. New Haven.

Layard, John. 1942. *Stone Men of Malekula: Vao.* London.

Leach, Edmund R. 1951. "The Structural Implications of Matrilateral Cross-Cousin Marriage." *Journal of the Royal Anthropological Institute.* 81:22–55.

———. 1970. "A Critique of Yalman's Interpretation of Sinhalese Girl's Puberty Ceremonial." In J. Pouillon et P. Maranda (eds.), *Echanges et Communications: Mélanges offerts à C. Lévi-Strauss.* The Hague.

Lévi-Strauss, Claude. 1949. *Les structures élémentaires de la parenté.* Paris.

———. 1962. *La pensée sauvage.* Paris. English translation, *The Savage Mind.* (Chicago, 1966).

Löffler, Lorenz G. 1966. "Klassensystem und Adoptionszeremonien bei den Aranda." *Zeitschrift für Ethnologie* 91:50–67.

Lounsbury, Floyd G. 1956. "A Semantic Analysis of Pawnee Kinship Usage." *Language* 32:158–94.

———. 1964. "The Structural Analysis of Kinship Semantics." *Proceedings of the Ninth International Congress of Linguists,* pp. 1073–93. The Hague.

Lovejoy, Arthur. 1973. *The Great Chain of Being.* Oxford.

Lowie, R. H. 1928. "A Note on Relationship Terminologies." *American Anthropologist* 30:263–67.

———. 1950 [1948]. *Social Organization.* London.

Marriott, McKim. 1976. "Hindu Transactions: Diversity without Dualism." In Bruce Kapferer (ed.), *Transaction and Meaning,*

A. S. A. Essays in Social Anthropology, vol. 1. Philadelphia: ISHI, 1976.

Mayne, John D. 1938. *A Treatise on Hindu Law and Usage*. Edited by S. Srinivasa Iyengar. Madras.

Meggitt, Mervyn J. 1965. *Desert People*. Chicago.

Meile, Pierre. 1945. *Introduction au tamoul. An Introduction to Tamil*. Paris.

Mencher, Joan P. 1966. "Nambudiri Brahmans: An Analysis of a Traditional Elite in Kerala." *Journal of Asian and African Studies* 1966/1:183–96.

Mencher, Joan P., and Helen Goldberg. 1967. "Kinship and Marriage Regulation among the Nambudiri Brahmans of Kerala." *Man* 2/1:87–106.

Morgan, Lewis H. 1871. *Systems of Consanguinity and Affinity of the Human Family*. Smithsonian Contributions to Knowledge, 17. Washington, D.C.

————. 1877. *Ancient Society*, pp. 424–52. London.

Mousset and Dupuis 1938. *Dictionnaire tamoul-français*. Pondicherry.

Murdock, George Peter 1947. "Bifurcate Merging: A Test of Five Theories." *American Anthropologist* 49:56–68.

————. 1949. *Social Structure*. New York.

Needham, Rodney. 1958. "The Formal Analysis of Prescriptive Patrilateral Cross-cousin Marriage." *Southern Journal of Anthropology* 14/2:199–219.

Nelson, J. H. 1868. *The Madura Country: A Manual Compiled by Order of the Madras Government*. 5 parts. Part 2. Madras.

Niggemeyer, Hermann. 1933. "Totemismus in Vorderindien". *Anthropos* 28:407–61, 579–619.

Pate, H. R. 1917. *Tinnevelly*, 1. Madras District Gazetteers. Madras.

Radcliffe-Brown, A. R. 1913. "Three Tribes of Western Australia." *Journal of the Royal Anthropological Institute* 43:143–94.

————. 1929. "Bilateral Descent." *Man* 29:199–200.

————. 1930. "The Social Organization of Australian Tribes." *Oceania* 1:34–63, 206–46, 322–41, 426–56.

————. 1950. "Introduction." In A. R. Radcliffe-Brown and Daryll Forde, (eds.) *African Systems of Kinship and Marriage*. London.

————. 1952. *Structure and Function in Primitive Society*. London.

————. 1953. "Dravidian Kinship Terminology." *Man* 53, art. 169.

Rao, M. Kodanda 1973. "Rank Difference and Marriage Reciprocity in South India: An Aspect of Implications of Elder's Sister Daughter Marriage." *Contributions to Indian Sociology* n.s. 7:16–35.

Rivers, W. H. R. 1907. "The Marriage of Cross Cousins in India." *Journal of the Royal Asiatic Society,* pp. 611–40.

———— 1914. *Kinship and Social Organization.* London.

Romney, A. K., and P. J. Epling. 1958. "A Simplified Model of Kariera Kinship." *American Anthropologist* 60:59–74.

Scheffler, Harold W. 1970. "The Elementary Structure of Kinship by Claude Lévi-Strauss: A review article." *American Anthropologist* 72/2:251–68.

————. 1971. "Dravidian-Iroquois: The Melanesian Evidence." In L. R. Hiatt and C. Jayawardena (eds.) *Anthropology in Oceania. Essays Presented to Ian Hogbin,* pp. 231–54. Sydney.

————. 1977. "Kinship and Alliance in South India and Australia (review article)." *American Anthropologist* 79/4:869–82.

Schneider, David M. 1968. *American Kinship: A Cultural Account.* Englewood Cliffs, N.J.

Schneider, David M., and Kathleen Gough, eds. 1961. *Matrilineal Kinship.* Berkeley.

Seligman, Brenda S. 1928. "Assymetry in Descent with Special Reference to Pentecost." *Journal of the Royal Anthropological Institute* 58:533–58.

Senart, Emile. 1896. *Les castes dans l'Inde: Les faits et le système.* Paris.

Service, Elman R. 1960. "Sociocentric Relationship Terms and the Australian Class System." In G. E. Dole and R. L. Carneiro (eds.), *Essays in the Science of Culture in Honor of Leslie A. White,* pp. 416–34. New York.

Srinivas, M. N. 1942. *Marriage and Family in Mysore.* Bombay.

————. 1952. *Religion and Society among the Coorgs of South India.* Oxford.

Stuart, H. 1891. "Madras Report." *Census of India,* vol. 13.

Tambiah, S. J. 1965. "Kinship Fact and Fiction in Relation to the Kandyan Sinhalese." *Journal of the Royal Anthropological Institute* 95, part 2:131–73.

————. 1973. "Dowry, Brideprice and the Property Rights of Women in South India." In Jack Goody and S. J. Tambiah,

Bridewealth and Dowry. Cambridge Papers in Social Anthropology, 7:59–166. Cambridge.

Thurston, Edgar. 1907. *Ethnographic Notes*. Madras.

Thurston, Edgar, and K. Rangachari. 1909. *Castes and Tribes of Southern India,* 7 vols. Madras.

Turnbull, T. 1895. "Account of the Various Tribes of Culleries; Customs of the Culleries." In B. S. Ward, *Geographical and Statistical Memoir of the Provinces of Madura and Dindigul* 3:5–9, 9–12. Madura.

Wallace, Anthony F. L., and John Atkins. 1960. "The Meaning of Kinship Terms." *American Anthropologist* 62:58–80. Repr. in Tyler, Stephen A. (ed.), *Cognitive Anthropology* (New York, 1969).

Webb, T. Theodor. 1933. "Tribal Organization in Eastern Arnhem Land. *Oceania* 3:406–11.

Winslow, Deborah. 1980. "Rituals of First Menstruation in Shri-Lanka. *Man* 15/4:603–25.

Yalman, Nur. 1962. "The Structure of the Sinhalese Kindred: A Re-examination of the Dravidian Terminology." *American Anthropologist* 64/3, part 1:548–75.

———. 1963. "On the Purity of Women in the Castes of Ceylon and Malabar." *Journal of the Royal Anthropological Institute* 93/1:25–58.

———. 1967. *Under the Bo Tree: Studies in Caste, Kinship and Marriage in the Interior of Ceylon*. Berkeley.

———. 1969. "The Semantics of Kinship in South India and Ceylon." In T. A. Sebeok (ed.), *Linguistics in South Asia*. Paris.

Index

Names of populations are in small capitals.

Unless specified otherwise, factual references relate to South India, and transcribed Indian words (in *italics*) are as a rule from the Tamil language, other languages being briefly indicated (S. = Sanskrit, H. = Hindi, Mal. = Malayalam, Mar. = Marathi, the last two in the relevant author's orthography).

Figures in italics following authors indicate quotations; those following subjects indicate definitions or key passages.